TRANSFORMING

E

Sh

Philip A. Woods

First published in Great Britain in 2011 by

The Policy Press
University of Bristol
Fourth Floor
Beacon House
Queen's Road
Bristol BS8 1QU
UK

Tel +44 (0)117 331 4054
Fax +44 (0)117 331 4093
e-mail tpp-info@bristol.ac.uk
www.policypress.co.uk

North American office:
The Policy Press
c/o International Specialized Books Services (ISBS)
920 NE 58th Avenue, Suite 300
Portland, OR 97213-3786, USA
Tel +1 503 287 3093
Fax +1 503 280 8832
e-mail info@isbs.com

British Library Cataloguing in Publication Data
A catalogue record for this book is available from the British Library.

Library of Congress Cataloging-in-Publication Data
A catalog record for this book has been requested.

ISBN 978 1 84742 735 9 paperback
ISBN 978 1 84742 736 6 hardcover

The right of Philip A. Woods to be identified as author of this work has been asserted by him in accordance with the 1988 Copyright, Designs and Patents Act.

Cover design by The Policy Press.
Front cover: image kindly supplied by www.alamy.com
Printed and bound in Great Britain by Hobbs, Southampton.
The Policy Press uses environmentally responsible print partners.

Contents

Acknowledgements   v

one   New openings   1
two   Driving democracy   15
three   Radicalising entrepreneurialism   31
four   The rise of plural control   45
five   A different view: organic meta-governance   57
six   The concept of adaptive strategies   77
seven   Embodying change   89
eight   Degrees of democracy   107
nine   Practice in the making   131
ten   Energies for change   155

Notes   165
References   183
Index   201

Acknowledgements

The ideas in this book are based on many years of research and study, a journey of enquiry enriched through professional and personal friendships and loving family relationships. I have been very fortunate to share time through research projects and other settings with many fine colleagues, too many to mention by name. I thank you all for being such an important part of my journey. Amongst these colleagues, I especially express my appreciation to two outstanding scholars for the insights I have gained from their work and for their friendship and stimulating intellectual exchanges over the years: Michael Fielding (Institute of Education, University of London) and Peter Gronn (University of Cambridge). My thanks also go particularly to members of the New DEEL (Democratic Ethical Educational Leadership) network, for their positive energy and inspiration and the value of their warm and scholarly conversations, especially Steve Gross (Temple University), Lisa Kensler (Auburn University), Mary John O'Hair (University of Kentucky) and Joan Shapiro (Temple University). Thanks are due to numerous people and institutions whose help and co-operation were vital to the research and preparation of examples discussed in Chapters 8 and 9. These include the staff and students of the schools whose co-operation enabled the research to take place which is drawn upon in Chapter 8, namely Michael Hall Steiner School, especially Ewout van Manen whose discernment and thoughtful reflections on Steiner education have been invaluable, the fictitiously named Urbanview Academy, and Sands democratic school; the British Academy whose grants funded the research at Michael Hall and Urbanview Academy; the headteachers of other schools I visited, and the staff and students I met, who gave insights into examples highlighted in Chapter 9 (Tony Billings of All Hallows Catholic College, Macclesfield; David Boston of Sir Thomas Boughey Co-operative Business School, Staffordshire; and Christopher Reynolds of Saint Benedict Catholic School, Derby; María Cecilia Fierro (Universidad Iberoamericana León, Mexico), who very generously wrote an English paper for me on the research study of initiatives which form part of Convivencia Democrática y Cultura de Paz en América Latina and which are highlighted as a result in Chapter 9, and to Charlie Slater (California State University, Long Beach) for alerting me to this work; Amanda Roberts (University of Hertfordshire) whose ideas and suggestions were so helpful; and Mervyn Wilson of the Co-operative College, whose work with others in the co-operative movement is such an important dimension of the emerging education system. My thanks to Patricia Broadfoot for the opportunity (during her time as Vice Chancellor at the University of Gloucestershire) to work with her on an article on plural controlled schooling which I re-worked, expanded and updated for Chapter 4 of this book. I am grateful to the School of Education, University of Hertfordshire, for its support which enabled my participation in the WorldBlu Awards 2010 conference in the US, and express my deep appreciation to WorldBlu and to all the awardees and participants at its conference who very kindly shared their views with me on organisational democracy, especially Sam Chaltain, Elannah Cramer, Roxanne Erdahl, Diana Fenton, Heath Mackay, Augusta Meill, Katrina Oropel, Anand Pillai, Aaron Ross and Fraser Wilson. Traci Fenton, founder of WorldBlu, deserves special mention for giving an insight into her energetic and growing campaign to enhance organisational democracy globally. I am very grateful to The Policy Press for the opportunity to publish this work and especially thankful for the sterling support of Alison Shaw during its preparation. Finally, my love and deepest thanks to my wonderful life-partner and co-researcher, Glenys – a fund of inspiration – for her constant support, critical acumen and stimulating conversation, and for her love and faith in me, as well as to our children, Stephen James and Elizabeth Lowri, who in various ways are sources of unending inspiration and holistic support.

ONE

New openings

Democracy serves neither society nor individuals. Democracy serves human beings insofar as they are subjects, or in other words, their own creators and the creators of their individual and collective lives. (Alain Touraine, 1997, p 19)

Sometimes we need to know when to catch the momentum of change: or, to be more exact, to distinguish normal and repetitive waves of newness from shifts of greater substance. After all, change is ubiquitous in modern society. Marx's famous observation captures that: society dominated by capitalist relations 'cannot exist without constantly revolutionising the instruments of production' and is characterised by 'everlasting uncertainty and agitation': '[a]ll fixed, fast-frozen relations ... are swept away, all new-formed ones become antiquated before they can ossify. All that is solid melts into air ...' (Marx and Engels, 1967, p 83). Where can we detect, to coin an inelegant phrase, solid change?

The proposition of this book is that the 'tectonic plates' that constitute the underlying structure of society are moving in the direction of democratic relationships which are the nurturing ground for the exploration and generation of enduring meaning; and that education is at the heart of this opportunity. There are structural opportunities for progressive change, and – crucially, in addition to that – our understanding of agency is evolving in a way that is especially conducive to taking advantage of those opportunities. Educational policy and possibilities for a paradigm shift in education are placed in the context of generic organisational trends that foreground participation and meaning. The argument is not that education should follow changes in the economy and other sectors: on the contrary, education has a sacred task that is not reducible to the demands of the economy or blind subservience to dominant ideas. Education, however, can and should be stimulated by innovations elsewhere, because it is both an ideal and an intensely practical activity. A good deal of the book, therefore, explores what is happening in other contexts, including some business settings, and interlaces education within the discussion.

New democratic times?

The hailing of more democratic times is not new. A 'sudden growth' of democratic and cooperative grass-roots organisations in the US during the 1970s and 1980s, for example, prompted great interest and an important scholarly study (recently re-published) (Rothschild and Whitt, 2009,[1] p 11). The study concluded that, whilst the 'master trend' in the 20th century had been towards greater concentration in economic and governmental power, this generated a counter-trend for 'self-determination': it signalled 'a shift from production for exchange value to production for use value, from a market calculus to a social utility calculus', creating spaces that 'integrate the world of work with the sentiments of play' and 'find a place for expressive impulses in an arena ordinarily reserved for instrumental activity' (pp 183, 191).

I should be more specific, therefore, about today. There is a confluence of institutional changes and cultural ideas that open possibilities for change. These constitute an influential context for education. Our opportunity is to build upon, renew and recreate for the coming times the democratising experience of the past; more particularly, it is to reshape the system of governance that emerged during the latter two decades of the 20th century – namely, the gradual adoption of a *steering* role for the state. This recasting of central governance combined markets, hierarchy and networks as modes of organisation, championed the perceived superiority of private business dynamism, and prioritised national competitiveness as the goal of public services, especially education. It has been criticised as giving the appearance of devolving power whilst in practice constraining and shaping local agendas and the 'souls' of professionals such as teachers[2]. Times are changing, however, and possibilities opening because of the distances (from the centre to the peripheries) entailed in that steering role, its own evolution to involve negotiation of values, meaning and relationships (Osborne, 2010, p 10), and as a result of contemporary trends.

Two factors particularly prompted the writing of this book.

A flawed model

The first is the denting of the superiority of the private business/markets model brought about by the financial and economic crisis begun in 2008. These economic upheavals burst a period of protracted 'capitalist triumphalism' and began to allow across the political horizon of feasible change 'a far wider range of possibilities ... than the established economic and political consensus had allowed us previously to entertain'

(Callinicos, 2010, pp 6, 16). It was rediscovered that markets 'can be shaped by vested interests, that economic players are not always rational, that markets are not self-correcting' (Brown, 2010, p 12). The 'credit crunch and fiscal crisis has freed our political imagination from the idea that this is the only game in town' (Craig et al, 2009, p 4). The state 'roars back' (Callinicos, 2010, p 95), albeit not necessarily in the same direct welfare role prior to the growth of its steering function. Most importantly, however, the crisis laid bare, as one headteacher put it to me, the 'spiritual emptiness of capitalism', and led, as another described it, to a renewed 'discourse around values'.

As a consequence, the superior private model no longer looks so superior. The idea that private business, markets and the role of people as consumers constitute the preferred model for all kinds of services and human activity is past its sell-by date. That does not mean that the entwining of private interests and bodies in education has ceased: these are still part of the policy community and the institutions and relationships that make up the education system (Ball, 2007; 2008a, p 37). The context that gave moral authority to the introduction of new private players, however, has begun to change. The danger to the social fabric of the ideal of relentless competitiveness, and all that was seen to go with it (quantification of progress, management through targets and managerialist cultural change), was made plain to see. As Stephen Green (2009), former Chairman of HSBC, put it, 'the world has looked into an abyss … [T]he manifest failure of market fundamentalism … will inevitably be the starting point for a new new [sic] world order' and 'a fundamentally renewed morality'.

What this latest economic crisis represented was a recurrence of the extreme turbulence that from time to time consumes the market system. Such crises are endemic. The depth and global scale of this one, and the unstoppable demand it placed on governments to act in the wider interest, however, have opened possibilities in political thinking. The crisis in the economy and the financial sector revealed (once again) the interdependence of business, government and everyone in society. It displayed in a dramatic way the interconnectedness that underlies social life, which is hidden by the apparent success of competitive individualism. Moreover, it shifted the dynamic of the power relationship between the private sector and the state (Callinicos, 2010).

How we understand this relationship between the state and capitalism matters, as the relationship between education and the surrounding capitalist-dominated society is framed by that understanding. If the economic crisis of the late 2000s demands a change in capitalism, what kind of change is needed? There is a range of options, summarised in Figure 1.1[3]. At the two extremes are liberalisation and abolition: liberalisation being a hard-line neo-liberal response, which is not to intervene but to let crises do their worst and purge the inefficiencies and pressures that build up; and abolition being the wholesale overthrow of the system, associated especially with Marxism. The second option (moderation) is acceptance of the occurrence of crises as characteristic of capitalism, but then to act to moderate their consequences as best possible. The next two options are variations on the creation of a 'better capitalism' (Callinicos, 2010, p 134). One (reform) is to go further than the previous option in constructing regulations and applying disciplines to the operation of markets. The other (transformation) is to apply systemic changes that embed alternative rationalities to competitive individualism – by introducing social goals, organisational democracy, more spiritual environments, and so on, into capitalist and bureaucratic organisations, and promoting and increasing alternative forms, such as cooperatives.

Figure 1.1: Changing capitalism

change	strategic aim	types of change
liberalisation	market regulation and control lessened further in the belief that truly free markets will correct problems	de-regulation
moderation	attempts made to curb the worst excesses	minimum new regulations
reform	regulations are reviewed and further modest changes are made to the system in the belief that these will curb future crises	more extensive regulations than with moderation and attention given to systemic change
transformation	systematic and deep changes are made to the economic system and the social and political environment in which it is embedded	as well as systemic regulation, enhancement of alternative rationalities (e.g. co-operatives, democratic organisations, workplace democracy, spirituality) and state activity
abolition	overthrow of capitalism	replacement with alternative system

Moderation and reform have been the immediate responses to the crises. The focus for longer term change – if it is not to be wholesale replacement of capitalism – is some version of the fourth, a transformation of capital. This is the terrain on which this book is focusing. It is a terrain that holds potentialities for varying degrees of radicalism, and it is one that is far from barren. The nutriments for transformation have been slowly nurturing. If transformation of capital is where we situate ourselves, it has radical implications for education and educational policy – i.e. for how it is shaped at school, local and national levels.

Meaning and participation in organisations

The second trend is the intense growth in recent years in attention to democratisation and greater meaning in organisations. This constitutes a key part of the potential for a renewed transformative approach to capital and a formative context for transforming education. One influential researcher and writer on business management concludes that successful contemporary organisations show the value of re-capturing and re-interpreting 'the very best of democracy' in the workplace and of recreating through today's technology 'the space, the feeling of time and the value of conversation and reflection which pervaded [democratic] Athens' (Gratton, 2004, p xiii). Reliance on the heroic 'Messiah' leader is giving way to recognition of the value of the quiet leader who is 'emotionally intelligent, sensitive and less rational, privileging the emotional and internal self' – the 'leader as Therapist', the 'leader-coach'; and beyond that, a more radical and democratic discourse of leadership is emerging which centres around connectedness (Western, 2008, pp 175, 195). There is renewed reaction to what some describe as a 'sense of spiritual bankruptcy within the corporate world', which requires democracy that gives recognition to 'the whole person, the spirit of who we are' (Roxanne Erdahl)[4]. Worldblu, a movement for organisational democracy established in 1997, captures the spirit of these trends with its aim of unleashing 'human potential and [inspiring] freedom by championing the growth of democratic organizations worldwide'[5]. One of the resources for change is the tradition of community and mutual ownership which offers different, more democratic models of social and business organisation. Whilst there have been times of decline as well as growth in these models, there is renewed interest in such alternatives and they have a significant presence already across society: in the UK the mutual sector includes multi-billion pound businesses and an estimated 23 million people are members of mutuals (see Woodin et al, 2010). As we shall see, national UK cooperative organisations are important 'critical democratic actors'[6], taking and making opportunities to advance cooperative and democratic principles in education.

In the 'third way' approach that has dominated educational policy, Andy Hargreaves and Dennis Shirley (2009) identify as a key 'distractor', the 'path of autocracy' which has turned a strategy of development into 'a slickly spun system of top-down *delivery*' (p 23, emphasis in original). At its worst, the third way policy of recent years has bred such a reliance on top-down direction that, in Churchill's phrase, it approaches a kind of dictatorship, but 'without either its criminality or efficiency'[7]. Out of a growing awareness of the limitations of this policy, and inspired by examples of better models of change, a new, more effective and sustaining course is emerging, according to Hargreaves and Shirley (2009, p 23), which is 'professionally engaging [and] democratically empowering'.

Organic change

These trends are, in fact, complex and multi-faceted and do not proceed with unquestioned inevitability; and nor are they to be embraced without critique. But it will serve us well to steer clear of the Scylla of 'insipid pessimism and dystopic thinking' and the Charybdis of 'jolly eutopianisms' (Sørensen, 2009, p 203). We must be careful not to indulge uncritically and too readily in the 'discourse of endings' in which diverse changes and pressures are seen as signalling the end of one epoch and the beginning of another (Ball, 2008a, p 193). When we talk of a paradigm shift, we should bear in mind Kuhn's (1970, p 175) definition of paradigm as 'the entire constellation of beliefs, values, techniques ... shared by the ... community'. Transformation of such a constellation involves deep change on many levels. Crucial to this is how the narrative of our self and social understanding is constructed. Writing in 2008 on the 'financial meltdown' begun that year, Slavoj Žižek observed that whether it will prove a 'blessing in disguise', or something else, depends 'on how it will be symbolised, on what ideological interpretation or story will impose itself and determine the general perception of the crisis' (Žižek, 2008). In other words, crucial are the ways in which the financial and economic events of recent years are seen and talked about, the narratives of where responses to it may be taking us and what pre-existing narratives they join with.

This is where this book comes in. It addresses the question of how emerging discourses and practices that promote forms of democratic education can be interpreted. It argues that there are discernible signs and signals of change that point towards a progressive paradigm shift in education; and it suggests what more can be done to promote and shape this shift – for example, through the power of reframing present practices as democratic components in order to encourage their growth and enhancement towards a more challenging, larger aim. In other words, it suggests a 'creative refashioning of [dominant] discourses' (Dryzek, 1996, p 154) and itself seeks to contribute to that refashioning. My contention is that we have the opportunity to consciously shape educational policy – at school, local and national levels – by understanding and growing the future in the most fertile ground we can find.

I argue that a fundamentally different way of envisaging the education system is called for today, one that will not necessarily fit well with left or right political perspectives. To that extent the argument is a continuation of the third way project. More deeply, it moves on from that project, because of the flaws that have been revealed through its practice. Changes are occurring in the policy frameworks that shape education and there is a need to regain a sense of agency, freedom and responsibility. People are organic beings, but everywhere they are subject to procedures and techniques, and corralled into impersonal systems. Echoing the arguments for democracy and meaning in Chapter 2, that is how a critic could polemicise against modern mainstream education. McCombs and Miller (2008, p 218), for example, caustically critique as fundamentally flawed the dominating 'Industrial Age' paradigm 'of viewing students as workers – and their achievements as products'.

During the period planning this book, while I was walking in a beautifully created organic garden, I was reminded of the longstanding metaphor of education as gardening. It was a lovingly nurtured garden with natural growth and meaning shaped by its owner, in ways designed 'to achieve a sense of harmony ... to blend the arts of imagination and architecture' and to create an environment 'which delights the eye, warms the heart and feeds the soul' (Prince of Wales)[8] – which indeed it did. The metaphor has long historical roots, evident in Lawrence's (1970, p 14) review of the philosophical history of modern education, referring to the growth of children like seeds and the 'common simile of the garden'. A school is more like the creative art of sustaining growth than the technical work of enhancing the effectiveness and efficiency of a mechanical organisation. It involves continual renewing. It requires responding to how things take in the 'soil' and 'climate'. The response of plants, or creatures, cannot be exactly predicted or controlled at an individual level (though patterns can be observed by the human observer): the growth of the individual occurs from within, in relationship with the environment. And, as you walk round the garden or school, what is revealed is the 'soul' of its creators: through layout, selection of plants/contents, features of celebration (including people, figures and ideas featured), themes and patterns. In other words, the garden is a symbolic environment, laced with many layers of meaning.

There is renewed recognition of the power of the garden or agricultural metaphor. Whilst the tendency of the 'engineering' approach is to 'erect one grand new solution after another', declaring the problem solved, 'gardening requires more patience and discipline' and more preparation (Hess, 2010, p 130). Sir Ken Robinson made an influential call for just such a model:

> I think we have to change metaphors. I think we have to go from an industrial model of education, a manufacturing model, which is based on linearity and conformity and batching people; we have to move to a model that is based more on the principles of agriculture. We have to recognise that human flourishing is not a mechanical process, it's an organic process, and you cannot predict the outcome of human development. All you can do is, like a farmer, create the conditions in which they will begin to flourish. So when we look at reforming education and transforming it, it isn't like cloning a system.[9]

Yet the agricultural model is only a metaphor, and has its limitations as a guide. People are not plants or livestock. They are creative actors and interpreters of their personal and social trajectories, and most significantly inhabitants and shapers of a *political* and *ethical* environment. They are conscious creatures who give answers – explicitly or implicitly – to questions of meaning. Indeed, there is a human impulse to find ways of orientating to ideals and the transcendent – the importance of love, truth, beauty, goodness. In his impressive analysis of the significance of the way the right brain has been marginalised to the left brain of logic, Iain McGilchrist explains how we need myth and metaphor (the sphere of the right brain) to understand the world. It is not an option to do without some kind of myth or metaphor. In the absence of any other we revert to the metaphor of the machine – which has been the experience of education and reduces everything to a linear process of manipulation, treating people as objects. We need something more: '... any mythos that allows us to approach a spiritual Other, and gives us something other than material values to live by, is more valuable than one that dismisses the possibility of its existence' (McGilchrist, 2009, p 442).

In the chapters which follow, the signs and potentialities of an emergent democratic self-organising system which is organic rather than industrial in its culture, and what needs to be understood in order to advance that change further, are explored.

Holistic democracy

Democracy attracts different meanings. In previous publications I have set out a view of what democracy is – a rich conception conceived as developmental or holistic democracy[10]. This conception underlies the analysis and discussion in this book. The intellectual roots of the holistic democracy model are in the tradition which includes the Oxford political philosopher, T.H. Green, and British Idealism. Hence it views human beings as possessing inherent capabilities – intellectual, aesthetic, spiritual and so on – which in combination enable people to make progress towards the ethically good. This grounding encourages a particular stance towards modernity. It encourages a discourse which draws on concepts and ideas such as creativity, self-transcendence and re-integration of human capabilities with the aim of challenging the dominance of instrumental rationality and the alienating character of the social order.

Democracy is about equal participation of all in the creation of their social environment and in the decisions which affect them. In holistic democracy, however, it is not the sole purpose. Integral to it is striving towards a way of living which aspires to values that represent the best of human progress. The inbuilt potential for each person to feel and understand what is truly meaningful and what should be counted as true and of highest worth, founded in a human capacity for spiritual awareness (see Woods, G. J., 2003, 2007), is at the heart of the model of holistic democracy. What comprises highest values, meaning and worth, how to prioritise between their often conflicting implications and the best strategies for trying to realise them, are all matters for debate. The great promise of democracy is that it aggregates differing perspectives and areas of knowledge, and thereby tests and enhances understanding of these matters and offers a better basis for practical decision making. In addition, according to the holistic model, democratic participation enhances the capacity to realise deeply embedded human potentialities.

There is a growing literature advocating organisational democracy – in organisations generally and schools in particular – on the grounds that it enables organisations to be more flexible, innovative and effective and that it has intrinsic value in creating a more ethical culture that respects the human needs and rights of organisational members. This is explored further in Chapter 2. Literature promoting democracy that involves more than consultation or voting rights defines it in terms of values (such as integrity and fairness), individual characteristics (such as sense of purpose and personal development), dispersal of power (through decentralisation, increased freedom and choice, accountability to organisational members and so on), and opportunities for debate and collaborative enquiry (involving dialogue, transparency, free information flows and so on)[11]. The value of the concept of holistic democracy is three-fold: it goes further in explicitly recognising the intimate relationship between participative decision making and the development of holistic capabilities that include spiritual awareness and involve inner transformation; it explicitly identifies, through four dimensions (defined below), the distinctive, complementary and essential components of a rich conception of democracy; and it provides a conceptual framework for considering the overlap and interplay between them[12].

At the core of the holistic democracy model are the four dimensions[13]: holistic meaning and holistic well-being (the expressive dimensions); and power sharing and transforming dialogue (the participative dimensions) (Figure 1.2).

Figure 1.2: Holistic democracy

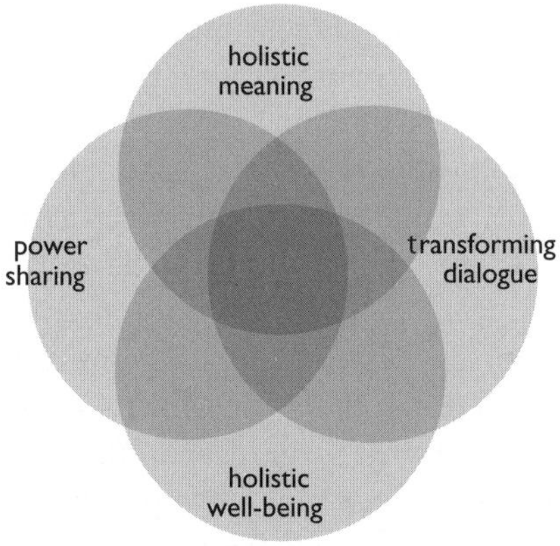

holistic meaning

power sharing

transforming dialogue

holistic well-being

These distinguish analytically the complementary and interacting dimensions of holistic democracy and have their own distinctive focus, priorities and consequences.

- *Holistic meaning* (pursuit of truth and meaning): aspiring to as true an understanding as possible not only of technical and scientific matters but also the 'big' questions of enduring values, meaning and purpose, through the development of all our human capabilities (spiritual, cognitive, aesthetic, affective, ethical, physical).

- *Power sharing* (active contribution to the creation of the institutions, culture and relationships people inhabit): includes exercising rights to participate in decision making and hold power-holders to account, and discretion to act freely and express identity within the parameters of agreed values and responsibilities.
- *Transforming dialogue* (exchange and exploration of views, open debate and transcendence of narrow interests): a climate where exchange and exploration of views and open debate are possible, reflecting the concern of deliberative democracy with individuals, in cooperation with others, seeking out the greater good for themselves and the community, by reaching beyond individual narrow perspectives and interests, and enhancing mutual understanding; aspirations to holistic meaning are thus tested through sharing, dialogue and constructive critique.
- *Holistic well-being* (social belonging, connectedness and feelings of empowerment embedded in democratic participation): the positive dynamic emergent from the other dimensions; it is about people being empowered and confident as organisational members, and the generation of belonging, connectedness, feelings of empowerment, self-esteem, happiness and participative capabilities through democratic participation and a sense of agency.

The most radical and rounded form of democracy occurs where the four dimensions overlap. This combination energises, in a social context that at its best is both critical and supportive, the personal capacity which makes holistic meaning possible. Their operation is intended to be developmental in the sense of the idealist tradition – a dynamic, social process of discovery, creative engagement, and movement from a limited perspective to wider, more worthy values. The ambition and scope of holistic democracy is summarised in this description which I wrote as part of my original exploration of democratic leadership:

> Where it is searched or struggled for, there is an energy behind democratisation that has much in common with the many religious, philosophical and political worldviews that people have created and thronged to over the centuries. This energy manifests itself in two ways. The first is the desire to consciously recognise, counter, challenge and overcome human weaknesses, both individually and as they manifest themselves in social injustices. Democratic ideals are based on an awareness and understanding of human fallibilities, particularly the capacity to abuse power ... The second is in

the striving to understand where a source of strength may be found to enable these weaknesses to be overcome and to provide (in religious terminology) salvation. [Holistic democracy] appreciates the strength of human creativity and growth in each person and the human potential for working together towards higher ends and overcoming disagreement and diversity of interests, without violence. If the term 'salvation' is not used in relation to democracy, there is still some sense of aspiration to an elevated life in company with others that is good for the person and good for society. Accordingly, the point of democratic leadership, grounded in the conception of [holistic democracy], is only partially to enable equal participation by all in the decisions that affect them. The primary point is to strive towards a way of living – in and through relationships – which is orientated towards the values that ultimately represent human progress and goodness. (Woods, 2005, pp 137–8)

Structure of the book

This chapter has set out the thinking behind the book and introduced the concept of holistic democracy. Subsequent chapters elaborate the argument concerning a democratic paradigm shift in education, placing it in the context of wider organisational and social trends.

Chapter 2 discusses in more detail trends towards democratisation and greater meaning in organisations. The triple drives underpinning these are examined – namely, instrumental incentives, the desire to express meaning and the intrinsic impulse to participation. The latter two – the expressive and participative drives – comprise the axes of holistic democracy.

Entrepreneurialism is a major theme within the rubric of the third way as a driver of change and innovation in private and public organisations. This offers scope for discretion and freedom, but also forges new expectations, anxieties and emotional commitments to goals that organisational members may have had no hand in formulating. Entrepreneurialism is examined in Chapter 3 through discussion of the concept of generic entrepreneurialism and more specific forms that make up a typology. Radical potentialities are highlighted, particularly the notion of democratic entrepreneurialism.

Chapter 4 provides a brief narrative of educational policy since the 1988 Education Reform Act in England, with particular reference to change in governance, highlighting the development of an education system that more and more resembles a governance model of plural controlled schooling. Although the focus is on England, the direction of change and the conceptual frameworks that are outlined in subsequent chapters will find resonances in other jurisdictions.

Chapter 5 is pivotal. In this chapter, the emerging system is conceptualised as a potential movement from marketising meta-governance towards organic meta-governance. The impetus of the latter is to create a democratic self-organising system. The argument that the centre of gravity of governance is shifting is represented diagramatically in a 'governance diamond' that shows different forms of governance (hierarchical, self-, co- and democratic governance[14]). The chapter concludes by considering the scale of the challenge to possibilities of a democratic paradigm shift.

The two chapters which follow consider the nature of change in shifting the centre of gravity and developing a democratic paradigm shift. Chapter 6 describes and commends the idea of adaptive strategies that build upon, utilise and challenge the present conditions in order to bring about change that creates environments more in line with democratic values and the human need for meaning and holistic development. The shift envisaged is not only about structures and strategies, but integral to it is the full development of the person and their capacity for agency. The importance, nature and strengths of the embodied social actor are explored in Chapter 7, in which ideas such as embodied learning, critical democratic actors and democratic consciousness are elaborated.

Chapters 8 and 9 in different ways provide practical illustrations of the ideas and concepts discussed in previous chapters. Chapter 8 sets out an analytical framework that enables exploration of 'degrees of democracy' and the diverse and messy reality that exists between the ideal-typical notions of the rational bureaucratic and the holistic democratic school. Data from three contrasting schools (democratic, Steinerian and an inner city Academy) are used to illustrate degrees of democracy and the elements of holistic democracy. Further illustrations of signs and potentialities of change are given in Chapter 9, which discusses a variety of examples of initiatives in the state sector that show aspects of the participative and expressive dimensions of holistic democracy and the work of critical democratic actors.

Chapter 10 summarises key points from the book and emphasises that the energies for change and the potential to forge a more democratic system are dispersed – not the product of centralised policy, but the combined influence of central and local government, professional bodies, teachers, students, parents, communities, sponsors and partners.

TWO

Driving democracy

When people are treated to freedom, equality and security, when they know that they are indeed the organization, when they believe passionately in the goodness of belonging to that organization, and when they take an active hand in steering justice and decision making through well-understood institutional processes, their organization will be capable of achieving truly astounding performance. (Brook Manville and Josiah Ober, 2003, pp 116–17)

Organizational democracy is a system of organization that is based on freedom, instead of fear and control. It's a way of designing organizations to amplify the possibilities of human potential – and the organization as a whole ... [T]he core of organizational democracy and political democracy is the same – allowing people to self-govern and determine their own destiny. What is different is the context – one is in the political arena, the other is in the realm of organizations. (WorldBlu[1])

The traditional organisational model is changing. There is a groundswell favouring more participative and meaningful organisational environments. An OECD study of governance concluded that a trend could be identified over a long period: '... a clear reduction in the absolute or unconstrained power of those in positions of power ... both at the macro-political level ... and at the micro level, where firms and families have experienced important changes in the exercise of authority' (Michalski et al, 2001, p 9). In his major examination of democracy, John Keane suggests that its nature is changing. He argues that we are moving into an era focused on scrutiny and control of decision makers – that is, one of monitory democracy, which is about watching and challenging power wherever it exists. The seeds of greater public accountability, according to Keane, are being planted everywhere – bedroom, boardroom, battlefield – so that 'all fields of social and political life come to be scrutinised' (Keane, 2009, p 695[2]). In the US, some kind of organisational democracy or employee empowerment is claimed to be adopted in some part of over 70% of organisations (Spreitzer and Doneson, 2005). The following is an example that conveys the optimism and enthusiasm behind much of the work, practice and study that make up this groundswell in organisational change:

> Collaboration, self-management, and organizational democracy fundamentally alter not only the way we work but the nature of work itself. Imagine organizations that behave like organisms, policies that are flexible and value driven, procedures that are instantly customizable and responsive to customer needs, goals that are challenges and contests, feedback that is received as a gift and a compliment, and conflicts that create opportunities for growth and learning. Imagine organizations that treat employees as artists and scientists, see complaints as suggestions for improvement, explore problems as objects of curiosity, and base motivation on love and self-actualization. Imagine work as play, communications as stories and metaphors, differences as welcomed, routines as rituals, and change as exploration and adventure. (Cloke and Goldsmith, 2002, p xii)

This is an important context for education to understand, especially as the boundary between private and public sectors blur and so much attention is paid to 'lessons' from private business (notwithstanding recognition that the private model has its flaws and limitations as a model). Many organisational leaders in business and other sectors are excited and passionate about democracy in the workplace. WorldBlu is a campaigning organisation for organisational democracy, founded in the US by Traci Fenton, that shares this excitement and passion. What caught my attention as I began to learn more about WorldBlu, were its energy and ambition, and its foundation, which Fenton (2002, p 4) articulates, in a commitment to 'freedom and self-expression' and to participation and 'creating meaningful work environments'. There is a resonance between these foundational commitments and the model of holistic democracy.

I went along to meet those who gathered to receive awards from WorldBlu in 2010 and who are engaged in bringing more democracy and meaning to the workplace[3]. They gave me an insight into what drives their moves towards organisational democracy. A mix of incentives and motivations was apparent. An important theme is a perception that more participation, respect and autonomy in the workplace will make it work better and be more successful in the market. One advocate said to me that his motivation was to avoid nightmares about metrics (achieving the targets and aims the company has): he wanted the staff on the frontline to understand what was needed and get on with it. A need to get away from micro-management was a marked theme, especially as a firm grows – though the micro-management mindset was seen as harder to leave behind. Awardee Augusta Meill, Vice President of Continuum, an innovation and design company based in Boston, US, with studios in four other cities around the world, explained:

> [F]or me organisational democracy is about being great at what we do. It's about a culture of collaboration and transparency and communication and empowerment and a lot of the words folks here [at the Awards event] have touched on, and creating the environment for our people to innovate in. Because we are talking about innovation it's a particularly kind of delicate sort of animal and we have to create the right kind of space both emotional and physical for people to behave in a way that allows innovation to nurture and grow.

Participants in the WorldBlu event also interlaced in their views about organisational democracy the importance of what they saw as its intrinsic benefits and its demands on people. Awardee Anand Pillai, senior vice principal of a large Indian IT company, HCL Technologies, explained that in his view organisational democracy was about giving employees voice and then, crucially, power – and that it has implications for the inner person who is part of the more democratic way of working:

> Giving voice to employees is one thing; empowering them is another, because if you don't do the second, and having only done the first, you'll create a lot of confusion. So empowerment, that's the first thing. The second one that we've also done is brought about a kind of culture of integrity, a culture of transparency with the management, so much so that they are open to listen to feedback, open to receive important suggestions rather than being defensive about it.

Another awardee, Fraser Wilson, President of Axiomnews in Canada, explained:

> I've given it some thought and there are all kinds of people that are looking for meaning in their lives. And a lot of people get meaning out of their workplace. Now some would say that it is the new generation – the gen Y that are really looking for meaning make a difference in the workplace. But I would beg to differ from that in that I believe it's all people regardless of whether you are gen X, whether you are gen Y, whether you are a baby boomer. Today people want to know that what they do with the majority of their waking hours is making a difference in life, that their values are aligned with that of the workplace. That they have an opinion, one that counts, one that is sought by an organisation and that democratisation of the workplace is enabling them to do more, to be more, to really embrace the human capital, the human potential that resides within the organisation, where everybody wins.

Among the companies winning an award was Namaste Solar (Boulder, Colorado), a cooperative entirely owned by its employees. They chose 'co-ownership over hierarchy, democratic decisionmaking over centralized leadership, sustainable growth over aggressive expansion, and collaboration over competition'[4]. For them, the well-being of the whole person within the organisation is a top priority and very much a part of what they mean by organisational democracy. Heath Mackay, a co-owner and commercial project developer of the company, said:

> Without a doubt one of the tenets of our company is managing the holistic health of the employees, the co-owners. We firmly believe that a company structure has a role of doing what we can to make sure that employees feel valued and empowered and are happy in their work lives as well as trying to make them happy in their life outside of work.[5]

An important practical dimension is recruiting the right people – i.e. those who will fit into the culture, or the new culture they are trying to create, and therefore be most effective in enabling a democratic organisational framework to work and will achieve what the company needs to achieve. This kind of control – 'third-level control' – has been found to be a typical characteristic of many cooperative organisations (Rothschild and Whitt, 2009, p 55). Elannah Cramer, then Vice President of Marketing, Personal Health Innovations[6], and consultant to one of the companies (Zappos) receiving an award, confided that organisational democracy is 'not something that everybody is going to be comfortable with. I think a lot of people won't be comfortable with it. Zappos for example hires people who very specifically fit in with their vision of what they want for their company'.

The discourse of those advocating organisational democracy places emphasis on a combination of rationalities, including commitment to community (in which identity is gained from being a member of the organisation conceived as a community), enhanced motivation through participation and feelings of autonomy and trust, and sharing of values (encouraging intrinsic as well as instrumental motivations). There are two spurs to this. The instrumental one: the old means–end, bureaucratic rationality, ensconced within a hierarchy, is not effective in creating the agility, efficiency and innovation needed. Features of democracy are better for creating more effective organisations and networks. The second spur is an intrinsic drive, seeing meaning and involvement in the workplace as important features in themselves. Traci Fenton, speaking at the WorldBlu event, identified as the essential point that we are most free when we are living our purpose, and that this applies in our working environment too: her call was that people 'Be not conformed to the world', but work for radical change in the working environment by choosing 'an operating system that works on the principles of democracy' based 'on freedom rather than on fear and control'.

Trends to greater democracy in the workplace should not invoke uncritical celebration, however. There are less attractive and dark sides to some of the changes taking place in the name of delayering and flexibilising organisations[7]. There is no master trend smoothly unfolding. There is, however, a discernible pattern of drivers to creating and sustaining organisational democracy which can be addressed under three headings – instrumental, expressive and participative (Figure 2.1) – each of which influences the form, character and priorities of democratisation. The expressive (meaning orientated) and participative drives form the fundamental axes of holistic democracy.

Instrumental drivers

There are impelling rationales in terms of efficiency and effectiveness for introducing greater participation and meaning in organisations.

Figure 2.1: Drivers to create and sustain democracy

These are the hard reasons which, for some, are most influential in driving change in this direction. Harnessing the benefits of more democratic styles of organisation to improve production has a long tradition. Efforts to involve employees to enhance organisational efficiency and effectiveness have a track record at least from the early 20th century, and cautious analysis of research studies on employee participation shows on the whole that they have positive benefits[8]. Long recognised motivating benefits for participation include reduction of the economic costs of illness and alienation consequent on soulless work procedures and the division of labour, improving efficiency levels through better information flow from frontline workers, more effective evaluation and correction of production processes through peer monitoring, and negotiated agreement on areas of activity outside the contract of employment (at the 'frontiers of control')[9]. These are what might be termed the linear benefits on production.

They have been enhanced considerably, however, in recent decades because of qualitative changes in the complexity of business and society. Moving 'to complex, highly interdependent, technological work within a rapidly changing environment and a mobile workforce is seen as a key driver', on the grounds that 'in complex production environments, workers are best-placed to make the decisions and that contemporary workers will be attracted by such models' (Flowers, 2008, p 15). Richard Sennett (2006, p 42) identifies as a key challenge to the pyramid model 'the development of new technologies of communication and manufacturing'. To meet these challenges, a different kind of organisation has been coming into being. Unlike the 'old-style corporation' in which activity 'occurs via a fixed set of acts', like 'links in a chain', the new flexibilised organisation operates more like an MP3 player enabling variation in the sequencing of production and 'task-orientated rather than fixed-function labor', and requiring a flexible mindset on the part of employees (pp 47–50). In this more fluid structure, 'sensitivity replaces duty' (p 51), as relationships, responding to change, team-building and team-working are so central to organisational activity. One line of argument is that in the knowledge economy, employees have more power and have to be coaxed and respected accordingly since they are the creators and repositories of knowledge. Lynda Gratton (2004, p 37, original emphasis), for example, argues that the relationship between the contemporary organisation and its individual members has fundamentally changed, from the industrialised relation based on the 'muscle power' of the worker to a more equal one based on knowledge and the capacity for generation of new knowledge which requires 'an organizational culture of trust and reciprocity in which employees *actively choose* to share their knowledge'. Entrepreneurial leadership is viewed as essential to improving the capability of organisations to innovate and improve performance in the face of 21st-century demands and turbulent times[10]. Companies 'encouraging spirituality or consciousness-seeking at work display smart, strategic, business intent' (Casey, 2002, p 178).

Changes emerging from the instrumental drive are both structural and personal (the latter concerning people's mindset, feeling, motivations and so on). Key changes are summarised in Figure 2.2.

Figure 2.2: Key changes emerging from instrumental drive

Structural

flexibilisation of roles, so they are focused on tasks and projects rather than defined by functions

team working

improving information flow upwards, from staff

knowledge sharing between organisational members

peer control and peer monitoring of processes

more creativity, choice and decision making by staff

Personal

introducing more meaning into work, e.g. by reducing the division of labour and through encouragement of expressive opportunities (discussed further below)

encouraging flexible mindsets

reliance more on 'soft' virtues, such as sensitivity, trust, reciprocity and relationship-building

The experience of the co-owned John Lewis Partnership shows the pressure to instrumentalise organisational democracy. One of the conclusions of a research study into the Partnership was that 'management have attempted to direct and define democracy in a highly constrained way, assigning it an instrumental purpose, and privileging the "business case" for democratic engagement' (Cathcart, 2009, p 1). Participation, in this analysis, is construed and used in a certain way in order to shape organisational members into the kind of people who would give the intense commitment the organisation wanted:

> The Partnership used the structure of 'co-ownership' to legitimise an emphasis on profit above all else, and to stress that although decisions may not be in the interest of individuals, they were in the interests of owners, and as owners of the business, Partners needed to concur. It was this disciplinary power which individualised Partners and constituted them as materially self-interested subjects ... In constructing the subjective position of 'Partner' as prioritising economic rewards above everything else, the potential for resistance was weakened. Ironically, Partners were individualised through their continuous engagement in the illusion of freedom that the construction of collective-ownership entailed. Further, Partners were told that they themselves wanted to show their uniqueness and commitment by working harder and pursuing higher targets and more demanding objectives. (Cathcart, 2009, p 275)[11]

What is often evident with moves to develop participation is that there is a combination of aims. The founder of the John Lewis Partnership, for example, 'saw co-ownership as a way to engage workers and instil a sense of responsibility, but also a way in which the excesses of capitalism could be constrained' (Cathcart, 2009, p 153). For Cloke and Goldsmith (2002, pp xiv, 97), arguing for the 'end of management', a shift to heterarchy, democracy and collaborative self-management is 'part of a larger historical transformation' in human needs and in the social nature of work. They see an intrinsic value to this shift, but also link it to humanity's interest in ecological survival and global economic and social challenges.

—

Expressive drivers

The expressive aspect of social life concerns the opportunity to find and create meaning, to give vent to spiritual, artistic and creative impulses, to enjoy the intrinsic value of relationships and the warmth of human bonds, to live ethically and to learn and grow as full human beings. The expressive function especially concerns the dimensions of holistic meaning and holistic well-being (Figure 1.2). The driver to enable an expressive dimension to organisational life is the recognition that people want more than mundane, repetitive lives. Modernity raises instrumental rationality to be the most valued mode of social action, one that pervades social life, and bureaucratic organisation and rationalising procedures become the dominant ideal. It leads to rationalisation and disenchantment, the diagnosis of modern organisational life associated with Max Weber which has been and remains immensely influential on understandings of organisational life. Implicated in this rationalisation is the disenchantment of the world: 'the ultimate and most sublime values have retreated from public life' (Weber, 1970a, p 155).

The social fact of disenchantment comes up against the human drive to search for and create meaning. It emerges in politics: reflecting on the future for the UK Labour Party, one commentator observed, 'The protest votes that we have seen ... are cries of anguish from people who are saying; we don't want to feel so powerless, and we don't know where we fit in. It's a plea for meaning' (Russell, 2009, p 83). It underpins renewals of cultures, such as First Nations in Canada and the development of Māori education in New Zealand[12] and engagement with the cultures of the nations within the UK.

The expressive dimensions of holistic meaning and well-being can be articulated and understood in different ways. Two kinds of interpretation (Figure 2.3) became apparent from developing the 'degrees of democracy' analytical framework and studying during this process data from three differing schools, as discussed in Chapter 8. (I do not suggest that these are exhaustive of all possible differences.) The first gives emphasis to affective feelings and ideas of *organic belonging*. This foregrounds the emotional aspect of identity and development and the nurturing of community and individuality in networks of supportive relationships characterised by human warmth, enjoyment and celebration. For organisations this involves stimulating 'the creation of personal networks and friendships that encourage others to value the relational element of the organisation and the maintenance of networks within and beyond the company' (Gratton, 2007, pp 146, 149). The second, and fuller expression where it augments organic

Figure 2.3: Interpretations of the expressive dimension

belonging, is around *connectedness*, which concerns the flourishing of everyone's innate capacity for a sense of unity and connection with the self, other people, nature and ultimate reality. Connectedness involves openness to energies which allow wisdom to grow and heightened spiritual awareness, and spirituality which stems from an inner quest that reflects a 'deeper, inner hunger for meaning and connectedness' (Murchú, 2000, p 192)[13].

A key marker of the importance of meaning and seeking re-enchantment is the growing participation in 'life spiritualities', a social phenomenon in the UK, the US and internationally which has been studied closely by Paul Heelas (2008). His investigation of participation in all kinds of spiritual development, healing and leisure activities addresses the question of whether this is simply reducible to another aspect of the consumer society; whether it is just a self-absorbed, commodified construction of the self driven by astute spiritual entrepreneurs. Whilst his study does not claim to evaluate the authenticity of all involved in life spiritualities, he makes a cogent case against explaining out of existence the substance of this important social phenomenon. His conclusion is that life spirituality is '... very much to do with the free expression, and thus the development, of what it is to be "truly" human', and that its emphasis lies not 'with the "good life" of materialistic utilitarianism', but with 'the "good life" of expressivistic humanism', infused by 'the ethic of humanity (owing a great deal to the Enlightenment and Romanticism) ... the "language" of expressivism ... the arts, poetry, music, the emotionally charged, the language, sentiments and sensibilities of the heart, the expressive ethicality of inner-wisdom' (pp 2, 3–4, 30). He goes on: 'The "freedom" component of the ethic of humanity fuses with self-expressive freedom. The "egalitarian" component of the ethic of humanity fuses with the theme of spiritual unity, and thus equality ... The voice of ethical authority is *experienced* as coming from within. (pp 30, 31, emphasis in original). The latter point is key to the relevance to democracy: the nurturing of this kind of spirituality is integral to holistic democracy which aspires to seek and move towards truth both in technical matters and in questions of meaning and purpose (Woods, 2005, 2006).

In this context, it is perhaps unsurprising that ways of introducing more meaning and values into organisational life and the mainstream economic functioning of society are receiving escalating attention. This includes practices and ideas concerning spirituality[14], associated with values, ethical sensibilities, higher purposes, qualities such as humility and balance, and inner meaning[15]. Some of this is being conceptualised as spiritual capital or spiritual enterprise, recognising the relationship between organisational life and the beliefs, commitments and traditions of the members of organisations. These include faith beliefs, but the area of organisational leadership and activity that spiritual capital points to is not only or necessarily about religious faith and belief. I define spiritual capital, broadening the approach of Theodore Malloch (2008, pp 11–12[16]), as the fund of belief, examples and commitments expressed through a philosophy or tradition, and people's capacity for spiritual awareness, which orientate people to the transcendental source of human happiness and meaning. It is both a resource for organisations and something which is capable of being generated within the organisation. Evidence suggests that in organisations across the world 'various new forms of self-expressiveness, meaning-making and spirituality' (Casey, 2002, p 152), including types of spiritual exercise such as meditation, opportunities for time in 'quiet rooms' and the 'gentle arts' of 'spirit-seeking, magic and divination', are growing (p 155). Catherine Casey (2004) suggests that organisational members through this kind of activity and perspective bring a 'potentially disruptive counterposition to bureaucratic and neo-rationalist organizational management' (p 75) and that the 'current of spiritual and self-expressivist explorations and demands among bureaucratic organizational employees, reveals ... signs of persons striving for subjectivation – for the accomplishment of becoming an acting subject ... [and] are efforts toward a freedom not reduced to an instrumental rationality of economic choice' (p 76).

These kinds of deeper concerns are associated with the energy and creativeness needed by successful organisations. In other words, they are seen as having instrumental as well as intrinsic value[17]. Gratton (2007, p 109), for example, concludes from her research that innovative networks are sparked by a vibrant culture of conversation where the 'vice-like grip of relentless pragmatism is softened by the invigorating spirit of Romanticism', embracing big questions about the meaning of life and fundamental purpose. Whilst the functional value would not be denied by proponents of the expressive aspect of democratised organisations, those like Cloke and Goldsmith emphasise and re-emphasise to business and organisational practitioners the intrinsic drive. The implications of organisational democracy 'extend far beyond enhanced productivity and employee job satisfaction'; it is, like political democracy, 'a statement of social values, a method of creating community, a recognition of our essential equality, a promise of fairness, an acknowledgement of the value of dissent, and a freedom to be ourselves' (Cloke and Goldsmith, 2002, p xiv). Play, intuition, aesthetics, humour and the panoply of human, social and personal living are encouraged in the democratic organisation (p 213).

The expressive dimension to organisational change is evident in understanding leadership. Tracing spiritual entrepreneurship in Western life over the past 200 years, Arthur Jue (2007, pp 3, 7) notes the increasing interest in 'holistic or whole-soul leadership' and concludes that 'the post-industrial milieu seems ripe for a reintegration of spirit in entrepreneurial life and leadership'. In education, democratic leadership is being encouraged to integrate issues of sustainability and ecology (Kensler, forthcoming). Simon Western (2008, pp 182, 195) suggests a new discourse is emerging in the field of leadership: one which is 'beginning to recognize that leadership now means re-negotiating what success means for an organization or company' (p 195), evolving a new paradigm that shifts the focus 'from functions and outputs and profits looking only at the closed system of the organization and business economy, to an ethical, socially responsible and sustainable ecological view' (p 196). Leadership discourses that grew up during the 20th century are under pressure from an emerging 'post-heroic' discourse concerned with 'more contemplative spiritual-human values' and environmental issues, and with 'a more compassionate, ethical and socially responsible and connected leadership' (p 182). This eco-leadership discourse, as Western calls it, at first taken up by environmental and social activists is 'being taken up by progressive leaders of business and politics' (p 182): it 'does not try to create strong cultures with homogeneous loyal employees, but the opposite; strong networks which enable difference to flourish' (p 196). Western summarises the emerging discourse:

> At the heart of [the eco-leadership] discourse is connectivity...
> There is an emerging sense that leaders of business, as well
> as social and political leaders are becoming eco-literate,
> which means applying systems thinking and 'spirit' to their
> organizations and beyond. This leadership discourse is not
> just about going green or taking an environmental stance...
> Eco-leadership... is about connectivity, interdependence and
> sustainability underpinned by an ethical socially responsible
> stance. (Western, 2008, p 183)

Participative drivers

The driver here is the intrinsic conviction that people have a right to
be involved in decisions that affect them, to have their voices heard and
their rights to freedom respected, and that those with power should be
accountable for its use. It includes democratisation that seeks to curtail
or abolish oppression and injustice. In its ideal form, the participative
impetus aims to advance power-sharing and transforming dialogue as
understood in the holistic democracy model.

There are several intellectual and practical roots to participation
in organisations and communities. These include the tradition of
participatory democracy – a direct and active process of involvement,
which also plays an important educational function by developing and
utilising skills and attitudes necessary for democracy and for democratic
citizenship. Underpinning this is the concept of self-organisation (or
anarchism in its original sense) – that is, 'organization without external
authority' achieved 'solely by internal discipline' and 'spontaneous order'
(Rothschild and Whitt, 2009, pp 12–18). Participatory democracy
contrasts with representative democracy[18].

Changing authority relationships

A more recent strand is monitory democracy. Keane's magisterial
study of democracy lays out its development to current times, though
he does not suggest any inevitable narrative of democracy. What is
observable, Keane (2009, pp xxvi–xxvii) argues, is progression from
an era of representative democracy to an era of post-representative
democracy, focused more on scrutiny and control of decision makers.
The key feature of this new phase is that 'all fields of social and political
life come to be scrutinised', spreading democracy into civil society
and beneath and cutting across state institutions (pp 695, 708/9).
Whilst Giddens (1994) proposed that a spread of dialogic democracy

was apparent, Keane (2009, pp 731–47) analyses and delineates forms of democratic activity that have the teeth to monitor, resist and challenge power – through new organisations and networks and through the spread of communication via technologies that include the internet – exposing injustices and defending human rights. It both requires and encourages a different kind of social subject: 'democracy requires colossal transformations of people's characters' (p 709), and a different relationship with the state. What needs to be imbued is 'a stronger sense that … citizenship could be lived by exercising options in addition to voting a few times' in one's life (p 824). Allied to this are the opportunities implicated in the new technologies of digital communication, highlighted by Alan Rusbridger:

> It's a trend about how people are expressing themselves, about how societies will choose to organise themselves, about a new democracy of ideas and information, about changing notions of authority, about the releasing of individual creativity, about an ability to hear previously unheard voices; about respecting, including and harnessing the views of others. About resisting the people who want to close down free speech.[19]

The idea of a changing relationship with the state is apparent in other reflections on the development of governance. Geoff Mulgan (2010, p 61) puts forward the idea of the 'relational state', one that does things with people rather than 'to or for' them. The driver to this change may not be the realisation of a better way to do government or provide services, but a recognition of the problem that governments have gaining and sustaining legitimacy. Mulgan argues: 'If legitimation is actually the heart of the state, government can succeed better by directly addressing the quality of its relationships with the public, rather than doing so indirectly through promises and their delivery' (p 62). Concerns about their poor legitimacy have motivated governments before to find new ways of enabling people to participate, an example being the development of parent participation in the 1960s and 1970s (Beattie, 1985). The idea of the relational state, and the interest in enhanced participation of which it is part, is tapping into widespread changes in governance – which is beginning to be explored as *new public governance* (Osborne, 2010). Predicated on a 'plural state and pluralist state', trends towards a new public governance are characterised by negotiation of accountability, values, meaning and relationships, recognition of power inequalities in networks and 'dispersed and contested' value bases, and a focus on the system level rather than the organisational level (pp 7–10). Renegotiation of power relationships is integral to the new modes of governance that are developing, as they entail greater involvement of users of public services as co-producers and new modes of accountability that build on social accounting traditions which incorporate assessments of issues such as social justice (pp 416-24).

In organisational democracy, dispersal of power is both a key and controversial aspect. The 'colossal transformations of people's characters', to which Keane refers, involve inner changes that concern the spiritual domain highlighted by expressive democracy. Speaking about organisational democracy, Anand Pillai of HCL Technologies observes:

> Personally I think there is a spiritual dimension because for us to receive feedback from somebody who's younger, we must learn to recognise that we are humble, and that can come only from a transformation from within. As the saying goes, with great power comes great responsibility, and with great responsibility comes great humility. All these things are deeply spiritual. I find it very difficult, even in situations where a person has not transformed within for him or her to be part of a system which is democratic, where everybody's equal.

Participation is most clearly obtained where rights to power and authority are secured through legal rights or equal ownership: 'Democracy is, above all, a sharing of power, and for organizational democracy to become consistent and widespread, employees need to become owners and not merely renters of their organizations, and of their work lives as well' (Cloke and Goldsmith, 2002, p 187). Examples are cooperative organisations, including large companies such as the John Lewis Partnership[20]. In the absence of such clear equality of authority, organisational democracy is open to the critique that power remains ultimately at the upper end of the hierarchy. Even with it, power is not a simple possession that can be shared around, as the research concerning the John Lewis Partnership, cited earlier, found. On the other hand, it is possible to envisage *degrees of democracy* in which influence and authority and the expressive aims of participation are dispersed to some extent (discussed in more detail in Chapter 8). One of the ways that proponents of greater organisational democracy try to overcome the critique that democracy is absent without shared ownership is to advocate forms of what we can call *simulated ownership*.

One approach sets out principles and ideas on how to turn 'employees into mini-CEOs' (Ross, 2009, p 21). Future Considerations, a UK-based company and WorldBlu awardee, which has worked to develop its internal democracy, places great store on the 'company circle' as a structured way of giving a sense of 'ownership'. The company has a constitution which contains its mission, vision and values and was ratified by staff members in 2009; and everyone in the company votes (on a one-member, one-vote basis) on all major decisions, including the company's annual budget, major variations to the budget and the election of its leadership. The company calls this process 'the company circle' and it 'is a major defining point of their workplace democracy approach because it emphasizes that certain decisions should be owned by the entire company'[21]. The rationale for this is that 'The organization is the sum of all its parts and stakeholders, not just the board or key shareholders and there are certain decisions that should be made by the whole organization ... It's not about eliminating hierarchy entirely; sometimes it's about reversing the hierarchy'[22]. Other organisations build in democratic spaces that are created temporarily for short periods, that suspend existing hierarchical structures and that 'foster stronger unity, creating informal ties that facilitate sustaining participative approaches' (Flowers, 2008, p 15).

This chapter has examined trends towards the creation of participation and meaning in organisational and community settings and identified three key drivers: instrumental (which includes longstanding perceptions of the benefits of participation and recent responses to qualitative changes in the complexity of business and society); expressive (which is about identity and individuality and has communal and spiritual dimensions); and participation (where differing relationships to authority are evident in trends such as monitory democracy and the development of new modes of governance). The next chapter focuses on the theme of entrepreneurialism, which interconnects with these trends, including the bubbling up of aspirations to meaning, and which also reflects the duality of control and autonomy (discussed in Chapter 4) as entrepreneurialism contains both radical possibilities for agency as well as subjecting people to particular kinds of demands and expectations.

THREE

Radicalising entrepreneurialism

Screw it, let's do it! (Richard Branson, 2007)

A politics of entrepreneurship is ... not (only) about 'the economic benefits certain successful entrepreneurs bring to our region or country, but about how citizens co-create the society they take part in ... Entrepreneurship can ... make a difference ... where existing situations have stiffened, in all fields of a society where we feel involved and want to contribute ... There is a saying that all the beauty of winter can be found in any single snowflake. Perhaps ... we have the potential to find the beauty of entrepreneurship in almost any interaction we see. Indeed, the space of entrepreneurship in society is about nothing less than beauty. (Chris Steyaert and Jerry Katz, 2004, p 182)

Entrepreneurialism and entrepreneurial leadership have come to be viewed as essential to improving the capability of organisations to innovate and improve performance in the face of 21st-century demands and turbulent times. Innovation is typically seen as 'the core capability for organizational success' (Gratton, 2007, p 5). As one educational analyst puts it, entrepreneurialism is advocated as 'a bet on human ingenuity', its 'secret' of success being 'to summon the best within us' (Hess, 2010, p 151). Governments, pulled by the promise of entrepreneurialism as an invigorator of organisational success and by perceived pressures of global economic competition, put a high priority on enhancing enterprise. Creating a more enterprising society has become an integral part of the dominant policy discourse in the UK to plug what is seen as an 'enterprise gap' (HM Treasury, 2004, 2008), with a clarion call being issued most recently to 'light the fires of entrepreneurialism in every corner of our country' (Cameron, 2010).

In the post-bureaucratic organisation (Maravelias, 2009), organisational members are expected to behave as if they are entrepreneurs and 'owners' of the organisation they work for. As a consequence, a new organisational and policy actor is being fashioned: the entrepreneurial subject, acting 'upon one's self and others in a specific, calculative and maximizing way'; and the employee is being 're-imagined ... as a strange hybrid, a mixture between "employee" and "entrepreneur" – an "entreployee"' (Weiskopf and Steyaert, 2009, pp 185, 186). This hybridisation is apparent in education, with the 'teacher of tomorrow' dubbed an 'edupreneur' (Breakspear et al, 2008, p 13). Such neologisms are symptoms of the pressure in the public sector over the past three decades to become more like private business and to operate in more market-like settings. The traditional public bureaucracy has come under sustained criticism, through works such as the seminal book by Osborne and Gaebler (1992), and the old regime of bureau–professionalism (Clarke and Newman,1997), in which the administrators and the professionals have their separate spheres of expertise, has given way to the advances of new public management (Osborne, 2010). Accountability – framed as the application of generic managerial techniques and measurement of effectiveness by quantitative targets and league tables based on these measures – has aimed to subject employees to the dynamics of market-like pressures. New creative thinkers and doers, and more agile organisations, are sought in order to create and replicate innovative solutions that go beyond, or creatively refashion, the traditional, accepted ways of doing things: excellence can be nurtured 'by keeping the field open to the skilful application of old models as well as smart efforts to leverage new knowledge, management practices, or technology' (Hess, 2010, p 150). Though for some this has not gone far enough[1], the political drive has been to make public sector organisations more flexible and much more entrepreneurial, and to re-align them around private ethics[2]. Consequently, the momentum of change is away from traditional hierarchy and bureau–professionalism towards *bureau-enterprise culture* characterised by:

- a dominating instrumental rationality embodied in flexibilised sets of organisational roles;
- a more entrepreneurial and consumer-responsive culture;
- a belief in flatter hierarchies, combined with reformed hierarchical structure and bureaucratic procedures;
- a visionary zeal to achieve system and organisational goals;
- the systematic monitoring and measurement of performance in formally rational ways.

One of the characteristics of bureau-entrepreneurial culture is the stress on the emotional aspect of leadership and behaviour. To put it in sociological terms, in order to maximise organisational effectiveness, instrumental action has to be supplemented by affectual action – that is, emotionally driven activity 'determined by the actor's specific affects and feeling states' (Weber, 1978, pp 24-5). The implication is that policies need to be followed which influence and shape those 'affects and feeling states' so as to obtain the kind of commitment and actions required to reach organisational and system goals. The entrepreneurial discourse, with its celebration of energy, dedication and continual change, answers a perceived need to make improving effectiveness and efficiency a constant organisational drive. Three factors associated with entrepreneurialism are particularly important in understanding its attraction and why it holds such promise for policy makers and organisational leaders: its focus on *energy, creative visualisation of change*, and the down-to-earth and essential activity of *mobilising resources*.

Generic entrepreneurialism

The expanding entrepreneurial discourse begs the question of what entrepreneurialism – or entrepreneurship[3] – is. If its applicability is seen as growing into new areas (du Gay, 2004), across the private, public and the third sectors, does its meaning also change and expand? One answer is to view entrepreneurialism as a generic phenomenon, defined in terms of skills and attitudes that are highly transferable. As a quality of an individual or of a systemic or organisational culture, generic entrepreneurialism is definable as the predisposition to and practice of achieving valued ends by creating, taking or pursuing opportunities for change and innovation and finding new resources or utilising in new ways existing resources (financial, material and human). Entrepreneurialism 'requires taking a view of the future, generating a vision around an idea, and then mobilising resources to achieve it' (Judge, 2005, p 53).

The generic approach is operationalised in terms of skills and tendencies such as risk taking, creativity, problem solving, teamwork, determination, achievement motivation, autonomy and internal locus of control, and in the school curriculum gives rise to attitude- and skills-focused enterprise teaching (Deuchar, 2007; Chell, 2009; Woods and Woods, 2011). In the running of schools, the case is made for a 'new enterprise logic' in education, with schooling being seen as 'an undertaking that is difficult, complicated and at times risky, often calling for daring activity... and is thrilling in its execution' (Caldwell, 2006, p 76). Schools are being called upon to value 'creative entrepreneurial risk-taking leadership' that is student-focused and capable of engaging in 'significant, systematic and sustained change' (p 194); and to engage in 'daring and disruptive changes' (Hargreaves and Shirley, 2009, p 109). The goal is constant improvement (Ofsted, 2002), by processes which 'constantly' generate and increase knowledge 'inside and outside the organization' (Fullan, 2001, p 8). A more entrepreneurial culture is valued as a way of overcoming the alleged stiffness, lethargy and unresponsiveness of traditional bureaucracy (du Gay, 2000), and is integral to the forging of bureau-enterprise culture which combines the dynamism of the private sector with the values of public bureaucracy.

Ethical questions are begged, if not necessarily answered, by the expansion of the entrepreneurial discourse. The question 'lurking in the background' – because entrepreneurialism lacks 'an account of ethics' – is the 'goodness of any social innovation' (Jones and Spicer, 2009, pp 145, 146). Questions of higher order values (social justice and larger purposes) have not been built into the concept of entrepreneurialism from its beginnings and notions of entrepreneurial practice can all too easily leave out difficult, critical probing on what is meant by the 'good' and 'ethical' life and how organisational and systemic structures and innovations support or hinder this.

Substantive meanings of entrepreneurialism

The practice and study of entrepreneurialism, however, is not devoid of ethical concerns and values. According to Campbell Jones and Andre Spicer (2009, p 146), much work to understand social and institutional entrepreneurship – by making 'social and institutional innovation into instrumental matters, so that we can know *how to do it*' – is out of step with the needs of social entrepreneurs on the ground who are 'actively concerned about *why* they are seeking to change social institutions'.

Practical interpretations of entrepreneurialism are often imbued with substantive meanings. In a study of Scottish teachers, Ross Deuchar found that they associated enterprise with business-related projects, but over time took a more socially orientated view, showing an increasing 'emphasis on the need for community perspectives, fair trading issues and a focus on global perspectives' that fitted well with their 'overall aims for school education as being about personal, social and moral development' (Deuchar, 2006, p 540). The co-operative movement in the UK is producing materials and support for schools which explains the value of cooperative enterprise as a different model of business, one which is 'owned and democratically controlled by [its] members', 'balance[s] the need to make a profit with the necessity of strengthening communities and protecting the environment'[4], and places the highest priority on doing business in ways that are ethical and values-led[5].

The expression of different aims, meanings and values through entrepreneurialism is apparent across diverse sectors – private and public. Entrepreneurialism may be promoted by business, but it is also in an ambiguous relationship with modernity. It launches into bureaucratic organisations and governance an impetus to innovation, change and lateral thinking that is in tension with the certainties and order of rational procedures. Entrepreneurial and bureaucratic rationalities vie with each other. Reflective advocates of greater entrepreneurialism candidly admit that 'the truth is that entrepreneurship is a headache' because it presumes that 'even smart, thoughtful, well-trained experts cannot anticipate needs, develop solutions, or ensure progress in orderly fashion' and many new enterprising ventures and ideas will fail (Hess, 2010, pp 150-1). In addition to this, entrepreneurs subvert or find ways round existing authority. The imperative for the entrepreneurial organisational member is to challenge the traditional and bureaucratically honoured ways of doing things and, therefore, to be motivated by their own initiative, conviction and sense of values and purpose. Entrepreneurship 'implies a revolt against fixed and stable hierarchies ... [and] hitherto taken-for-granted rules and the active creation of new ones, altering the lives of those involved' (Beyes, 2009, p 95).

Entrepreneurialism therefore has radical potentialities. Entrepreneurialism can be challenging to power, forging and tapping into democratically based collective energies. It engages the a-rational side of being (Beyes, 2009; Warren and Anderson, 2009) and shares to some degree the postmodernist challenge to the Weberian thesis of rationalisation[6]. Its potential is to allow openness to new ways of understanding meaning, purpose and ethics. It celebrates *agency* (personal and collective) and is capable of reinterpretation as a dynamic model of change through democratic participation in and by communities and organisations.

The issue is in what values, worldview and priorities for change are different versions of entrepreneurialism embedded. I formulated a typology to chart some of the key differences in interpretation (Woods et al, 2007a; Woods and Woods, 2009), based on literature on entrepreneurialism and, particularly, the burgeoning attention being given to social entrepreneurialism. Three of the types (business, social, public) are familiar in literature on organisational innovation and change; the fourth (cultural) is an additional type, identifying a distinct form of entrepreneurialism (Figure 3.1). In this chapter, I develop below the notion of democratic entrepreneurialism, which is a particular configuration of public and cultural entrepreneurialism.

Figure 3.1: Typology of entrepreneurialism

Business entrepreneurialism is concerned with achieving competitive advantage and success as defined in business culture – in short, innovation with a *competitive mission*. It involves application and advancement of values, principles and practices of the private business sector, which is 'greedy for new things' and where innovation is perceived as 'the healthy, normal, necessary course of action' (Drucker, 1985, p 142). Entrepreneurial success is measured systematically against market criteria, ultimately sales and profits.

The term 'social entrepreneurship' is used in a large variety of ways (Dees, 2001: Roper and Cheney, 2005). In the typology, it is distinguished from public entrepreneurialism and defined as innovation with a *social mission* aimed at making a specific change with a social benefit to a targeted population – for example, reducing disadvantage, deprivation and social exclusion through schemes such as provision of housing, support for learning and self-help, and bringing health care to deprived areas. It consists of action and drive, originating outside the traditional public sector (the private and third sectors), which mobilise ideas, practices and resources and utilise entrepreneurial flexibility and creativity.

> Social entrepreneurs can be anyone; young or old, educated or illiterate, an accountant or unemployed ... Muhammad Yunus gave entrepreneurs in areas of poverty access to loans with his micro credit. Jamie Oliver is transforming the lives of young people by giving them careers through his restaurants. Emma Spiegler changes lives by developing support for young people affected by someone else's addiction ... The variety is endless. (Emberton, 2010)

There is much interest in social entrepreneurialism for several reasons. It offers enormous promise for politicians assailed by high expectations and finite public resources; it appeals to the logic that sees capitalist rationality as the most successful model for bringing about human advancement (notwithstanding the knocks to the market model, already noted); it tends not to challenge or ask fundamental questions about structural inequalities embedded in the existing system and assumptions of income distribution; and it harnesses the potential for affectual action, giving a drive and energy to ideas for increasing the social good.

> Social entrepreneurs sit up and take action, they do things most people don't even think about. They are more than just active citizens; they are entrepreneurial-minded passionate individuals who change the world around them. They are people driving real-life solutions for society through the form of social ventures. Social entrepreneurs have real-life solutions ... fuelled by personal drive ... A social entrepreneur is someone who recognises a social problem and uses enterprising approaches to organise, create and manage a venture to make social change a reality. (Emberton, 2010)

Cultural entrepreneurialism advances ideas and values that give purpose to individual and social action – in short, innovation with a *mission to bring meaning*. This is concerned with creating and taking opportunities to innovate so as to advance values and understanding of the deepest importance to personal and social development and to sustain certain norms and values. Its focus is on meaning which gives purpose to individual and social action. Examples include the foundation of the Salvation Army (which is also an example of social entrepreneurialism as it was established to give aid to the poor as well as to preach the gospels), taking opportunities provided by the Academies programme in England to sponsor schools with alternative educational philosophies and widen their accessibility, as with the Steiner Hereford Academy, and finding creative ways of raising ecological awareness[7].

There is no agreed meaning of public entrepreneurialism in the literature (Bartlett and Dibben, 2002), though considerably less attention is given to this concept than social entrepreneurialism. One way of defining it is as the pursuit and development of innovative ways of providing high quality public service 'products' (Zerbinati and Souitaris, 2005). There are, however, distinctive features to a civic, public orientated form of entrepreneurialism which gives a central place to values such as equality and public welfare. Public entrepreneurialism involves asking the fundamental questions about meaning, purpose, ethics and power that are often lacking in thinking about social entrepreneurialism[8]. The typology, therefore, draws a clear distinction between social and public forms of entrepreneurialism. Public entrepreneurialism involves the application of entrepreneurial flexibility and creativity in order to operationalise, advance and sustain public aims and values, which include public welfare, equality, accountability and respect for diversity (Woods and Woods, 2004). In other words, public entrepreneurialism involves innovation with a *public and community-orientated mission*. Public entrepreneurialism is, therefore, more complex than improvements in a specific product or service.

The typology of business, social, cultural and public entrepreneurialism has been used in research with schools and found to be useful in orientating to different meanings of entrepreneurialism (see Green, E., 2009; Slater, 2010). Whilst it may look like a neat instrument for classification, the typology is a device for abstracting from the complexities of practice and helping to make sense of people's complex and fluid constructions of meanings. Attitudes and actions cannot necessarily be neatly classified. Constructions of meanings around entrepreneurialism interconnect and overlap the categories of the typology and need to be placed in the context of underlying motivations and principles (Woods and Woods, forthcoming). Box 2.1 gives an example of entrepreneurialism as combining the go–getting dynamic and flexibility associated with business, with a social goal of enhancing opportunities in state funded education.

Box 2.1: Case study: entrepreneurship enriches teaching

The 'financial genius' of headteacher Sylvia Libson has allowed Oakington Manor primary school to extend and enrich its teaching. Courtesy of her entrepreneurial skills, the large primary near Wembley Stadium generates substantial sums from letting. The building is almost always open and no corner is left unused, says Simrita Singh, the senior deputy head. As a result the 720-pupil primary is able to employ support teachers for each of the year groups, essentially meaning one additional teacher for every three classes. Sometimes they work with groups of children outside the classroom, sometimes they team teach inside – it depends on what the children need. With two teachers knowing each class inside out, continuity and progression are guaranteed, says Simrita Singh. There is the flexibility for staff to move between being class teachers and support teachers. And some teachers have moved from the classroom to become specialists. Oakington Manor employs four specialists – in PE, modern languages, ICT and music. Three of the four were grown in-house. The ICT specialist is a former class teacher, as is the

---

PE specialist who now also runs courses for the local authority. The languages specialist is a recent development. 'Two years ago a class teacher said he was keen to learn Spanish. We supported him and he is now absolutely brilliant at teaching the language right through from reception through to Year 6,' says Simrita Singh. 'While we do have subject leaders to support class teachers where they need it, we would love to have specialists in all subjects. The children get a much richer experience.' (Hofkins and Northen, 2009, p 37, reproduced by kind permission of the University of Cambridge)

Conceptions of enterprise in education are usually imbued to some degree with some sense of its having an ethical and communal purpose. Analysis of data from an inner city Academy in England, which I undertook jointly[9], found a predominant focus on generic entrepreneurialism in the approach developed by senior leadership and staff. At the same time, other, more specific meanings were evident in the curriculum and the leadership activity of staff. There was a strong undertow towards business entrepreneurialism, with successful business people being projected as role models and students encouraged to see themselves as potential business entrepreneurs. Equally, views were expressed that showed a more public-orientated model of enterprise, concerned with helping to develop and sustain values such as community participation and social justice. Amongst students in the Academy, whilst enterprise was often associated with business and trading, there was also a strong philanthropic and ethical component in most constructions of meaning around enterprise. The data suggested that *individualistic* motivations to do with enterprise were likely to be found in a small minority. The large majority of students took a more *relational* perspective, which could be seen as taking two forms: a *relational/business view*, associating enterprise with business and trading *and* with a concern for others' welfare, feelings and quality of experience; or a 'purer' *relational view*, where enterprise is more specifically conceived in terms of altruistically orientated change and innovation motivated by the good it does for others. The picture that emerged was a complex one of different strands involved in the approach to enterprise. Reflection on the findings led us also to highlight that understandings of entrepreneurialism involve (explicit or implicit) 'architectonic' principles – i.e. principles which 'relate to the fundamental structuring elements of a person's overall view of life' (McLaughlin, 1996, p 12), which may be economistic, religious, democratic, spiritual or secular (or a mix of elements from more than one of these). The detailed content of these principles is crucial to how entrepreneurialism is operationalised. In light of the strands that emerged, it was proposed that constructions of entrepreneurialism are the product of different layers of meaning and of the weight and interpretations that people and organisations give to those layers: the significance placed on a broad concept of generic entrepreneurialism; the predominant motivational perspective (the emphasis given to individualistic or relational perspectives); the associations made between enterprise and values and practices connected with business, social, cultural or public approaches; and the nature of the architectonic principles underlying identity and practice. The levels of meaning are represented in Figure 3.2. Democratic entrepreneurialism emerges from a particular combination of meanings.

Figure 3.2: Levels of meaning around entrepreneurialism[10]

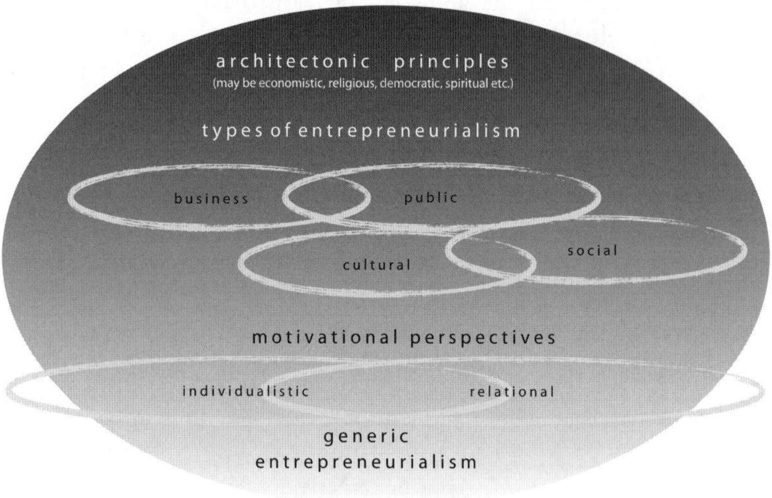

architectonic principles
(may be economistic, religious, democratic, spiritual etc.)

types of entrepreneurialism

business   public

cultural   social

motivational perspectives

individualistic   relational

generic
entrepreneurialism

Democratic entrepreneurialism

Entrepreneurship has begun to be developed as a model for 'innovative thinking, reorganizing the established and crafting the new across a broad range of settings and spaces and for a range of goals such as social change and transformation far beyond those of simple commerce and economic drive', becoming 'visible in multiple sites and spaces' (Steyaert and Katz, 2004, p 182). One example is a city-wide initiative, led by the city council, which is described as 'structured self-organisation' – that is, public leadership exercised to devise self-organised solutions (Leadbeater, 2006). Rewritten in a specific way and a critical spirit - with values of democracy, community, freedom and the search for meaning paramount – entrepreneurialism is capable of taking on a radically different meaning than that embedded in competitive individualism. This is exemplified in a series of events and books – 'movements in entrepreneurship' – which has sought to act as a 'disruption in the development of entrepreneurial studies' and to 'appropriate a place in the world of business schools' (Hjorth and Steyaert, 2009, p 1). In its most radicalised form, entrepreneurialism is the innovative and practical formation of conditions which nurture active participation, individuality, dispersion of freedoms to take initiative and the co-creation of meaning in which people are involved as whole human beings. It is my view that efforts to radicalise entrepreneurialism will benefit from defining it as the creation and renewal of holistic democracy. In this section, I therefore conceptualise and outline this form of radicalised entrepreneurship as democratic entrepreneurialism.

The idea of democratic entrepreneurialism (Figure 3.3) combines the drives to participation and expressive democracy encountered in Chapter 2. It brings together, therefore, public entrepreneurialism and a particular, holistic vision of cultural entrepreneurialism. As conceived here, democratic entrepreneurialism is grounded in the architectonic

Figure 3.3: Democratic entrepreneurialism

the quest for innovative change:

framed in... a fundamental view of people as capable of freedom, equality and substantive liberty, flourishing best in conditions of organic belonging (in other words, holistic democratic architectonic principles)

tapping... the energy, creative visualisation and mobilising capacity of entrepreneurialism

in service of... innovation to advance:

participation (power sharing and transforming dialogue), which includes
- challenging power and authority structures to enhance spaces and scope for participation, advance social justice and enable people's freedom of exploration and risk-taking (mindful of costs to others and the environment)
- openness and transparency (multiple communication flows) as opposed to a 'behind closed doors' approach
- transforming awareness through dialogue
- moving beyond masculine images of 'creative destruction', saying 'yes' to life-enhancing change

expressive democracy (holistic meaning and well-being), which includes
- finding and creating meaning by encouraging holistic knowledge goals, embodied learning and co-creation across boundaries
- living ethically and learning and growing as full human beings, giving expression to spiritual, artistic and creative impulses and rescuing the social and personal from being appendages to the market
- nurturing mindful practice (the capacity to be guided by aesthetic, affective and spiritual sensibilities, as well as cognitive knowledge), creating harmony and balance and a culture of care for the natural environment (connectedness)
- enjoying the intrinsic value of relationships and the warmth of human bonds (organic belonging)

principles underpinning holistic democracy. This grounding views people as not only fundamentally *equal and free* beings (principles that run through all conceptions of democracy) but also as living to their fullest where *substantive liberty* is able to thrive (fulfilling an inherent potential for growth – intellectual, aesthetic, spiritual, and so on) – that is, in conditions of *organic belonging* ('unity in diversity' that values both difference – cultural and individual – and the profound bond that connects human beings *qua* human beings and calls forth an acknowledgement of fundamental equality) (Woods, 2005). Democratic entrepreneurialism innovates in ways that place highest value on the flowering of the person and their *humanistic potential* in a social order in which they are actively and self-consciously engaged.

Thus, democratic entrepreneurialism is guided by a commitment to innovation which translates into practice the dimensions of holistic democracy – namely, power sharing and transforming dialogue (participation), and holistic meaning and well-being (expressive democracy). It harnesses the openness, creativity, energy and mobilising capabilities of the entrepreneurial mindset (which are the features of generic entrepreneurialism); and, crucially, it rewrites the driving aim of entrepreneurialism as innovation for *challenging power* (to create more equal relationships and opportunities for freedom and transforming dialogue) and *creating meaning and growth as full human beings*.

The impetus behind democratic entrepreneurialism is the generation of imaginative ways of advancing the sorts of organisational aims and practices associated with holistic democracy described in the 'degrees of democracy' analytical framework discussed in Chapter 8. This involves creating innovative opportunities and conditions for individual freedom, genuine community participation and democratic decision making; looking for ways to eradicate, avoid or mitigate repressive pressures, to work towards social justice, and to form spaces where authentic freedom can be exercised; encouraging multiple communication flows which create cultures of openness and transparency; and exploring innovative ways in which the personal and the social can be rescued from being an appendage to the market – from being an area of life to be seen in instrumental terms in which individuals make choices and conduct and educate themselves so as to better fit into the economic system. Democratic entrepreneurialism challenges the historical growth of the idea of a private world of individualism defined sharply against the public world dominated by the state, and gives life and energy to a civic realm which is neither subsumed within or subservient to the state, nor restricted to economistic relations and values, by creating 'new forms of sociality' (Hjorth and Bjerke, 2006, p 109). Rather than being a 'slave' or 'silent rebel', in post-bureaucratic systems the person 'emerges as an *opportunist* who must constantly fight against any form of subordination, even the subordination to his or her self' (Maravelias, 2009, p 26).

Radicalised entrepreneurship is a specific response to 'context-specific limitations ... a specific way of dealing with, and of *problematizing* and *transforming* them ... [by creating] distance to what is seen as normal and habitual ... [revealing] the becomingness of the world'. The point is to put to the fore a positive and life-affirming approach. Think not so much in terms of 'creative destruction' with its masculine and negative overtones, but in terms of grasping what the present is and imagining it otherwise, powered by experimentation and openness to new connections (Weiskopf and Steyaert, 2009, pp 196-7). Elannah Cramer, a senior company leader[11], puts it more prosaically, linking individuality, creativity and risk taking and talking about the people and environment she admires and associates with organisational democracy:

> ... people who are open and excited about making their own decisions, that don't need to be told, aren't sheep, but rather are excited to go out there and risk making a mistake and risk failing, in an environment in which failure is actually celebrated and not necessarily embraced for the failure itself but for the learning experiences that can come from that. I love the idea of a work environment in which people are allowed to be themselves and aren't afraid to just be themselves and bring their own strengths.

Democratised enterprise includes ensuring that entrepreneurialism moves beyond the masculine image it is often associated with of imposing change and conquest and that it develops entrepreneurial approaches that respect local and existing values and priorities whilst exploring the potentialities and issues of new ways of doing things (Lindgren and Packendorff, 2006). Key aims are the achievement of harmony and balance and a culture of care. Say 'no' to what negates life and limits the possibilities of life (Weiskopf and Steyaert, 2009, p 200); say 'yes' to the life-enhancing effects of discourses and practices that liberate people to aspire to their full human potential. Founded in the holistic democratic perspective, this means living ethically through the nurturing of mindful practice (Woods and Woods, 2009c), an approach to living in which the person is responsive to their aesthetic, affective and spiritual sensibilities, as well as cognitive knowledge, and to their integral connection to the natural environment. Entrepreneurial spaces that are democratised are potential areas to be, or to become oneself, in which it is possible to create roles which are 'open and generative' (Hjorth and Bjerke, 2006, p 101). These are areas where connected leadership and spirituality in organisational settings and networks can be, and are, found room. Democratic entrepreneurialism is not only about emotional commitment and energy, but draws from the deep well of personal and collective potentialities that are opened by fully embodied learning (discussed in Chapter 7).

This chapter has addressed entrepreneurialism as a pervasive theme in private and public sector change. The notion of bureau-enterprise culture describes the entrepreneurialising of traditional bureaucracies and ways of working, without the abandonment entirely of bureaucratic processes and relationships. The meaning of entrepreneurialism is not given, but is open to various interpretations, and is capable of a radicalisation that puts participation and aspirations to holistic meaning to the fore. This democratic entrepreneurialism is a great conceptual and practical resource for the adaptive strategies discussed in Chapter 6, because it offers a different narrative than individualistic entrepreneurship and harnesses energy, creative visualisation for change and the skills needed to mobilise resources in the service of larger purposes and co-creation for the greater good.

FOUR

The rise of plural control[1]

> [G]overnance is the positive acceptance of diversity by the state – pluralistic forms of organising, multiple lifestyle choices, flexible work patterns, free markets. It is therefore tempting to represent it simply as a straightforward and necessary adaptation to a changing world. In fact, it is not as easy as that. There may be an affinity between the flexible economy and social diversity, but the new technology and the politics of identity have different points of origin and do not necessarily work in unison. (Martin Albrow, 2001, p 164)

The 1988 Education Reform Act (ERA) in England was a turning point in educational policy. To put it in summary terms: before that, the system was conceived as a tripartite partnership model between central government, local education authorities and schools and the teaching profession, providing governance through the 'assumptions of professional expertise reinforced by the orderly controls of rational bureaucracy' (Ranson, 2008, p 205)[2]; from that point, central government took a much more active role through steering and direct intervention. Governments since then – Conservative, Labour and Coalition (the latter taking office in 2010, involving the Conservative and Liberal Democratic parties as partners) – have used their central role to give a specific character to the education system.

The 1988 ERA ushered in a national curriculum, a national system of student testing, publication of schools' test results in the form of league tables, a tougher regime of school inspections operated by a newly created organisation (the Office for Standards in Education, Ofsted), more open enrolment of pupils (giving parents the right to express a preference for which school their child should attend), funding of schools based on numbers of pupils, and devolution to schools of responsibility for managing their income. These were modified, but not altered in their essentials, by the Labour Government which took office in 1997, and since then there has been an extension and in some ways radical development of some of the key policy directions established by that time.

Central government extended its influence over pedagogy – through initiatives such as the national numeracy and literacy strategies in which schools were pressed to follow a particular teaching approach, and the promotion of priorities like personalised learning, where the particular needs and current knowledge of the individual learner is supposed to be at the centre the teaching strategy. The organisation and conditions of school staff (teaching and non-teaching) have been changed too, through a systematic process of 'workforce remodelling' driven by central government. This has been about shifting bureaucratic burdens away from teachers in order to free them up to focus on teaching; but the changes are also about creating a flexible and easily deployable workforce and making more visible the role of support staff, coordinating more effectively their work with that of teachers – thus raising issues about the position, status, cost and expertise of the teacher.

Diversity of schools has increased and continues to increase significantly through deliberate central government policy. Specialist schools (schools with an emphasis on or expertise in a particular curriculum area, such as business and enterprise, sport or language) have been created, and new kinds of faith schools, like Islamic schools, admitted into the state sector. A major policy strand is the enhanced role given to new actors in the state education system. A key example of this is the greatly increased involvement of the private sector through use of consultants and outsourcing (contracting service provision to private companies).

The creation of new types of school is at the forefront of moves to facilitate diversity, innovation and the blurring of the public/private boundary. In 2002, the first batch of a new organisational type of school – known as Academies – opened. Academies are state-funded schools. Outside the local authority system, they are intended to be innovative and entrepreneurial. When first introduced they usually replaced existing schools, and initially were meant to be opened in disadvantaged areas and to be a means of tackling stubborn educational inequalities. From 2010, the opportunity to convert to Academy status was offered to all state schools and the programme is part of the Coalition Government vision of 'freeing' education from unnecessary controls. Those opened under the Labour Government are managed by independent sponsors, such as businesses, faith groups, educational institutions (including universities and colleges) and charitable organisations. In the current system, the emphasis is on ensuring sponsors for 'low-performing schools' converting to Academy status: these are required to have a sponsor who, in the words of the Department for Education, 'will bring added drive, expertise and capacity'[3]. In fact, it is central to the

Coalition's school improvement strategy to ensure that schools deemed to be 'low-performing' convert to Academy status and to connect them to 'strong sponsors' and 'outstanding schools' (Department for Education, 2010, p 56). There is continuity between this and the Academy policy of the previous Labour Government, in that outside sponsors are seen as a force for change and a source of dynamism and expertise where improved performance is most needed.

The Coalition Government's cri de coeur is to give power back to the people through its policy of localism, and autonomy for schools is a driving rationale in its education policy. Amongst the first actions of the Coalition Government in 2010 were rapid moves to create more of these types of 'quasi-autonomous schools'; first, as we have seen, by extending the Academies programme: all state schools are invited to become Academies, with the aim of doubling the number of Academies during the academic year 2010/2011[4]. (By January 2011, there were 407 Academies, including 371 secondary school Academies, comprising 11% of all secondary schools in England; more than 200 had become Academies since September 2010[5].) Secondly, they aimed to do this through the creation of a new type of school – Free Schools – modelled on Sweden's Free Schools. These can be started and run by teachers, charities, parent groups, existing Academy sponsors and others. By November 2010, the first 25 Free Schools were announced, the aim being that a number of these should open in 2011[6]. The Free Schools programme includes University Technology Colleges (formed in partnership with universities, colleges and businesses, specialising in subjects such as engineering) and Studio Schools ('14–19 institutions with an entrepreneurial and vocational focus, catering for students of all abilities who are disengaged by an entirely academic curriculum') (Department for Education, 2010, pp 60-1).

Additional to Academies and Free Schools is another organisational innovation, begun under Labour, which is the opportunity for state schools to adopt trust status. Existing schools can apply to become Trust Schools, which are state funded and supported by a charitable trust of external partners, including further and higher education, business and the voluntary sector. By August 2010, there were over 340 Trust Schools (primary, secondary and special)[7]. Trust partners include companies such as Land Rover, the children's charity Barnardo's, the Midlands Co-operative Society and universities such as the University of Exeter and Liverpool John Moores University.

Control and autonomy

Current policies on 'quasi-autonomous' schools are very much an extension and enhancement of policy initiatives begun by the previous government. With this there is a continuation of certain tensions, in particular that between autonomy and control. The waves of reform over the past years constitute a complex, dual process of centralisation and enhancement of autonomy. The Coalition provides a new twist with its stress on freeing schools and, in the words of Michael Gove, Secretary of State for Education, 'a determination to give school leaders more power and control'[8]. 'Ministers are committed to giving schools more freedom from unnecessary prescription and bureaucracy. Ministers have always made clear their intentions to make changes to the National Curriculum, to ensure a focus on the basics and to give teachers more flexibility than the proposed new primary curriculum offered'[9]. The challenge for a government committed to giving more freedom is to step back from the powers that it has, which have grown up over many years, and to restrain itself from defining in growing detail the 'basics' that are to be prescribed.

Central control

Central government powers have been enhanced (at the expense of local government powers over education), and state-level priorities and rationales cascaded down the system. Central control has been exercised through *content change*, i.e. modifications and transformation in curriculum, pedagogy and so on, through both direct and indirect pressure from central government. The rationale for this fits with a *quality control* model of governance, in which government seeks 'to secure some control over the quality of key school processes and products' through bureaucratic 'laid-down rules and requirements' and 'set procedures, controls and monitoring arrangements' (Glatter and Woods, 1995, p 161). There are prescriptive elements to attempts to bring about content change, such as the national curriculum, pupil tests and assessment and regular school inspections by central government inspectors. From 2006/07, central government took to itself (away from local authorities) the power to determine the level of funding allocated to individual state schools (Levačić, 2008, p 230). There has also been a host of initiatives which, whilst not being statutory requirements on schools, seek to shape the discourse, identities and practices of education. These include the creation of the National College for Leadership of Schools and Children's Services and schemes that come with earmarked funds and much persuasive back-up from central government, its agencies and consultants to encourage schools to take them up (p 228), such as the national literacy and numeracy strategies.

Initiatives such as these are aimed at shaping the 'deep structure' of education, the 'underpinning cultural epistemology which quite literally defines the taken-for-granted assumptions about education at every level' (Broadfoot et al, 2000, p 206). The purpose of education has been framed principally as a means of developing in young people the skills and attitudes, including a more entrepreneurial mindset, required to ensure a competitive economy; supplemented by attention to development of citizenship and learning the difference between 'right and wrong', especially during periods of 'moral panic' generated by incidents of violence in society. Although citizenship is now a statutory curriculum subject, it does not necessarily generate critical understanding of issues of social justice (Fielding, 2009). Generally, at national level, deeper conceptions of education have been eclipsed, and schools are most strongly judged against examination grades and test scores. Although nationally there was a period of activity aimed at developing spiritual development in schools in the mid-1990s, this came to an abrupt end when government decided to subsume spiritual and moral development within higher priority curriculum areas of citizenship and PSHE (personal, social and health education) (Woods, G.J., 2003).

The second way that central control is manifest is through *structural change*. A key component of this is bringing in new organisational structures, new agents of change and new relationships in order to facilitate enterprise, innovation and the dissolution of traditional boundaries of education (Woods et al, 2007a; Woods, 2010b). A critical innovation is structural reform through the creation of 'quasi-independent' state schools, such as Academies, Free Schools and Trust Schools. These are at the leading edge of change which brings private organisations, groups and individuals into influential roles in the public education system. They are controversial, with Academies for example being criticised for taking schooling out of the local democratic framework and transferring too much influence to unaccountable sponsors. The scale and complexity of private participation in state education – through sponsoring of schools, contracting out of public functions, the increased use of private consultants and so on – has grown markedly (Ball, 2007, 2008b), leading to 'an incremental process of breaking up established assumptions and modes of operation and taken for granted practices and replacing these with new "freedoms", new players and new kinds of relationships and new forms of service delivery', so that 'the private sector is now thoroughly intertwined in the day-to-day business of decision-making, infrastructural development, capacity building and services delivery' (Ball, 2008b, pp 195, 196). The outcome of this centrally driven change is a shift of control and influence – 'control of education seeping from the public to the corporate sector' (Ranson, 2008, p 206) and to other groups.

The degree of that shift is, however, difficult to specify. Certainly what can be seen is a sustained change in the character of the English education system as a result of central government's ability to exercise power and influence through the mobilisation of both material resources (which include legislative change and funding allocations) and symbolic resources (which include agenda-setting and shaping the discourse about education)[10]. The extensive consultations and research of the Cambridge Primary Review in England found 'widespread and growing disenchantment with the extent to which government and its agencies have tightened their grip on what goes on in local authorities and schools since 1989, and particularly since 1997. Centralisation was the key complaint' (Hofkins and Northen, 2009, p 40).

Autonomy

Waves of reforms have also generated a mix of policies aimed at, or rhetorically advocating, autonomy. A major component of this are reforms that attempt to replicate a *competitive market governance* model (Glatter and Woods, 1995), i.e. the creation of a market-like environment in which schools are intended to act more like small or medium-size businesses responsive to consumer preferences. A key structural change in the creation of such a quasi-market is the principle of student-led funding which has underpinned allocation of resources to schools since 1988. The competitive environment for schools has undoubtedly increased as a result of policies advancing the competitive model.

A second major component is made up of changes which in different ways empower, or are advocated as empowering, educational stakeholders. Some of this is consistent with a *local empowerment model* of governance, which enhances opportunities for parents and the local community to be involved and participate in decision making (Glatter, 2003). Strongly to the fore have been changes which follow a *school empowerment model* of governance whereby authority is devolved to the school on finance, staffing and other issues (Glatter, 2003). Financial delegation to schools, for example, represented a real and significant shift (Levačić, 2008, pp 222, 224). More recently too there is an increased emphasis on 'professional empowerment', in which schools are explicitly encouraged to lead reform and increasing numbers of senior professionals are enabled to give system leadership (Hopkins, 2007, pp 169-70).

Caldwell celebrates England as a leading nation in adopting the self-managing school model, which at its simplest calls for schools 'to determine goals, formulate policies, make annual plans, allocate resources, and implement plans of learning and teaching, and evaluate outcomes' (Caldwell, 2006, p 18). Indeed, England is going beyond the original model, according to Caldwell, by which he has in mind developments such as building on internal self-management to blur external boundaries and connect with local communities, agencies, businesses and so on – in the manner of extended schools, for example (Caldwell, 2006, p 25). Caldwell's perspective is not one, however, that confronts the issues of managerialism and economism that more critical analysts have identified as integral to the policy changes in England.

A plural model

It is clear that there can be no simple celebration of enhanced autonomy. In line with an overarching emphasis on network governance, which deploys a mix of markets, hierarchy and networks, there are, inherent in the English education system's changes, strands of both control and autonomy. Policies that can be seen as enhancing autonomy have to be understood in relation to and in the context of the centralising framework. Educational professionals and schools are constructed within the changes emanating from the centre that have sought to change content and bring about structural change.

The governance frame created by central government has opened spaces and opportunities for different kinds of agency through its 'empowerment' agenda and the introduction of new players as sponsors and partners of schools, by no means all of whom are from the business sector. There is a great deal of activity from a variety of non-business groups in taking advantage of opportunities to sponsor or partner Academies, Free Schools and Trust Schools. The promotion of localism, discussed in the following chapter, also sets a different rhetorical space for local groups wanting to become involved. This suggests that a further, emerging governance model for the school education system can be discerned: *plural controlled schooling*. Plural controlled schooling is characterised by multiple sources of control and influence on education. Whilst central government retains significant levers of control, there is also a multiplication of educational players and partners, drawn from business and other sectors. These are not necessarily or typically local community stakeholders. Many have their roots beyond the community in which the school is situated. This is distinctive, therefore, from the local empowerment model. New educational players may have their base in geographical areas away from the school, have a national or international presence, and be from a different socio-economic environment than either the school or its local community (such as higher or further education, the private sector, faith groups, or the charitable and voluntary sector). The emphasis in plural controlled schooling is on diversity of sources of control and influence, the consequent necessity for networks and partnerships, and on processes of relationship-building between educational players which involve negotiation and attention to the nurturing of connections across traditional local community, organisational and sector boundaries.

What is driving the move towards plural controlled schooling? The emergence of plural controlled schooling is bound up with the policy trajectory of the third way. It is both a product of the third way and a force for change that presses towards a different meta-governance frame. The third way can be seen as an attempt (whatever one's view of its success or otherwise in doing so) to face two fundamental questions[11] – namely:

1. What alternative exists which enables avoidance of subservience to capitalism and markets on the one hand and the command-and-control state (through forms of welfarism, socialism and communism) on the other?
2. How can the Weberian challenges of rationalisation and disenchantment be addressed in contemporary times? (See Woods, 2010a.)

The modernising agenda pursued in the 1990s and into the new century aimed to alter radically the old regime of bureau-professionalism, in which the administrators and the professionals have their separate spheres of expertise (Clarke and Newman, 1997). New Labour since 1997 attempted to chart a new way between what it saw as the old dichotomy between state control and individualistic autonomy, summarised by Tony Blair, Prime Minister from 1997 to 2007:

> There will be no return to the old centralised command and control systems, which stifled innovation and responsibility, and we reject the creation of bureaucratic and pointless internal markets. Instead we favour partnerships at local

level, with investment tied to targets and measured outcomes, with national standards but local freedom to manage and innovate. (Blair, 1998, p 15)

Current Coalition policy openly acknowledges its debt to Tony Blair – 'it is a pity that [his] trajectory was stopped', says the Secretary of State for Education[12]. Plural controlled schooling is a logical policy direction to pursue from the basis of a third way belief in the entrepreneurial dynamism of private business. As a model of governance it follows the promise of entrepreneurialism. Professionalism is recast around the idea of the entrepreneurial leader, aping private sector rationality. Entrepreneurial leadership is identified as a key issue for the successful development of Academies (Davies with Macaulay, 2006), and the kind of leadership it entails is integral to the system redesign being applied to schools (Hargreaves, 2008, p 4). Bringing in different players and agents of change through plural controlled schooling is another dimension of the agenda to engender entrepreneurial dynamism in the public sector of education.

A further way of looking at the development of plural controlled schooling is to see it as a response to certain of the problems that the third way has steadily run into. In summary, the following are the main problems that have been identified with the third way:

- the limitations of the private sector as a model for the public sector, including the inapplicability of private sector techniques (Osborne, 2010, p 4)[13], and concerns about the weakening of a distinctively public ethos with values and priorities beyond those of business;
- too much faith in technocratic solutions (the 'engineering' approach which was noted in the Introduction leads to 'technocratic distractions' which become 'more subtle and more diffuse' – Hargreaves and Shirley, 2009, p 40);
- narrowing of public service focus and quality, associated with technocracy; too much of an intra-organisational focus; too little on inter-organisational working (Osborne, 2010, p 4);
- too much emphasis on simulated, heightened emotions to drive motivation, leading to 'a carnival of collegiality' and 'hyperactive professionalism' (Hargreaves and Shirley, 2009, p 41);
- too much central control (the 'path of autocracy' – Hargreaves and Shirley, 2009, p 23) and the inherent deficiencies of micro-management; failure to live up to the promises in terms of delivery, including the stubborn continuation of social and educational inequalities.

Third way policy was not a tightly defined phenomenon, either in theory or practice. Some of these problems and challenges were recognised by its policy leaders, such as the importance of inter-agency working and the value of collaboration between schools (Woods et al, 2007b). On the other hand other policies, especially the reliance on central initiatives, were consistent themes and came to be more and more questioned. This is where plural controlled schooling has an attraction as it promises a way of moving from tight central control and of tackling intractable problems in terms of delivery (though it certainly is not a coherent answer to the diverse issues raised by third way policies). A momentum has grown concerning the inherent problems of micro-management, recognising that the (apparently) more business-like way of disciplining education is not what is needed for the modern economy: that 'while standardization, micromanagement and tightened inspection systems may ... have been adopted in large part as a consequence of global pressures, it is likely that they are exactly the opposite of what is required to meet the challenges of this global future' (Bottery, 2004, p 86). Fear and 'punitive accountability' will not get you very far, as Michael Fullan (2008, p 13) concludes succinctly: perhaps it will reap 'short-term and fleeting results', but '[b]ullying backfires when it comes to complex change'. Central direction alone is unable to achieve the goals (like raising standards and narrowing the educational achievement gap between social groups) that the centre sets itself: 'top-down approaches to reform based on short-term target setting' yield little success (Hopkins, 2007, p 24). The Cambridge Primary Review's consideration of national testing, for example, leads it to conclude:

> the evidence is mixed. Claims about improvements in reading, science and numeracy are, up to a point, reasonably secure – though they are based on Year 6 test scores which represent a very narrow concept of standards. Against this positive ... [there is] evidence of the loss of a broad and balanced curriculum; the stress that testing inflicts on teachers, parents and children; the limited impact of the expensive literacy strategy; and the failure to close the achievement gap. (Hofkins and Northen, 2009, p 40)

Moreover, not only has the entitlement to a 'broad and balanced curriculum' been compromised, it is possible that 'because standards in the basics and the availability of a broad and balanced curriculum have been shown empirically to be linked, the narrowing of the curriculum in pursuit of standards in "the basics" may have had the opposite result to that intended, *depressing* standards in "the basics" rather than raising them' (Alexander, 2010a, p 6).

Signs have been apparent in England of the target-driven culture having run its course, with mandatory national testing in England being significantly reduced, a head of steam growing for curriculum reform and increasing opportunities for creativity and flexibility, and evidence of creative change taking place in some schools, and renewed interest in the democratic role of school governors[14]. The Specialist Schools and Academies Trust has been pursuing a remodelling of education – 'system redesign' – which owes more to teacher-led innovation and 'Wikipedia' style modes of organisation than top-down change (Hargreaves, 2008). The leader of a federation of schools describes it as 'a culture shift' which, at its core, 'is the belief that the next steps in school transformation will be shared across the school system and not from the government of the day down'[15]. Change is driven by networks, 'often short lived and without traditional hierarchies of power and control' (Vacher, 2008, p 33), and by use of interactive, web-based technologies, which includes students working together in groups and councils within their schools and in partnership with other schools: the idea of 'co-construction' is to the fore in the redesigned system as students are recognised as 'a major resource in the redesign of learning, schooling and leadership' (Vacher, 2008, p 29).

The policy trajectory set by the third way led to a recognition (through analysis of its own performative measures) that educational inequalities were stubbornly continuing; and gave it an apparent way of addressing the problem of central control and micro-management – namely by following the promise of entrepreneurialism and forging a culture of innovation. The move to pluralism and further celebration of innovation and enterprise in some ways reinforced some of these problems (such as continuing the privileging of private business concepts and language) and in other ways opened possibilities to challenge others (such as reliance on centralised views and knowledge and narrowness of conceptions of educational achievement, by enabling different players to enter state education). Conceptualising the system that can be seen as emerging from this trajectory of change, and setting out critiques of such a possible paradigm shift, is the subject of the next chapter.

FIVE

A different view: organic meta-governance

> [U]nless the paradigm at the heart of the culture is changed
> there will be no lasting change. (Richard Seel, 2000, p 3)

A progressive response to the structural changes in the education system requires a transformation in the way we relate to and conceive the system. The creation of more sponsored and quasi-independent schools brings dangers of fragmentation and subjection of education to private interests. These remain, nevertheless, within the socialised sphere of relationships, i.e. within a sphere that remains in public ownership and/or funded collectively by state finance. The system being created is not a monolithic vehicle for business values, but an arena where contending influences and ideals are being played out.[1] The policy developments we are in the midst of are a response to the limitations of a centralised socialised system – not socialised systems per se: '... the principal cause of the failure of what we might call the social democratic model to achieve its objectives is not the size of the state but the intellectual framework in which it operates' (Ormerod, 2010, p 10).[2] We need, therefore, to 'think constructively beyond the pressures of the present', as Stephen Ball observes, and 'to struggle to think differently about education policy before it is too late' (Ball, 2007, p 191). From a school improvement perspective, David Hargreaves argues, 'In an era of diminishing centralisation, accelerating the rate and depth of school improvement ... requires a new vision' (Hargreaves, 2010, p 3).

The dynamic of the emerging system is a self-organising one – a recasting of the mutualist tradition (Rothschild and Whitt, 1986/2009, p 15) in a systems context, which involves individual and organisational actors who bring diverse kinds of capital. It is bubbling up in various ways, from diverse perspectives. One way is through the initiatives, such as those promoting 'system redesign', alluded to in the previous chapter. Another is that of community organising, which in the US shows 'how positive educational change often starts beneath or beyond government policy', in church basements or union offices, on street corners or the internet, and 'how parents and communities can be so much more than objects of political intervention or recipients of government services' (Hargreaves and Shirley, 2009, p 62). Richard Hatcher makes a socialist case for local, community involvement in the new diversity of schooling. It is a way of promoting mass participation where people feel they can make a difference; and new and different approaches to challenging social inequalities in education need to be tried out locally to see what succeeds: 'the potential benefits of "bottom-up diversity" (as against centrally driven diversity) resulting from local popular participation greatly outweigh the dangers' (Hatcher, 2009).

There is an overlap between the political left and right that can and needs to be exploited, continuing in a new phase the striving to move 'beyond left and right' which Tony Giddens (1994) encapsulated in the 1990s. We have the opportunity to learn from experience since then. The essential goal remains – to achieve better education (effectiveness) and ethical change, social justice and participation (democracy) – but to also broaden the vision of education, which is encapsulated in the notion of holistic democracy. The shifting discourse around governance offers a favourable climate. We are within a flow of change which can be understood intellectually and felt. The new public governance, encountered in Chapter 2, is 'both a product of and response to the increasingly complex, plural and fragmented nature of public policy ... in the 21st century' (Osborne, 2010, p 9); and a response to new public management running out of credibility. Systemic problems are pushing in the direction of certain structural opportunities. Key drivers were highlighted in Chapter 2. The instrumental drive, which sees the value of more freedom and participation for organisational effectiveness, is powered by the necessity to respond to qualitative changes in the complexity of business and society. This gives a strong impetus to experiments and initiatives in organisational democracy and localism. At the same time, social and human concerns push in the direction of opportunities which can interrelate with instrumentally generated change. Expressive drives seek to make space for organic belonging (the socio-emotional dimensions of happiness, community, identity, individuality) and connectedness (spiritual awareness with a profound ethical character), helping to forge alternative rationalities. Drives to participation are boosted by the perception that over-centralisation neither succeeds nor is consistent with a free, democratic society. This is in the context of the restless evolution of democracy (generating monitory democracy, for example) and the renewing of older forms of participatory democracy. Democracy in practice is not a single kind of animal – unchanging with set and agreed characteristics. It evolves and its defining features are contested, and the problems and context for democracy alter. The challenge of responding to climate change, for example, requires democracy to progress: '… we need a different way of doing democracy. We need to involve citizens beyond their quintennial visits to the ballot box. We need to engage them in actively defining the problem and the solutions to it' (Burrall, 2010, p 22). This resonates with Churchill's exposition on post-war democracy alluded to in Chapter 1, though now we have new tools and technologies.

Spirit of change

The concept of localism has come to the fore in political governance and policy, acting as a focus in the search for a different discourse and policy direction. With the ideas of cooperativism and mutualism, it has emerged, or re-emerged into the policy and political discourse, embraced by all the major parties in Britain. (See Harrington and Karol Burks, 2009, and Conservative Party, 2009, for example.) The idea of localism is capable of targeting both the power of the state and that of capitalist markets, though it is also capable of being focused more on one than the other[3]. The state-focused strand is prominent in the UK Conservatives' localism agenda, which champions 'radical decentralisation' against an 'over-centralised state' and 'target-driven, top-down government which is trapped in the bureaucratic age and micro-manages all they do' (Conservative Party, 2009, p 2). The Coalition Government is foregrounding the idea of the 'Big Society', which is rooted in a rhetoric of spreading power to people:

> [T]he best ideas come from the ground up, not the top down … when you give people and communities more power over their lives, more power to come together and work together to make life better – great things happen.[4]
>
> We will support the creation and expansion of mutuals, co-operatives, charities and social enterprises, and enable these groups to have much greater involvement in the running of public services.[5]

The Coalition's focus is on reducing 'big government' (HM Government, 2010, p 7), however, rather than tackling the systemic inequalities and power differences created by market-driven economies. The Coalition agreement states that:

> We share a conviction that the days of big government are over; that centralisation and top-down control have proved a

failure. We believe that the time has come to disperse power more widely in Britain today; to recognise that we will only make progress if we help people to come together to make life better. In short, it is our ambition to distribute power and opportunity to people rather than hoarding authority within government. (HM Government, 2010, p 7)

It goes on: 'there has been the assumption that central government can only change people's behaviour through rules and regulations. Our government will be a much smarter one, shunning the bureaucratic levers of the past and finding intelligent ways to encourage, support and enable people to make better choices for themselves' (HM Government, 2010, pp 7–8). This is not a brand new idea, but it does give a renewed emphasis to a trend towards some kind of distributing of power and to the case for a more democratised society. This ambition, paradoxically, fits with the uncertainties that arise from the necessity of forms of decisive government intervention – that is, the problems that arise from recognising that governments cannot simply execute change in a linear model of efficacy. As Callinicos puts it: 'As a result of the economic upheavals in the late 2000s, we are likely to see both a stronger state and a more unstable state system' (Callinicos, 2010, p 127).

What is one person's instability is another person's opportunity, however. A longstanding critique of third way policy has been its blindness to the importance of freedom – its preference for the 'path of autocracy'. More than a decade ago, Ralf Dahrendorf (1999) highlighted the fact that 'liberty' seldom appeared in third way literature and never in a central place. Since then there has been growing criticism of an over-intrusive state. From this perspective, the growing interest in localism and cooperativism, from left and right, can be seen as a way of refocusing on the dispersion of power and participation.

Another way of looking at localism and mutualism is to focus on the inequalities and deficiencies of the private market and capitalist relationships – to see this as an alternative way of organising services and enterprises so that citizens and consumers are in control. In fact, the radical view of localism sees it as both an alternative to individualistic capitalist relations and a way of renewing the public realm. This is the thrust of one Labour argument as part of attempts to renew itself after almost 13 years in power.

> In the wake of the credit crunch, the public have made it very clear that they are unwilling to put their trust in large organisations that they feel are not run in their interests and

operate too far outside their control ... [T]he public have signalled the need for wide-ranging democratic renewal that will provide them with greater power over the issues that matter to them most.[6]

A report by the Innovation Unit concluded that 'There is certainly real potential in cooperative and mutual governance models for our public services' and that 'we may for too long have been in thrall to big business, corporate structures and transactional services' since they 'can improve services' cost-effectiveness' through 'the way they harness the creativity and energy of staff and citizens and their ability to contribute to local communities and economies' (Craig et al, 2009, p 5).

The spirit of change is abroad in education, as is apparent from the development of plural controlled schooling and the moves away from micro-management. Many would echo the call that 'Government should return power to schools for the sake of education and democracy' (Hofkins and Northen, 2009, p 40). The work of David Hargreaves (2007, p 2), influential in England, promotes a profession-led culture of innovation, replacing the 'culture of compliance', and sets out a vision of a 'self-improving system', building on the autonomy allowed so far, in which 'much (not all) of the responsibility for school improvement is moved from both central and local government and their agencies to the schools' (Hargreaves, 2010, p 5). The spirit of this is apparent in current government policy:

> [T]he timetabling, educational priorities and staff deployment of schools cannot be decided in Whitehall. And the attempt to secure automatic compliance with central government initiatives reduces the capacity of the school system to improve itself. Instead, our aim should be to support the school system to become more effectively self-improving. (Department for Education, 2010, p 13)

Hargreaves and Shirley (2009, p xii) argue that in education internationally, 'in the depths of crisis, a new spirit is emerging in which service and sacrifice in a commonwealth of hope can elevate us to a higher purpose and a humane exercise of powers'[7]. They point to components of a sea-change in educational reforms. The sustained growth of student voice, distributed leadership and acknowledgement of the key place of teachers and professional capacity in school improvement arguably creates the potential for genuinely participative and collegial relationships (Hargreaves and Shirley 2008,

2009).They argue that a 'fourth way' is opening up, the principles of which comprise: an energised profession; an engaged public; a guiding but not controlling government; interactive partnership of equals; and dedication to serving and improving the public and educational common good (Hargreaves and Shirley, 2009, p 69).

This spirit of change resonates with key elements of a general shift to a new public governance, and with what was described some years ago as a move from government to governance, which involves decentring, flexibility, professionalisation, and forms of authority that rely on reputation and demonstrated competence rather than coercive control. Leadership is achieved through exemplary performance and encouragement of others.At the same time information flows laterally, not only within government and within corporations and associations, but across their boundaries (Albrow, 2001, p 161).

In summary, the theme of the decentralising logic is renewed or rediscovered faith (at least rhetorically) in:

- professional responsibility
- less central direction
- local control and community/public involvement
- negotiated relationships, values and goals
- bottom–up innovation.

A democratic paradigm shift

Whilst such a list of currently favoured features of a new logic sounds progressive and promising, a genuinely democratic shift means going further.The posited fourth way, for example, whilst progressive in many ways, needs to be grounded in a much deeper vision and analysis of democracy. Otherwise it is in danger of allowing senior leaders and government to remain patriarchal forces of ultimate wisdom, steering and intervening as needed. It needs to be made explicit that education, grounded in a rich vision and analysis of democracy, means more than a narrow focus on cognitive abilities and skills and more than a form of system redesign in which co–construction concentrates on 'intellectual capital (knowledge and skill, core competences)' (Hargreaves, 2010, p 10).

There is much to do to achieve this. Localism sounds attractive, but depending on how it is pursued it may mean more democracy and empowerment and more meaning for people's lives; or its consequences may be transference to the local level responsibility for dealing with the effects of spending cuts (passing the buck) and greater scope for assorted, unaccountable players with money and influence to control education (privatisation of education) – creating fragmentation and exacerbation of inequalities. In any case, rather than a radical attenuation of the *influence* of central government, there will be a change in its nature. If the idea of localism is to have beneficial results, it will require, therefore, not the absence of steering, but the plotting of a new course. Mass localism 'depends on a different kind of support from government and a different approach to scale. Instead of assuming that the best solutions need to be determined, prescribed, driven or "authorised" from the centre, policymakers should create more opportunities for communities to develop and deliver their own solutions and to learn from each other' (Bunt and Harris, 2010, p 5).

The thesis behind this book is that there are structural opportunities for a democratic paradigm shift, and that our understanding of agency is evolving in a way that is especially conducive to taking advantage of those opportunities (the latter point to be explored in Chapter 7). In the bigger picture it is a further phase in a long story of attempts to transform capitalist rationality (Figure 1.1). Two developments are needed (Figure 5.1).

Figure 5.1: Key changes

organic meta-governance

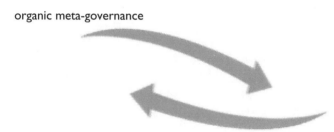

democratic consciousness

Organic meta-governance

The first one is a re-framing of the way in which policy is constructed and operationalised. To put it technically, it requires the construction of a specific kind of *meta-governance* which explicitly works towards enhanced democracy and frames education in a people-orientated educational philosophy. When thinking about educational policy, we need to ask a basic *political* question. Karl Popper (1971, p 121) argued that the basic political question is not 'who should rule?', but 'how can we so organise political institutions that bad or incompetent rulers can be prevented from doing too much damage?'. Popper's argument is that we should be prepared for bad government and build in checks and protections. In this spirit, if we are concerned that powers concentrated too much in government hands, or indeed in other institutions and interests, are capable of leading to education destructive of true learning and freedom, then we need to address a question something like this: 'how can educational policy be framed so that it is prevented from doing too much damage?'. One of the implications of this question is that educational policy should concentrate on meta-governance, i.e. governance directed at 'controlling the environment of action' rather than action per se (Peters, 2010, p 38). But, what kind of meta-governance? Not all forms of meta-governance are benign or sufficiently measured in exerting power. The idea of steering from a distance has been part-and-parcel of the neo-liberal educational agenda. This kind I term *marketising meta-governance*, which is about controlling from a distance so as to steer education in the direction of people-formation for the economic system: 'the transference of methods for the standardization of inert objects to the governance of people' results in 'narratives that are about technical improvements to a measurement system but have little to say about social justice' (Gunter, 2010, p 115). The marketising model of meta-governance is what has underlain dominant policy trends in the UK, the US and elsewhere.

A second kind is *organic meta-governance,* which fosters a democratic self-organising system and – returning to the garden metaphor for a moment – is about nurturing the environment for good growth to take place, i.e. diverse approaches to the encouragement of holistic-democratic relationships, practices and ways of working that respect human flourishing and freedom. The theoretical basis for this organic meta-governance is one that views optimistically the capacity and potential in contemporary society for agency, innovation and difference[8]. It also draws from the evolution of governance beyond new public management, which promoted private sector techniques and generic management, to a new public governance in which 'multiple interdependent actors contribute to the delivery of public services' and accountability shifts decisively from reliance on narrow metrics to incorporate public values such as equity and social justice (Osborne, 2010, pp 9, 424-5).

Democratic consciousness

The second development concerns education in its broadest and most basic and truest sense. This is a renewing of an innate sense of liberty and agency in the people who live and work within the framework of meta-governance: 'Man's self-esteem, his freedom, has first to be reanimated in the human breast ... [in order to] create once more out of society a human community, a democratic state, in which men's highest purposes can be attained' (Karl Marx, quoted in Lowith, 1993, p 108). It underlies the operation of a self-organising dynamic of bottom-up initiatives that marry, with a progressive agenda, creativity and dispersed energies and action. Integral to this is an understanding of the roots of democratising initiatives, which include traditions such as that of mutualism and the relationship with new mass participative activities like 'life spiritualities' (Heelas, 2008) and how they connect with democratic change[9].

We cannot tackle education without addressing the fundamental issue of what it is for and about. The underlying question for educational policy in the past three decades has been, 'what is the best policy for ensuring maximum educational attainment?'. The deeper question underlying this, however, is, *'what should young people learn?'*. This is to pose a people-orientated rather than system-orientated question. As Marx put it, 'We set out from real, active men, and on the basis of their real life process'[10]; or a student in a democratic school, 'In state schools children have to adapt to the system; here ... it's the other way'. To the question about what young people should learn, there are numerous answers. Some might say it is the skills they need to survive in and contribute to the economy, and the knowledge and capabilities required for the 21st-century economy; others might say it is the knowledge, beliefs and predispositions required to be true to a community's faith. Others could say it is about learning to live tolerantly in a diverse society and to be a responsible and active citizen. What is constant is that a view has to be taken.

The answer underlying the analysis in this book is that what it is most important for students to learn is how to be free persons, capable of unfolding their full potentialities as people and creatively engaged in creating the world around them. It is integral to the concept of democratic leadership which I believe to be most relevant to education (Woods, 2005). Democratic leadership in education fosters people as creative agents, capable of dealing with the pressures of modernity and moving towards 'self-conscious self determination'[11], the antithesis of alienation. Education with this in mind is integral to democratic society: hence the reference earlier to democracy involving 'colossal transformations' of people's characters (Keane, 2009, p 709). In more recent work that I have been involved with, it has increasingly made sense to sum it up as the development of democratic consciousness. By that I mean a free-thinking mindset, a predisposition to cooperation operating with virtues such as compassion, capabilities like articulacy and criticality, a sense of innate equality in relation to those in authority, awareness of the claims you can rightfully make on others and they on you, and 'mindful practice' (the capacity to be guided by aesthetic, affective and spiritual sensibilities, as well as cognitive knowledge)[12] (see also Figure 7.2).

In short, the second development that is demanded is the nurturing and strengthening of democratic consciousness, which is not only an inner change (which cannot be imposed) but also creates practical, outer change through democratic entrepreneurialism. Combined with the answer to the first question (posed on p 64), what is important to develop is organic meta-governance which aims to shape an educational terrain where democracy and free agency are protected and cultivated.

Overviews of governance

Two ways of setting governance approaches in context are set out here. The governance frame (Figure 5.2) sets in the context of different forms of governance, organic meta-governance as the progressive possibility beyond third way policy. Each of the models in Figure 5.2 is an ideal-type, abstracting from the complexities of reality. The welfare state represents the pre-1988 position: provision of welfare by governmental authorities, a bureau-professional regime with professionals and administrators having their own spheres of expertise, a mindset of compliance in traditional hierarchy, but with claims to professional autonomy; and separate dynamics from these two – one constructed around ideals of professionality, the other being about administration which values distance and bureaucratic procedures.

Marketising meta-governance represents a break with this. It is about controlling from a distance so as to steer education in the direction of people-formation for the economic system. It is infused by

Figure 5.2: Governance frame

	welfare	marketising meta-governance	organic meta-governance
organisational regime	bureau-professional	bureau-enterprise	holistic-democratic
mindset	compliant / professional autonomy	entreployee	democratic consciousness
dynamic	administrative distance / professionality	business / social entrepreneurialism	self-organising, co-operative, democratic entrepreneurialism

market values, blurs public/private boundaries, and simulates markets within the public sphere. The regime sought is bureau–enterprise culture and the model organisational actor being encapsulated is the idea of the 'entreployee'. The dominant dynamic of the system is entrepreneurialism (business and social) and increasing pluralisation.

Organic meta-governance also incorporates a more distant, but not inactive, governmental role, though with a very different vision and values. It explicitly seeks to nurture democratic ways of working and the development of people's 'substantive liberty'[13] – that is, the flourishing of all their capabilities as human beings. The favoured organisational approach is that of holistic democracy, with a recognition that there are degrees of democracy. Progress is not reducible to narrow, measurable metrics, but involves deep reflection on meaning and purpose as well as the organisation and techniques of learning. The mindset fostered is democratic consciousness and the dynamic is innovation and change that is shaped by self-organising energies and democratic entrepreneurialism. Its pluralism protects against dominance by an economised state and imposition of orthodoxies.

Another way to gain a perspective on the changes we are seeing is through the 'governance diamond' shown in Figure 5.3. This provides an overview of approaches to governance based on the nature of the interactions, which shape relations of power and influence and degrees of independence. It is formulated from Jan Kooiman's distinction between hierarchical, self- and co-governance (Kooiman, 2009), and integrates into the scheme the concept of democratic governance, so providing, arguably, a more complete overview.

Figure 5.3: Governance diamond

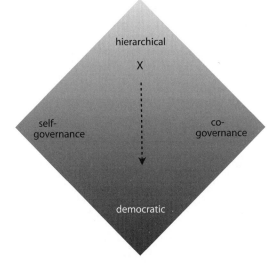

Hierarchical governance is made up of vertical power relationships in which 'top-down' influences and decisions predominate, whether through steering or direct control. Self-governance occurs where social actors (people and/or organisations) are able to be and act with substantial independence: they have capacities to develop and sustain their identities and 'a relatively high degree of social-political autonomy' (Kooiman, 2009, p 79). Co-governance is where social actors see that they have something significant which they share (interests, identity, and so on) and which they advance by working together: 'the essential element [with co-modes of governance] is that the interacting parties have something "in common" to pursue together' (p 96). Kooiman identifies various modes of co-governance, ranging from less formal ways of sharing information and developing common understandings of problems to institutionalised relationships where responsibilities for agreed areas are formally shared – so co-governance includes networks as well as types of formal partnership, such as public/private partnerships and federations of organisations.

I add democratic governance to these as it represents the idea of governance grounded in the participation and consent of social actors. Neither self- nor co-governance is identical with democratic governance. The latter brings with it a kind of legitimation which is distinct from the rationales of hierarchy, and a specific combination of dimensions with demanding implications for practice: in holistic democracy, these are conceptualised as power sharing and transforming dialogue, together with aspirations to holistic meaning and well-being[14].

The modes of governance in the governance diamond are not exclusive. Elements of each may be present to varying degrees. For example, degrees of self-governance and co-governance are apparent in the plural model of education that is growing in England, with the creation of Academies, Free Schools and Trust Schools. The centre of gravity of the schools system is shifting – from around point X in Figure 5.3 (where the centralising reforms of Thatcherism and third way policies took it) towards more self- and co-governance, and (as argued in this book) with signs and signals of change in democratic directions too. The dotted line in the governance diamond shows a trajectory. How far it can and will go is a question which in part will be answered by the extent to which the adaptive strategies and the fuller conception of 'embodied change', addressed in Chapters 6 and 7, are pursued and turned into effective practical change.

Challenges to the possibility of a democratic paradigm shift

Before turning to these matters, let us consider the scale of the challenge. The idea that contemporary organisations should embrace more democracy, encourage enterprise and freedom amongst organisational members and be more meaningful spaces is a beguiling one. It drives a powerful discourse in contemporary times, as we have seen. The feasibility of the idea that a paradigm shift is occurring or possible is open to powerful critiques, however.

Operational problems

Democratic approaches face operational difficulties. One concerns *democratic capacity*. This is a question of civic and personal capacities, which are interrelated. The argument with civic capacity is that marketising meta-governance and the growth of networks has marginalised local democratic institutions, reducing the capacity in the system for the genuine exercise of democracy. The recent history of educational policy has simultaneously enhanced central power and devolved power and responsibility to schools, diminishing the powers of elected local authorities. This atrophies the organs of effective local democracy and community empowerment. The argument concerning personal capacity is that the kind of education and society we currently have limits the development of the skills and attitudes necessary for democracy. Against this, however, it should be possible to take some comfort from the growth of monitory democracy.

Another, oft-repeated operational challenge is that of inefficiency. This critique asserts that democracy makes organisations, including schools, inefficient. Democracy takes time and requires attention and efforts that, the critical argument goes, would be better spent on increasing effectiveness.

Growing evidence, however, suggests that this is not a zero-sum game. Participation, enhanced engagement and positive feelings of identity and well-being materially improve the work of organisations. Analysis of Finland's educational success in terms of international measures suggests that 'Co-operation and networking rather than competition and disconnectedness should ... lead the education policies and development of education systems' (Sahlberg, 2006). Evidence has accumulated of the positive effect of shared leadership on schools and educational attainment. The largest and most extensive study of school leadership conducted in England to date highlighted the 'positive associations between the increased distribution of leadership roles and responsibilities and the continuing improvement of pupil outcomes' (emphasising also that it is a combination of strategies, sensitive to the specific needs and context of school over time, which influence student outcomes) (Day et al, 2009[15]). A study of the operation of democratic principles[16] in 79 schools in the US, involving more than 3,000 teachers, found them to be positively correlated with teachers' professional learning: where these principles – which include shared intentional direction (developed collaboratively) and a participative approach to leadership – are put into operation, teachers are more likely to experience professional learning which is continuous and shared amongst the teaching staff (Kensler, 2008). The accumulating research suggests the importance of shared leadership being coordinated and operating within a clear organisational structure and culture[17]. In addition, there is a strong case that how schools are run and how staff and students are treated and treat others are in themselves powerful models that affect students more broadly than narrow attainment targets: learning to be together in an environment that operates ethically and participatively is an environment in which everyone has the opportunity to learn important things about themselves that are not easily learnt in other ways.

Socio-political critiques

Another type of challenge is more profound and intractable. This is concerned with deep-seated socio-political critiques, summarised under four headings.

Clash of rationalities

First is the thesis that there is an inherent clash of rationalities: 'The argument is that the rationality of modern organizations is fundamentally different from that of the governance of society, for the main foundation on which "organization" rests is contractual, particularly in relation to the engagement and deployment of an employed workforce' (Woods and Gronn, 2009).

Dominance of economistic and performative culture

The second, and the strongest, concerns the dominance of economistic and performative culture. At a societal level, this argues that individualistic capitalism has too much staying power. Callinicos suggests that the world will see both capitalism in many forms and stronger nation states as a consequence of the financial and economic crises: according to this analysis, recurrent crises are inherent to capitalist economic systems and each crisis requires renewed state intervention to support capital, which state managers are prone to provide as their power is bound up with the success of capitalism (Callinicos, 2010). This is reflected in the UK Coalition Government's focus on reducing 'big government', rather than tackling the systemic inequalities and power differences created by market-driven economies. From this perspective, diminishing the role and reach of the state is an easier option.

A major critique of educational policy since the 1980s is that it has too readily been driven by an uncritical, positive valuation and celebration of the private market and priority to education aimed at improving the stock of human capital available to serve in the market economy – in short, by 'market servitism'. The prime goal of marketising meta-governance is the forging of people who will best fit the needs of the economy; and its preferred process of change is deployment of the principles and methods of contemporary business, as perceived by policy makers. Waves of reform have resulted in the 're-narration of schooling and learning through innovation and enterprise' which is 'part of an adaptation to a particular version of the economic and social context of globalization and post-modern society' (Ball, 2007, p 136). For all the moves to devolution and rhetoric of freedom to come, education has become suffused with an economistic and performative culture; the economism associated with marketising meta-governance is too steeped into the system to allow freer alternatives to nurture[18].

To be more successful according to the performative criteria that dominate the education system (Ball, 2006a), educational organisations need to work in a much more entrepreneurial way in order to facilitate innovation and rapid knowledge transfer, to enact change and to be agile – i.e. 'to respond faster, to move quicker' as external requirements and conditions change (Gratton, 2004, p 207), with staff able to 'steer a zigzag course and cross old boundaries' and create new combinations of knowledge through 'multiple weak networks' (pp 7, 92). This requires – the critical argument goes – 'greedy work' (an intensification of the demands on staff) (Gronn, 2003, p 5) and the construction of loyalty and commitment to organisational goals ('responsibilisation' – Gewirtz, 1999, p 152). The needs and interests of the organisation demand that attention be given to forging emotional integration, through which emotions and commitments are approached methodically and harnessed in a rationally calculated way, enacting a form of subtle instrumentalism (Woods, 2005). Accordingly, 'irrational emotional factors are rationally calculated' (Weber, 1970b, p 254). The resultant culture resembles that of Fielding's 'high performance learning organisation' in which the 'significance of both students and teachers is derivative and rests primarily in their contribution, usually via high stakes testing, to the public performance of the organization', compliance is ensured 'through a sophisticated psychology of emotional assent' and 'the personal is used for the sake of the functional' (Fielding, 2006, pp 304–5). The large and growing literature on spirituality in organisations attests to the capacity for modern organisational policies to seek to engage the deepest desires and energies for productive purposes (Casey, 2002: Poole, 2009).

This suggests that despite the development of plural controlled schooling, there is overwhelming pressure towards *convergence*: the dominant and ultimately effective press is to conformity around an instrumentally driven business model of entrepreneurialism and innovation. From this point of view, policies like the Academies programme are a further twist in the subordination of education to the economy, instrumental rationality and the worldview of individualistic private business. There may be some interesting initiatives that appear to challenge the materialism and instrumentalism of a profoundly economistic society – but these remain (according to the convergence thesis) marginal and junior partners in the dominant educational rationale.

The instrumentalising agenda is pursued through a variety of 'policy technologies' – such as the application of management techniques – which 'insinuate themselves into the lives and "souls" of teachers' (Ball, 2006b, p 79). Ultimately, what is distributed through distributing leadership within the organisation, according to this critical perspective, is the scope for tackling technical questions – involving 'rational selection of instrumental alternatives' in a context where goals and values are given (Habermas, 1974, p 3) – rather than genuine empowerment. The 'scope of dispersed initiative' (the terrain of issues and organisational activities open to independent initiative) (Woods, 2004, p 6) is therefore radically attenuated and restricted to operational matters. 'Higher-order' concerns, such as the basic values, conditions of employment, strategic policies or ethics of the organisation are off-limits as the main concern is to encourage staff to apply their creativity to operational matters that help the organisation succeed in improving its performance according to the measures imposed by the market or government funders. More than this, the rules and social artefacts created by the instrumentalist agenda constrain the type of freedom and individuality that people see themselves as valuing. From the perspective of this critique, education is but a part of a wider danger that threatens the public and third sectors, including social entrepreneurialism. If a democratic paradigm shift is to happen, it needs 'to happen sooner rather than later, as ... the drive of a market and managerialist culture and agenda is set to infest the [public and third sectors with] ... potentially catastrophic consequences ... for the social and ethical capital foundations in society' (Bull et al, 2008, p 11). What is in prospect, in other words, is yet another defeat in the long struggle against the encroachment of commodification into all areas of social life and the spread of Weber's disenchanting instrumental rationality.

Endemic power and social inequalities

A third critique is that of endemic inequality. The charge is that typical kinds of democratising initiatives do not disperse power; they only alter the way power is exercised. The more fluid organisation that puts emphasis on participation, sensitivity and mutual respect is still run from a central point. Sennett (2006, pp 51, 53) puts it like this, continuing his metaphor of the organisation as an MP3 player: flexible performance is possible only because 'the central processing unit is in control of the whole', and the flip side of flexibility is uncertainty about the future which creates anxiety acting as a discipline. At most, the critical argument goes, there may be only small, inconsequential shifts in power and influence throughout the organisation.

More generally, participation means more effective socialisation into goals and culture determined by those with power. This critique sees participants deprived of their capacity to think for themselves as they become so wrapped up in the beguiling claims of organisational solidarity and equality. They work harder because they believe, but their work does not in reality constitute an opportunity for true expressive activity. They are taken out of themselves by an artificial effervescence: 'a carnival of collegiality', 'evanescent "high"' and 'hyperactive professionalism' (Hargreaves and Shirley, 2009, p 41). They are seduced into becoming the entrepreneurial employee – being innovative and risk-taking and feeling freer – but do not exercise genuine control.

In plural controlled schooling, the scope and capacity to join the new, influential 'plurality' and take on the role of new educational players and partners are not equally distributed. Sponsors and partners tend to be individual and institutional actors who already have existing structural advantages in their field, be it business (financially privileged and/or well-connected business people, or successful companies) or the cultural sphere (universities, colleges, churches and their agencies, and so on). Plural control does not equate with democratic control, unless there are specific policies and procedures in place to ensure transparency, principles of equity and fairness, and community participation. The policy is prey to 'the political and economic interests invested in advocacy groups' and 'the exclusion of dissenting views within extensive but ultimately tight-knit policy networks' (Ball and Exley, 2010, p 165).

Another concern in relation to inequalities is the vocationalisation of the curriculum, especially in schools serving mainly disadvantaged communities. This is a process of increasing access to vocational qualifications at the expense of the traditional emphasis on academic qualifications. By adopting curricula and examinations that critics argue are less academically demanding, schools in areas of disadvantage increase their (historically relatively poor) headline examination results. This selective curriculum change, arguably, compounds educational inequalities, however, by systematically skewing the opportunities open to different social groups and providing an education for the less advantaged which gives qualifications which tend to steer them into particular types of employment that tend to be less rewarding and/or of lower social standing.

The socio-political critiques have to be taken seriously. The critiques sharpen our antennae for the very real problems and limitations that potentially affect such initiatives. But they do not mean that democratising initiatives are to be written off, or do not form a significant movement for progressive change. Regarding the 'clash of rationalities' critique, it is hard to see why this assertion should be accepted. Life is seldom reducible to simple incompatible and exclusive binaries. More often the neatness of the concepts does not reflect reality. Practice has different dimensions, with different rationalities intermingling, which may conflict but which may engender also creative tensions and openings for change. Organisations are not monolithic, framed by bureaucratic and hierarchical relations, but can and are created according to alternative models, such as cooperativism and value-led philosophies.

Concern about the immense pressure to follow economistic and performative priorities has to be countered by awareness of the capacity of individuals to imagine and sustain different realities in their souls and appreciation of the fact that there are resources which can be mobilised to offer alternatives. Expressive democracy, where it is able to gain an outlet, has a virtue and a worth of itself in so far as it is experienced as authentic by its participants. And inequalities can be addressed and diminished in real and practicable ways. The discourse of innovation, participation and localism is capable of being appropriated by participants for higher and progressive ends. Just such an example of this is entrepreneurialism, which not only has been re-defined into social entrepreneurialism but, as we have seen, is being radicalised further as way of generating community-based and democratic change with agendas of social justice. The possibility of adaptive strategies to build and develop a democratic paradigm shift, and the strengths of the embodied social actor integral to this, are the subject of Chapters 6 and 7 respectively.

SIX

The concept of adaptive strategies

> What provides hope ... is that by enhancing the value of the values it excludes [like the value of freedom is enhanced by the experience of prison], capitalism fuels its own opposition. (Paul Heelas, 2008, p 2)

> Complex goals necessarily involve more room for agency on the part of policy and managerial actors operating across organizational and bureaucratic boundaries and building alliances between different tiers of governance. Such actors confront a field of plural goals, multiple stakeholders and conflicting values and aspirations ... struggling to manage the resulting tensions, but at the same time exploiting those very tensions to enlarge the space for agency around 'social' agendas. (Janet Newman, 2005, pp 728–9)

There are two easy (well, relatively easy) options for the policy analyst. One is to take the critique-laden road which encourages pessimism, even cynicism, and endless critical questioning. The products of this road are the despair of policy makers who want answers so they can enact change and reform. They charge that this path brings questions but no solutions. This is the cry of the school effectiveness and improvement movement, for example. For this road, we need only assent to the socio-political critiques outlined in the previous chapter. The other road is the solutions-rich road in which answers are plentiful and the feeling is often one of heady optimism (as well as recognition of the necessity of hard graft to bring about the touted solutions). The products of this road are the despair of the critical thinkers and analysts. They charge that this path brings only the illusion of solving problems and systematically overlooks the deeper issues that superficial change and reform do not address. So, we need both then. Correct? Would that it were so simple. If we are to avoid the extremes of 'insipid pessimism' and 'jolly eutopianisms', as declared in Chapter 1, we need something more than a simplistic combination of the two roads. The critiques of the possibility of a more democratic future for education – especially charges that instrumental and economistic priorities have become ingrained into the system – do not simply fade away. The 'generative power of hope' (Sørensen, 2009, p 218[1]), which comes with the positive road, has to hold realistic possibilities of transforming the profound problems which the critiques identify. That involves a dialectical movement between the two roads.

The plural controlled model of education – in which government retains significant levers of control, but equally there is a multiplication of educational players and partners, drawn from business and other sectors – is a part of an unfolding governance transformation. One of the drivers behind it is recognition of the failures and limitations of central control and micro-management. Plural controlled schooling involves the intertwining of powerful private and economistic rationalities with other kinds of perspectives and interests and, with the advance of managerialism and technocratic strategies of school improvement, is open to the critique that the effective drive is to convergence around a narrow, performative model of education (Woods, 2010b). Stephen Ball's studies of the education system shine a light on the complex networks and interrelations that create a heterarchy of people, organisations and interests. Two points that Ball makes are important to bear in mind: that the heterarchical system is a political construct – it arises from numerous political and policy decisions about education; and that it is characterised by power differences. It is no level playing field. But Ball also expresses a tentativeness about what it all points to. His analysis leads him to resist conclusiveness. Whilst he is prepared to suggest that the changes we are witnessing represent a 'dislocation', changing the 'underlying set of rules governing the production of discourses and the conditions of knowledge' and transforming 'the meaning and experience of education', he also wants to see his analysis, rather, as 'a set of starting points and methodological possibilities' (Ball, 2007, pp 184–6). His analysis is not a deterministic one. The ambiguity of these reflections reinforce the view that the education system which is emerging is a territory over which social forces encouraging a larger view of education are contending with economistic perspectives on the purpose of schooling; and that some of these represent credible attempts to provide opportunities for re-enchantment – that is, education that fosters meaning in contemporary life and capabilities and predispositions to challenge domination by rationalising forces (Woods, 2010a).

This recognition gives rise to the idea of an alternative to the convergence thesis – namely, the hypothesis of *diversification*. In this, meanings and practice show significant variations, ranging from models and rationales that serve business and instrumental rationality to fundamentally different models and rationales of human development, particularly those seeking progressive change. The diversification hypothesis is consistent with new openings theory[2], which emphasises the capacity and potential in contemporary society for agency, innovation and difference. Key features of society characterised by new openings include personal reflexivity, construction (rather than inheritance) of identity, cultural diversity, active individual agency, collective action (the latter not confined to social class but active through new social movements for example), and choice and participation in groups and organisations (challenging traditional hierarchy). New openings theorists take the view that 'increased diversity, openness, and participation herald a more inclusive, freer and sustainable democracy' (Antonio,1998, pp 46, 47). This theoretical perspective is akin to the idea of holarchy, as an alternative to hierarchy, which describes the ideal or aspirational state of a self-organising system and its constituents. David Spangler's definition captures the essence of a holarchic system, 'in which different and unequal participants nevertheless enhance each other and co-creatively make a larger wholeness possible'. Holarchy honours

> each participant and looks not to their relative ranking as in a hierarchy, but to what they can contribute by virtue of their differences. Thus in a hierarchy, participants can be compared and evaluated on the basis of position, rank, relative power, seniority and the like. But in a holarchy each person's value comes from his or her individuality and uniqueness and the capacity to engage and interact with others to make the fruits of that uniqueness available.[3]

Plural controlled schooling opens spaces and opportunities for different kinds of agency through its 'empowerment' agenda and the introduction of new players as sponsors of academies and partners of trust schools, by no means all of whom are from the business sector. All of this introduces some degree of indeterminateness in future developments. Central government is not in control of all of the consequences of everything that it controls. One of the ways in which the indeterminateness of plural controlled schooling is institutionally present is in the entrepreneurialised spaces that are integral to bureau-enterprise culture. Signs of what new openings look like are running through the education system and are illustrated in Chapter 9. They include developments in teacher leadership founded in inclusive, participative principles and efforts to extend student voice so that students are engaged in generative activity that affects the school and community.

There are dangers. One of them is that localism and the dispersion of influence and power gives some people and ideas more power than others. A laissez-faire approach, or one that simply has not thought through and made clear the key values that should guide the system, leaves the question of who is allowed into the educational arena to the free play of individual and institutional decisions. It therefore cedes formation of the consequent pattern of education to existing social forces and the inequalities and power differences that are represented in them. A lack of clear public purpose and simple rules that back that purpose leaves the way open for 'the disparate authority of charitable or corporate purpose' (Ranson, forthcoming). The entrepreneurial spaces and structural opportunities in the new openings are not simply free spaces, tabula rasa, as we saw from the sociopolitical critiques of the possibility of paradigmatic change outlined in the previous chapter. They emerge within a specific structural and policy framework. They emerge in a policy climate which is attracted to the promise of entrepreneurialism, grounded in the kind of business entrepreneurialism celebrated in much business literature and practice. Even advances in creating teacher-led innovation, less hierarchical, network-focused ways of working, and student co-construction can remain fixed in their aims on the measurable rather than reflecting on what constitutes true education[4]. The pervasive power of instrumentalism and economism does not ebb away of its own accord. A strategy of response is therefore needed to the emergence of a system that increasingly has the characteristics of self-organising governance.

Strategy of adaptation

Faith in the power of agency drives the second of the two roads – the 'solutions-rich' road prone to over-optimism. The power of imagination is indeed just that – a power to be reckoned with. On its own, however, it is vulnerable. It needs to be embedded within a strategy of adaptation which understands the force of the socio-political critiques, seeks ways to counter the dominance of instrumental rationality and recognises that there are degrees of democracy which make progressive change achievable. The task of the strategy is to shape the spaces that provide openings for change at national, local and institutional levels.

The strategy of adaptation means the intentional process of countering the 'asymmetrical operation of instrumental and substantive rationality' (Davies, 2006, p 6) and expanding the zone of participative discretion that exists in contractual employment relationships[5] – that is, making the most of the leeway that exists in formal organisational and inter-organisational relationships. The feasibility of this strategy rests upon the possibility for adaptive rationality, a concept proposed by Richard Bolan and whose value is highlighted by Sabine Hotho and David Pollard (2007, p 597) who explain that it is

> an expanded, socially grounded model of rationality which is crucially linked to the notions of adaptation and mediation ... This is not only fundamentally social in the goals it aims to achieve, but also a means to mediate between instrumental rationality, e.g. the means-ends calculation rationality of modern management thought, and substantive rationality or, in Weber's terms, value-based rationality.

Adaptive rationality 'stresses the co-existence of rationalities' within people and within organisations and 'the need for mediation' between them (p 597). Recognising their coexistence does not mean absence of struggle. Part of the reason that there is struggle is that the substantive purpose is the one that gives meaning and direction, and is not reducible to calculative processes which tend to reduce evaluation and success to numeric measures. Discussing the influx of the kinds of expressions of spirituality, meaning and identity into organisational life discussed in Chapter 2, Catherine Casey (2002, p 173) observes that these are signs of 'a wider cultural reaction against the totalizing ideology of modern, and post-industrial, productivism. The reduction of humans and their potentialities to instrumental resources as organizational producers and consumers is, in these new ways, being challenged from within, and beyond, the organizational sphere'. They reinforce 'the contested and always limited rationality of social systems – and ... the competition between instrumental rational achievements and cultural and identity demands' (p 176).

The other reason for struggle is that adaptive rationality cannot just be about talk but comes up against material and symbolic constraints. There are underlying modes of authority and controls over material and symbolic resources that have to be recognised and addressed. For example, critical study of the marketising meta-governance system in England warns that political analyses 'of new governing relations may reveal discursive shifts, but it is important to be attentive to the underlying systems thinking that is data driven and data dependent' (Ozga, 2009, p 160); and that 'with the development of an increased reliance on "self–administered" policy communities, the "core executive" retains a substantial authoritative and coordinating presence over policy' (Ball, 2009, p 96). Adaptive rationalities, therefore, have to take a considered and realistic approach. It is suggested here that adaptive rationalities require four elements that combine to create a strategic impetus to progressive change in the direction of holistic democracy (Figure 6.1).

Figure 6.1: Elements of adaptive strategies

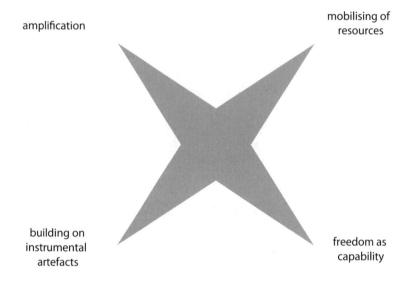

amplification

mobilising of resources

building on instrumental artefacts

freedom as capability

Amplification

The first is amplification. This is the explicit and systematic articulation of substantive values of holistic democracy, the deepening of commitment to these and identification of what these mean in the local context of a particular organisational or inter–organisational setting. It is a process of self–consciously placing in a wider set of priorities the performative goals and constraints of an economistically dominated culture.

Amplification is about depth of change, which is absolutely crucial to the possibility of a paradigmatic shift. It is more than adding a statement of values or renewing them every so often. It would be very difficult to find a school that did not describe itself as and was not to some degree values-led. It is also more than giving attention to people's feelings and emotions. Recent trends in leadership and organisations have brought to the fore the salience of affectual action, particularly the emotional energy that is needed to generate intense commitment and entrepreneurial activity amongst organisational members in service of organisational goals. In other words, instrumental rational action has been supplemented by action led by feelings. It is important to be clear, however, on the difference between affectual action and values rational action. The latter involves systematic ways of working dedicated to the pursuit of specific values, whilst affectual action concerns emotional motivations. Values rational action therefore relates to the discourse and literature focused on making organisational life genuinely and consistently committed to values beyond profitability and/or success measured in performative goals.

Corporate citizenship is one context for this. Expression of corporate citizenship does not in itself signal a real commitment or allay the institutionalised ways in which employees or stakeholders may be disadvantaged or marginalised by the operations of the organisation. Corporate citizenship raises issues of power in relation to interpretations of its meaning (Adler et al, 2007). Quanta is a London-based company which works with other organisations on their corporate citizenship development. Its approach illustrates the considered reflection that is evident in some parts of the field. Quanta draws attention to the value of and need for a 'structured soul searching exercise within the organisation' and the difference between instrumentally meeting minimum legal obligations and the hard work involved in establishing a 'firm moral commitment' (such as to organic food, to employee welfare and so on) which builds from 'empathy [based on] recognising those near and far as part of the same group as ourselves, and [sharing] their perspectives and plights without having to be in the same situation as they are'[6]. This strategic reconstruction of an organisation's fundamental rationality involves emotions – but, in addition, a deeper sense of dedication to higher values. A study of ethics and social entrepreneurship conceives the process as proceeding through levels[7]. The penultimate level in its framework is that in which 'business ethics are revised to re-frame the concept so that it is measured in more than economic terms – beyond bottom line accounting, to a point of looking at what the purpose of multi-bottom lining has to offer and what is represented along the line' (Bull et al, 2008, p 14). The deeper (fifth) level embraces 'charity' (literally 'love') which in its purest form removes 'economic thinking completely from decisions regarding social action' (p 7).

Willingness to engage in self-scrutiny and soul-searching is crucial in order to navigate to deeper levels of organisational commitment to specific values. Lisa Kensler, who researched the WorldBlu democratic principles in schools[8], points out the importance of understanding the basic assumptions (the architectonic principles, we might also say) that underlie organisational life and relationships. She observes, however, that 'we don't articulate our deeply held assumptions very often in organisations or in political systems, and many of our policies at the national level, international level, local level, organisational level are inconsistent with the core assumptions of true democracy'; yet, if we were to bring those assumptions to our workplaces, we would have a 'much higher level intentional practice'[9].

Key substantive values that orientate people and organisations to deeper commitments are enshrined in the notion of holistic democracy. These are higher order values, such as democracy, social justice and connectedness. They are distinguishable from procedural values, such as honesty and trustworthiness, which – whilst important – only have their complete value in service of higher goals and are capable of being deployed in service of lower and malign aims and values. The higher order values also place into context the importance of social or organic belonging, which again is crucial for a moral and good life, as well as having wonderful, intrinsically valuable energies. In its best form, organic belonging is characterised by fellowship and human warmth in which individuality and freedom flourish, within a culture animated by higher order values and connectedness (Figure 2.3). The 'degrees of democracy' analytical framework discussed in Chapter 8 can be used to support a deepening of reflection as a participative exercise in a school or other setting. The framework illustrates how amplification entails reflection on differing aspects of organisational activity.

Building on instrumental artefacts

Operationalising the amplified understanding that emerges involves working out how this can be advanced whilst also taking into account the demands of performative culture[10], which includes building on the artefacts and organisational changes arising from the instrumental drive to participation and meaning. Carolyn Shields (2010, p 570) draws attention to the fact that transformative educational leaders 'must be able to work from within dominant social formations to exercise effective oppositional power, to resist courageously, and to be activists and voices for change and transformation'. Hence, the second element of adaptive strategies is drawing out the democratic possibilities from changes emerging from this instrumental drive. These were summarised in Figure 2.2. They include structural changes, such as flexibilisation of roles and team working, as well as changes centred on people –

introducing more meaning into organisational life, encouraging flexible mindsets and developing 'soft' virtues such as sensitivity and reciprocity. These offer opportunities for deepening reflection and practice in democratic directions.

Opening these opportunities may be prompted by critique. An example is asking questions about the limitations of team working and collaborative relationships, in terms of who is excluded or marginalised: whose voice counts most, and what leads to some participants exercising more informal authority than others? Teachers who are working together as co-leaders do not necessarily equally share leadership, but differences in role and influence emerge between co-leaders, arising from institutional, cultural and personal logics. These logics may be about assumptions concerning who works best together and may involve gendered assumptions about who takes the lead (see Paredes et al, 2010, for example). The instrumental intention to use collaborative work to make the organisation or inter-organisational setting work more effectively can be amplified by conscious attention to hidden inequalities and ethical questions about the meaning of the work. It provides the potentiality for multiple voices to be heard, to raise critical questions informed by democratic principles and to change practice. Initiatives established with an eye to instrumental goals may be extended through intentional enhancement. For example, collaborative teacher groups may be not only a vehicle for raising student attainment but also a basis for widening student involvement and action – as discussed in Chapter 9.

Valuing freedom as capability

The third element is giving particular attention to freedom as capability. This approach to freedom emphasises it not as an individualistic quality, but as an outcome of being and cooperating with others. It is not simply about a person or group being able to do what they wish to, but understanding that achieving what we want depends as much on the support or collaborative effort of others as on ourselves. Freedom is not an expression of the isolated individual, conceived as the ability to do what one wants independently and without interference. Rather, 'effective freedom', as discussed by Amartya Sen, is constructed through relationships in which others – colleagues and institutions (including the state) – give help or work in cooperation in order to achieve desired ends.[11]

Freedom as capability is integral to adaptive strategies that seek to challenge the dominance of instrumental rationalities and hierarchical power, because it concentrates on people as social beings who are intrinsically interdependent and who must have ways of expressing their needs and wishes if they are not to be the products of agendas imposed upon them. Freedom as capability is also fundamental to education which is about nurturing in others the capabilities that will enable them to feel and think for themselves. If freedom as capability is taken seriously it has very practical implications: it requires ways to be devised that enable personal and professional development to explore personal and organisational goals as equally valid aspirations. Such development is about shaping them together and facing any tensions between them, rather than the one dominating the other.

Mobilising of resources

The fourth element of adaptive strategies is the mobilising of resources. This is a continuous process and includes the re-shaping of entrepreneurialism for holistic democratic ends. The capacity to forge 'new openings' depends on the availability of varieties of resources or capitals and the ability to draw these together and utilise them. In broad terms there are two forms: *symbolic resources* and *material resources* (Figure 6.2). (In the examples in Chapter 9 we will see deployment of both forms allowing different approaches to be developed and sustained.)

Symbolic resources are made up of cognitive-technical, social, emotional, aesthetic, ethical and spiritual 'capitals'. Adaptive rationality takes sustenance from alternative sets of ideas and values within available symbolic resources and these constitute the basis for action and innovation that do not conform to the convergence thesis. Mobilising of symbolic resources includes the evolution of identity, constructed over time from different sources – not just those handed down from the state – but also local identities, 'grand narratives' and prospective 'stories' of how the future can be. The mix is forged locally, and includes orientations to ideals as well as social and material identities[12]. It involves the balancing of strong identity within the organisation or inter-organisational setting, an identity that is firmly rooted internally and is *oppositional* to instrumentalising rationalities[13] – with an identity with a wider movement of like-minded people and organisations and system-wide aims (Rothschild and Whitt, 2009, Chapter 4). The employee-owned company, Namaste Solar, describe their path as an 'extraordinary experiment, drawing on intellectual, philosophical, and political models that inspire us, while crafting something uniquely our own'[14].

Material resources include funding and the availability of personnel and facilities which players outside the state system may provide. Included in this is access to expertise supportive of holistic democratic aims which provides a 'supportive professional base' (Rothschild and Whitt, 2009, p 121). Approached with a strategy of adaptation, entrepreneurial spaces offer a structural potential which, according to local circumstances, can be used in ways that transcend subservience to rationalised social authenticity and create free democratic space that allows interaction and deliberative exchange without the usual constraints of hierarchical and bureaucratic relations or the social and competitive pressures and distinctions that characterise performative and market cultures. Apple and Beane (2007) in the US identify lessons from attempts to create schools that are more democratic: they show that it is possible for educators to give education a more democratic character by engaging students in learning that is important to them and maintaining a whole-school or system-wide perspective.

Figure 6.2: Symbolic and material resources

cognitive
technical

spiritual

social

ethical

emotional

aesthetic

material
(funding, facilities, people)

In summary, adaptive strategies understand the force of the socio-political critique of the possibilities for paradigmatic democratic change, based on an appreciation of the tensions between instrumental and substantive rationalities in education. They are grounded in clear priorities: at the top are higher order values (democracy, social justice, connectedness), then organic belonging (fellowship and freedom), followed by the material aims of measured performance and income[15]. The ultimate aim, however, is to forge a unified practice, integrating these priorities by giving ideal aims a practical cutting edge that amplifies the possibilities emerging from current educational policy.

SEVEN

Embodying change

> Each self is unique, and therefore incomparable. It is a single
> wellhead of creation ...The living self has one purpose only:
> to come into its own fullness of being, as a tree comes into
> full blossom, or bird into spring beauty, or a tiger into lustre.
> (D.H. Lawrence[1])

Who are the change-agents for this progressive adaptation? They are
embodied actors, a concept which contrasts with the idea of the 'empty
self' that is generated by consumerism and filled up with the consumer
products and the shallow, passing ephemera of externalised identities[2].
This chapter gives attention to the nature of this embodiment.
Conceptions of the person and holism are part of the paradigm shift
that this book looks towards. Underpinning organic meta-governance
is the nurturing and strengthening of democratic consciousness. This
involves critical, analytical engagement as well as strengthening, on the
basis of the reaction against centralisation, a renewed sense of agency,
freedom and responsibility. It is also about democracy as a holistic way
of being together.

Holistic capabilities

The power of agency and imagination is not to be underestimated.
Recognition of this is integral to the growth of appreciative inquiry,
for example: 'the co-operative, co evolutionary search for the best in
people, their organizations, and the world around them', substituting
for managerialist intervention 'inquiry, imagination ... innovation ...
discovery, dream, and design' (Cooperrider and Whitney, 2005, p 18).
If imagination and optimism soar too high or without any sense of
reality – remembering the story of Icarus – they come to nothing,
however. Hence, the call for what Bent Sørensen (2009, pp 207–8) calls
immanent utopias. In a diverting account of entrepreneurial utopia –
orientated around an art installation event involving a naked woman
in a bathtub in a dimly lit bar – he calls for regained faith in the body
as 'a site of sensuous, affectional and political thinking' and of 'struggle
for life': the utopianism that radical entrepreneurialism potentially may

unfold 'must be sought for in immanence' and located in the world (p 211). The question is what makes up the body in which imagination and optimism, and personal agency, are grounded. Change that builds on the power of imagination taps into the creative ability of people that is embedded in their make-up. It requires, therefore, not only analytical capabilities (the sphere of the left brain), but also the capabilities of the right brain, and full appreciation of the range of capabilities – cognitive, emotional, physical, aesthetic, ethical and spiritual.

Logic-dominated rationalistic dialogue, on which Habermas's concept of communicative action exclusively relies, replaces an 'incarnate and differentiated moral subject with a generic, hyper-rational being' (Gardiner, 2004, p 34). This leads to the argument that 'Habermasian distinctions, such as between public and private, communicative and corporeal action, or rationality and non-rationality have to be thoroughly revised' (p 44), leaving behind the idea of a disembodied subject acting in an 'abstract space disconnected from experiential, embodied and affective human qualities' (p 43). Instead we need to operate with 'the notion of multiple counterpublics endowed with diverse rationalities and modes of interaction and expression' (p 44). In other words, adaptive rationality must mobilise all the resources and capabilities people have. For genuinely new openings to be generated, change must be initiated and sustained by embodied actors. The embodied actor is key to any meaningful response in the emerging system.

Yet education is deeply implicated in passing on the dominant, narrowed conception of what it is to be an educated person and the privileging of rationalistic approaches to human development. As noted in Chapter 5, people's emotional and spiritual aspects are capable of being harnessed to instrumental ends and subject to rational calculation. When education draws upon brain research, for example, it often does not examine in depth the implications of left-brain dominance, but draws on interpretations that apparently offer adaptable techniques, comfortably set within the linear, left-brain paradigm, in order to increase conventional learning[3]. Another example is data-driven decision making, which has a continuing, strong momentum, reinforced by the current government[4]. I am not arguing against the value of research and the intelligent use of data to inform understanding of education: the problem, rather, is the dominance of rationalised thinking and the idea of being 'driven' by data without combining systematic research with other kinds of understanding. As Hargreaves and Shirley (2009, p 87) put it, we need 'effective use of data by teachers who know how to blend creativity and intuition'.

McGilchrist's (2009) study of the divided brain shows the effect on society and culture of dominance of one part, the left brain. In the Western culture the left and right brains are engaged 'in a sort of power struggle', with repercussions for our society (p 3). It is worth quoting him at length on what we should expect the social consequences of left-brain dominance to be (p 433):

> We would expect there to be a resentment of, and a deliberate undercutting of the sense of awe and wonder ... Religion would seem to be mere fantasy. The right hemisphere is drawn forward by a desire for power and control: one would expect, therefore, that there would develop an intolerance of, and a constant undercutting, ironising, or deconstructing of such exemplars, in both life and art ... It would become hard to discern value or meaning in life at all; a sense of nausea and boredom before life would be likely to lead to a craving for novelty and stimulation. Experiences or things that we would normally see as having a natural, organically evolving, flowing, structure would come to seem composed of a succession of frames, a sum of an infinite series of 'pieces' ... As a culture, we would come to discard tacit forms of knowing altogether. There would be a remarkable difficulty in understanding non-explicit meaning, and a downgrading of non-verbal, non-explicit communication. Concomitant with this would be a rise in explicitness, backed up by ever increasing legislation, de Toqueville's 'network of small complicated rules'. As it became less possible to rely on a shared and intuitive moral sense, or implicit contracts between individuals, such rules would become ever more burdensome. There would be a loss of tolerance for, and appreciation of the value of, ambiguity. We would tend to be over-explicit in the language we used to approach art and religion, accompanied by a loss of their vital, implicit power.

The description echoes the disenchanted world of Weber's ideal-typical rational bureaucracy and is based in the argument that a habitual or normalised use of one part of the brain is implicated in this social reality. Other studies have illuminated the consequences of excessive rationalism. For example, emphasis on the cognitive has had immense repercussions for the religious sphere, as Charles Taylor has examined. It has led to 'excarnation' – 'the steady disembodying of spiritual life, so that it is less and less carried in deeply meaningful bodily forms, and lies more and more "in the head"' (Taylor, 2007, p 771).

The rationalised approach is also enmeshed within a way of thinking that sees control and the exertion of interests as the overriding way of the world. Instrumental rational action is a way of sustaining the power embedded in hierarchical organisation. If disinterested analysis and decision making of rational policy making is an ideal, then it is frequently bent to the wills of contending players in the micro- and macro-politics of organisations and systems.

Whilst the impulse to rationalisation is strong, we should not take the description above as a static picture of where we are. It is not the only robust force. We are living in a time of reconstructing and unifying understanding about the embodied person. Paul Heelas has shown, for example, how important and pervasive are 'life spiritualities'. These and other trends seem to illustrate the observation that '... the obvious inauthenticity of the left-hemisphere world we have come to inhabit may in itself lead us to seek to change it' (McGilchrist, 2009, p 449). Moves away from this have significant implications for practice: 'In the real, practical everyday world ... the "return of the right hemisphere" is of ultimate importance' (p 437). Scholars of public policy are fundamentally extending the parameters, 'moving beyond self interest as the fundamental motivator of political action, and beyond bounded rationality as the primary mode of reasoning' (Schneider and Ingram, 2007, p 1). Policy analysis is recognising increasingly the importance of admitting into policy debate different forms of knowing – whether that be through differing kinds of experience or the various ways (psychological, spiritual and cultural) that people come to perceptions and ideas on matters of debate. One outcome is the emergence of 'boundary organisations' that bring perspectives together from their different spaces and, where they are successful in being collaborative and inclusive, can act to 'blur boundaries and create new ways of knowing ... that [introduce] new elements ... into the policy space and [refocus] attention away from the elements unique to each of the original ways of knowing' (pp 13–14).

There is of course in education a tradition of responses and challenges to the limitations and distortions of industrial, rational-bureaucratic models of schooling and cognitive, left-brain dominated learning. An example is Montessori education, which more recently has been studied in connection with psychological theories of flow (Rathunde, 2009); and there are other educational approaches, many outside the state sector, which prioritise attention to the creative and spiritual dimensions of education from Steiner, Buddhist and other perspectives

(Woods and Woods, 2009b). Another trend – affecting state education in recent years – is the increased attention given to emotional awareness and different kinds of intelligence, symptomatic of 'a growing awareness of the absences that sit at the heart of the predominantly technical and managerial paradigms of educational change and reform' (Goodson, 2003, p 67). This includes work on multiple intelligences – including emotional, musical and spacial intelligences – which has been influential in widening thinking about the range of intelligence that student education and educators' own professional development needs to be concerned with (Gardner, 1999; Goleman, 2005). Within this trend the idea of spiritual intelligence has also come to have some purchase on professional development in education (Zohar and Marshall, 2000). In amongst the numerous publications and reports of the National College for Leadership of Schools and Children's Services can be found recognition of the value of incorporating right-brain faculties: 'Breaking outside the box of the rules and thinking laterally to meet a specific need is a more creative activity of the right brain ... [and emphasises] the importance of drawing from all one's mental powers in being an effective leader and manager' (Green, 2002, p 8). The Cambridge Primary Review, which reported in 2009, highlights contrasting views of expertise in teaching: an official, rationalistic perspective, compared with a richer, alternative view (Hofkins and Northen, 2009, p 35[5]). The first is the perspective of the Training and Development Agency for Schools, a government agency: 'Excellent and advanced skills teachers should have a critical understanding of the most effective teaching, learning and behaviour management strategies, including how to select and use approaches that personalise learning to provide opportunities for all learners to achieve their potential'. The second perspective the Review quotes is that of David Berliner, which reflects the Review's case that teaching involves tacit knowledge and includes much artistry, flexibility and originality, which is much closer to right-brain approaches:

> If the novice is deliberate, the advanced beginner insightful, the competent performer rational and the proficient performer intuitive, we might categorise the expert as being arational. Expert teachers appear to act effortlessly, fluidly and instinctively, apparently without calculation, drawing on deep reserves of tacit knowledge rather than explicit rules and maxims.

The sorts of moves in the direction of recapturing a fuller sense of the body and learning go only so far, however, towards the need for 'feeling intellects' (Rowe, 1973, p 23). A holistic view of the embodied learner (adult and child) conceives the person in terms of the full range of human capabilities – spiritual, cognitive, aesthetic, affective, ethical, and physical. Education in skills that are important for work is important. In the holistic view, education (including professional development) is placed in an infinitely broader context. If we draw on the poets to express this, skills and even emotional intelligence are placed in a larger perspective that nurtures higher faculties in order 'to render... feelings more sane, pure and permanent ... more consonant ... to eternal nature, and the great moving spirit of things'[6] – since 'in the soul are many lesser faculties that serve Reason as chief'[7].

In examining reflective leadership, work that I have been involved in has proposed successive levels of embodied learning (Figure 7.1[8]). Disembodied learning is learning which is dominated by cognitive reflection. Partially embodied learning recognises the importance of physical and emotional experience as well as cognitive faculties for learning: it includes intuitive capabilities in so far as they are derived from psychological capabilities. Fully embodied learning extends the understanding of the body to embrace spiritual capabilities which nurture and enhance an inner state that is in tune with a transcendent reality and the supreme values of connectedness and compassion. These capabilities are integral to holistic democracy and the aspiration to truth and meaning which is essential to it. They are a resource for handling the 'lesser faculties' that can get in the way of cooperative power sharing and transforming dialogue, and if we are to achieve 'open-minded engagement in public reasoning [which] is quite central to the pursuit of justice' (Sen, 2009, p 390). Should we take the proposition of transcendent reality and a human spiritual capability seriously? The idea that we should (however different people or groups describe its details and whether or not it is understood theistically or religiously or otherwise) is based on three key arguments. First, accounts of transcendent spiritual awareness are widespread and these provide indicators that such awareness is a particular and distinct kind of phenomenon, not reducible to other experiences or explanations. Secondly, there is enough evidence to show that such accounts cannot, as a group, be dismissed as irresponsible or untrustworthy. Thirdly, if spirituality is granted to be an activity which is concerned with relating to and appreciating the transcendent, logically there must be a human capability to enable that[9]. This is not simply about feelings and emotions, but about learning 'to open the heart as well as to illuminate the mind' (Cottingham, 2005, p xii).

Figure 7.1: Embodied learning

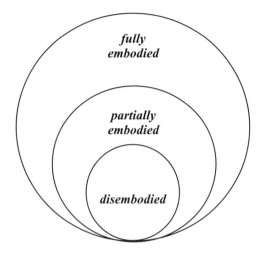

This figure is (c) Copyright Reason in Practice Ltd 2010

Various illustrations are possible from different walks of life. Tony Hsie (2010, p 79), CEO of a company which received an award for its democratic character in 2010 and was bought by Amazon for over $1billion, describes an unbidden spiritual experience. He writes of an occasion (at a dance) where, unexpectedly: 'I was surprised to feel myself swept with an overwhelming sense of spirituality – not in the religious sense, but a sense of deep connection with everyone who was there as well as the rest of the universe'[10]. In a completely different context and kind of life, Eric Clapton (2007, pp 259– 60) had brought himself to the point where, to rid himself of his addictions, in the privacy of his room and on his knees, he 'surrendered' and asked for help: 'Within a few days I realised that something had happened for me. An atheist would probably say it was just a change of attitude, and to a certain extent, that's true, but there was much more to it than that. I had found a place to turn to that I'd always known was there, but never really wanted, or needed, to believe in ... Before ... I found my God in music and the arts ... In some way, in some form, my God was always there, but now I have learned to talk to him.' The point is that these awarenesses have real and practical consequences, and profound meaning, for people and their lives. They entail learning.

Research into the spiritual awareness of headteachers of state schools in England (both religious and non-religious believers) found that a majority reported experiences of this type and were inspired or supported in their leadership by some kind of spiritual power (Woods, G.J., 2003, 2007). One described profound experiences in his early life, including 'mystical' experiences of overwhelming beauty in nature, as well as powerful sense of a guiding hand, which had a lasting impact on his continuing sensitivity to finer feelings. Another talked of the sense of being in touch with a 'bigger feeling' which she felt was difficult to explain and articulate, but that it was a 'sort of feeling of continuity and being part of the whole ... I feel embarrassed talking about it to be honest ... It's something that's very, it's very deep inside' (Woods, G.J., 2003, p 316). Others talked about being aware of a larger power, that they called God or Christ, or of feelings of being part of nature. These examples of spiritual awareness had lasting, positive effects for these school leaders. They helped to 'strengthen a focus on ultimate ethical values, underpinned a sensitivity to higher needs and the well-being of others, and encouraged a special value and priority to be placed in the educational life of the school on that which engages, enhances and respects higher feelings' (p 149). Such strengthening of substantive values is significant for sustaining effective adaptive strategies in the face of instrumental pressures.

Jack Whitehead offers another kind of illustration of the importance of spiritual energy in education. His reflection on his work on action research and lived theory provides an example, directly relevant to professional development, of the importance of recognising fully embodied learning. I believe it has resonance with numbers of practitioners, from those with non-specific conceptions of the spiritual to those with more particular or faith-based understandings. The reference to social and non-social, cosmic energies – both important but distinguishable analytically – echoes the distinction between organic belonging and connectedness. Whitehead writes that:

> ... my explanations for my educational influences include the non-social flows of life-affirming energy that distinguish my social relations as educational. Whilst expressing this life-affirming energy in my social relations I want to emphasise that I bring energy that flows from outside the social through the cosmos into my educational relationships. I use the expression of this energy in my accounts to distinguish what is educational from social relations. Hence I do not subsume my understanding of what is educational to a

concept of 'social' in the improvement of practice and in the generation of knowledge. (Whitehead, 2008, p 109)

… I feel that two affirmations have been most significant in my practitioner-research: The first affirmation is the experience of an energy that I feel is flowing through the cosmos. This energy is life-affirming for me and I associate this energy with the state of being affirmed by the power of being itself. When I read these words in Paul Tillich's work in *The Courage To Be* (1962, p. 168), I understood that this affirmation referred to a theistic experience in a relationship with God. Having no theistic desires myself I use the words 'state of being affirmed by the power of being itself' to communicate my experience of a flow of life-affirming energy that when combined with my values provides me with explanatory principles to explain why I do what I do. I believe that a similar energy is informing an Ubuntu way of being as this is expressed by Nelson Mandela … The second affirmation is in relationships with others when mutual recognition evokes a flow of life-affirming energy. (Whitehead, 2008, p 114)

The term 'sacred' describes something of the depth of what we are dealing with here and how it *calls* upon our attention. Gail Davies writes interestingly on debates concerning biotechnology, drawing on Habermas and critiques of Habermas's conceptualising of ideal speech and communicative action. The profane and the sacred are evident in such debates – appeals to reason on the one hand and 'gut' concerns about 'playing God' on the other. Habermas's reliance on rational argument is open, as we have seen, to the criticism that it creates a subject who is disembodied and abstracted from their relationships and context, and restricted to 'only certain forms of expression [which] are seen to constitute the required openness to communicative rationality' (Davies, 2006, p 8). Humour, irony and parody are excluded, and so 'laughter, outrage and [reliance] on colloquial categories to present persistent arguments about the "unnaturalness" or "yuk factor" of biotechnology … are frequently dismissed as unreasonable and irrational' (p 9). Yet they are ways of expressing something that restricted rational argument is unable to. Spiritual awareness is often difficult to articulate exactly because it touches profound truths and insights through a direct, heart-centred approach. Consequently, people rely on other forms of communicative expressions – such as poetic phrases, metaphors or apparently irrational utterances – to give vent to the deep sense of sacred and inviolable concerns that are difficult to communicate in 'objective' language. (This is not to say that they trump all other contributions to debates; rather, that the instinctual and intuitive contributions can be vehicles for deeper perceptions and orientations highly relevant to practical action.)

The point is profoundly relevant to education. Ultimately, the care and nurture of young people's growth is a sacred concern, in the sense that it pertains to the most precious period of growth as a human being. It needs, therefore, to be expressed in myth, metaphor and poetic forms, as well as rational analysis. A principal of an Academy described the students 'as my angel children'. There is a metaphoric power in this kind of appreciation. This comes from people as fully embodied subjects, whose understanding includes but goes beyond conventional rationalism. In full recognition of that point, the following is one way of expressing educational purpose in contrast to narrow economism: education should enable the student to discover 'his or her "calling": an occupational choice directed by the individual's inner guiding spirit', where the ultimate aim is to 'perpetuate the concept of sacred trust – so that it will carry over into the child's adult years ... and to cultivate an integrated cultural identity and holistic personality' (Mitchell, 2005, pp 298–9).

On democracy, we are still in a dialogue with the Athenian democratic society of Ancient Greece. It is apparent in texts about modern organisational democracy (Manville and Ober, 2003; Ober, 2008, for example). There may be suggestions from anthropological explorations that democracy in fact pre-dated that time (Keane, 2009; Sen, 2009), but our knowledge of Athenian democracy is much greater and our connection with it in the world of ideas considerably closer. In Athenian democracy, both spiritual and cognitive education were significant for the nourishment of democratic consciousness. Spiritual sensibilities, fostered by the natural environment as well as belief in deities, co-mingle with dialogue and democracy[11]. A 'subtle blend of mystical and rational perceptions of reality' fostered 'a sense of responsibility for maintaining a harmonious cosmos balanced between the metaphysical and physical realms of reality' (Mitchell, 2005, pp 16-17). In contemporary times, this observation begs the question of how and whether spirituality and democracy can be interrelated. For some, they – or, more specifically, religion and democracy – are seen as antithetical. In fact, spirituality and democratic forms of organisation have a strong connection. In summary, there is an interconnectedness of spirituality and democracy for two prime reasons.

1. Spirituality is a source of strength for the person and their democratic consciousness. This is to do with developing human potentialities – not the imposition of rules, ways of life and cultural assumptions, or using spiritual authority to sustain unjust economic, political and military authority, which religions have often sought to do. It was a strength to the imprisoned Nelson Mandela, who 'began to discover depths of resilience and spiritual attributes that he would not have known he had' (Tutu, 2005, p 73). In the long history of democracy, and in governance through assemblies that predated Ancient Greece, the sense that it is right for the many to be involved in decision making grew from people's divinely given capacity (Keane, 2009, p 147). Assembly government was encouraged before Athenian democracy by myths in the East (p 114): it was the 'very possibility of merging with the powerful gods that gave human beings courage to pick themselves up, to stand erect and shift for themselves in the world' (p 116). Absolutely key to democracy is the question of what faculties people have as human beings to draw upon, and development of the full extent of human potentiality is exactly the focus of true spirituality. The Reformation and the political revolution across the countries of the British Isles in the 17th century were one of the early forging grounds for modern Western democracy because the personal relationship with God seized so many people as the bedrock for a life of meaning and eventual salvation. And if each person carries that responsibility and capacity, they surely can rightfully claim to be co-creators of the mundane social world they inhabit. Spiritual development nurtures a protective capacity which democracy needs – that is, a sense of people's own strength and capacity for discernment and judgement[12]. Spirituality feeds creativity through intuition (Woods and Woods, 2002).

2. Democracy requires us to understand the limitations of human knowledge, as well as our strengths. This could also be termed humility. Hugh Bowden has argued that accounts of Athenian democracy that leave out or marginalise the importance of spiritual rituals and observances and frequent use of the oracles fail to understand it. Integral to Athenian democracy was the significance attached to finding out what the gods knew and wanted (Bowden, 2005, p 85). Fundamentally, this was a recognition that human wisdom only went so far. Socrates explained the importance of divination. People can learn the skills and requirements to work as a farmer or carpenter, or as a manager or ruler, as these can be 'grasped by human reason', but 'the most important aspects ... of these things, the gods kept to themselves' – matters such as how different choices

will work out; so, 'what was not clear to men we should try to learn from the gods through divination: for the gods give signs to those to whom they are gracious'[13]. Bowden's point is that, empirically, this was not only integral to democracy then, but that it is also entirely consistent with self-governance. Divination was about seeking the highest advice possible to contribute to collective deliberations. We would not revert to the religious ways of Ancient Athens today. The point that Bowden emphasises, nevertheless, carries a contemporary message. There are matters that we cannot discern and judgements we are unable to make without tapping into sources greater than our cognitive, physical and emotional capabilities – whether we call these life-affirming cosmic energies (as per Whitehead), life spiritualities, God, Spirit, Allah or other names.

This reinforces the importance of spiritual capital, not only as a part of the drive to meaning and expressive democracy but also as a resource and energy that helps to displace economistic motives and thereby aids the process of amplification and sustaining the focus of adaptive strategies on higher order values.

Critical democratic actors and democratic consciousness

Particularly important to social change are critical actors, and for the purposes of the specific focus of this book, critical democratic actors. Critical actors have crucial effects in networks, influencing the cascading effect discussed below. 'Highly connected agents have enormous potential influence in spreading behaviour across such networks' (Ormerod, 2010, p 30). Much attention is being given to the notion of system leaders in education – effecting change throughout systems (Hopkins, 2007) – and to 'nodal systems leaders' who have strong levels of commitment, skills, understanding and inspirational qualities to make partnerships work (Hargreaves, 2010, p 17). These notions have democratic and radical potentialities. In the new public governance, local authorities, even in their diminished roles, have the potential to act as community leaders (Martin, 2010, p 344). Critical actors for social justice initiate change and policy proposals and 'embolden others' to action[14].

Democracy, and especially holistic democracy, asks a great deal of participants. They are asked to act authentically, in the comprehensive sense of being true to and shaping progressively the self, society and ideals[15]. Capabilities for this are variably distributed amongst organisational members. Those with greater capacity and who are active in the organisation are critical democratic actors: they display greater capabilities for engaging in fully embodied learning, develop greater understanding of the democratic philosophy, and encourage and coordinate collaborative activity, fostering transformation through their own holistic participation and facilitating others' involvement[16].

The spaces opened by enterprise and plural schooling are the operating areas of critical democratic actors who can re-make and shape new possibilities within it. They are 'entrepreneurial bridge builders' (Ober, 2008, p 153) – influential agents in organisational and inter-organisational spaces, operating at nodal points in networks, who take advantage of the possibilities in entrepreneurial spaces – mobilising resources and meanings across boundaries. They 'create and cultivate democratic space', even within 'an educational setting that is predisposed to non-democratic practices' (Johnson and Hess, 2010, p 7). Critical democratic actors apply and work through adaptive strategies, facilitating conceptual and experimental innovations[17]. The first (conceptual innovation) reframes the way people think and feel. The second (experimental innovation) brings about incremental practical change. Both take effect through micro-genesis (Holland et al, 1998), the capacity of people to make differences in their everyday worlds which, through copying and influence on others, can have wider implications throughout larger organisational and social settings. Inspiring and motivating others and enacting change (though conceptual and experimental innovation) are features of the influential notion of transformational leadership. The concept of transformative leadership, however, advocated by Shields (2010), whilst also about change, is explicitly concerned with critique of inequalities and testing taken-for-granted assumptions (or, to put in another way, the architectonic principles underlying entrepreneurialism, highlighted in Chapter 3), with the aim of advancing social justice and democracy. It is much closer, therefore to the leadership offered by critical democratic actors.

Johnson and Hess in their advocacy of democratic leadership offer examples in the US of critical democratic actors who cultivate democratic spaces. These include a Nebraska Commissioner of Education who followed critique of the standardised national tests with successful implementation of a more teacher-led and locally responsive system that was eventually approved by the US Department of Education, and a principal whose vision of high school as 'democracy's finishing school' led to changes that facilitated students' engagement in their own education and in the school's governance (Johnson and Hess, 2010, p 6). There are numerous other examples of such actors[18]:

insights into selected examples are featured in Chapter 9. It is worth emphasising that critical democratic leadership is not the sole preserve of those in high authority positions, but is possible from differing institutional and non-institutional positions.

The action of critical democratic actors is grounded in democratic consciousness. By this I mean an interacting set of capabilities, predispositions and insights that animate the person to act within and shape a democratic culture (Figure 7.2). This 'inner dimension' makes progressive change in a democratic direction more than the contentious pursuit of individualistic and divisive interests.

Figure 7.2: Democratic consciousness

Mindset

free-thinking, independent minded, co-operative predisposition, sense of innate equality

Virtues and values

compassion, holistic democracy, social justice

Skills and capabilities

articulacy, criticality, mindful practice, creative visualisation for change, skills for resource mobilisation, network logic

Democratic consciousness is an ideal-typical construct of the characteristics of the critical democratic actor. As well as a commitment to the values of holistic democracy (power sharing, transforming dialogue, holistic meaning and well-being), it includes a free-thinking mindset, a predisposition to cooperation, virtues of which compassion is the most important, capabilities like articulacy and criticality, a sense of innate equality in relation to those in authority, awareness of the claims you can rightfully make on others and they on you (social justice), and mindful practice which draws on aesthetic, affective and spiritual sensibilities, as well as cognitive knowledge, and a capacity to nurture connectedness (Woods and Woods, 2009c). For good measure it also embraces the energy, creative visualisation and skills for mobilising resources of the democratic entrepreneur. It is awakened by exposure to and engagement with critical thought (consciousness raising as advocated by Freire, for example) and deepening engagement with values and how they can be amplified through adaptive strategies to change practice.

One of the aspects of democratic consciousness developed by practice and training is the capacity to engage in 'network logic' – a 'core thinking skill' which enables individuals and groups to be part of a dialogue between the whole and the parts in a holarchy. Network logic facilitates reflexivity, planning and awareness of one's self or group as a whole in itself and as a part of a larger whole. Each part or level of the organisation or network possesses its own integrity and is equally valued for itself, whilst being an active and integral contributor to the larger context[19].

Aspiration to holistic meaning and the creative visualisation of democratic change – aspects of democratic consciousness – are awakened not only by cognitive reflection but also in response to myth and metaphor. In exploring the possibilities of entrepreneurialism, Richard Weiskopf and Chris Steyaert frame their exploration in a parable taken from Nietzsche, which leads, *inter alia*, to recognising both the 'no of critique' and the 'yes of becoming'. A sentence from Nietzsche, which Weiskopf and Steyaert quote, and their explanation of the parable which opens their discussion is reproduced in Box 7.1[20].

Box 7.1

I name you three metamorphoses of the spirit:
how the spirit shall become a camel,
and the camel a lion,
and the lion at last a child
(Nietzsche, *Thus Spake Zarathustra*)

In the story of Zarathustra and the three metamorphoses, Nietzsche starts rather at the end, as human and educational development is not seen so much as a matter of a tabula rasa or a fresh beginning but rather as a condition of being loaded by (scientific and worldly) tradition, as an exercise in getting familiar with (the history of) ways of thinking. He creates the image of the camel or of all those who move around with heavy loads of conventions and values that might help them to take part or function in a certain context but that also retain them in thinking and doing anew. The metamorphosis from camel to lion creates the possibility of questioning the many things one has dressed oneself with and to problematize the many assumptions one is working from. The third metamorphosis from lion to child brings along the possibility of new affirmations and the active affirmation of power as reactive values are transformed. (Weiskopf and Steyaert, 2009, p 183)

The point of interest here is not so much the idea, but the mode of presentation (the parable) from which their discussion unfolded – and the kind of responses that this way of communicating encourages. It is not simply recognising myth, metaphor and story as devices of communication: they are often used to get over ideas. The significance is the arational nature of these modes of expression that is beyond or under the 'visible' communicative signals of the explanatory, propositional points that emerge from it. In this case, it is the innocence of the child which resonates with the idea that the emergent self-organising system must be seen differently. This is not only an idea to be stated but a consciousness to be awakened. Amplification is not simply about techniques for change, but about awareness.

Democratising networks

Networks are characteristic of the governance that has developed into the 21st century and integral to organic meta-governance. An understanding of how social networks work and an appreciation of their influence on people is essential to developing effective policies, argues Paul Ormerod (2010). Understanding and using them 'can make a significant contribution to tapping into civic capacity ... and meeting public policy goals ... [though they are] complex and the way they operate is unpredictable' (Ormerod, 2010, pp 36–7). They also have, however, a weakness – a deficit of democratic accountability. Reliance on networks tends to be characterised only by 'thin democracy', relying on distant mechanisms of representative democracy (such as a national parliament) which do little to facilitate accountability and participation throughout the system (Woods, P.A. 2003, p 153). Network theory of governance 'neglects the continuing power of the state over the system frame, and the regulation of resources' (Ranson, 2008, p 208: see also Martin, 2010).

Ormerod's contemporary recognition of the ways in which people take cues and learn from those in their web of relationships makes sense. It is prefigured in democracy as a mode of governance in Ancient Athens. The context in democratic Athens was the operation of temporary teams (Athenian boards) and extended social networks (tribes and so on) within a culture clearly communicating and reinforcing its values and ways of working as a democracy. There were, therefore, strong specific and shared norms embedded in how people behaved and interrelated, specifically valuing active democracy – which of course differentiates it from many of the myriad networks that populate modern society (though some networks are avowedly about democracy and social justice[21]). One of the great values of democracy in Athens was how it aggregated the diverse experiences and perspectives of citizens, whilst not requiring every individual to be an expert of every decision and detail. This was done by individuals recognising issues where they were not knowledgeable and building up an awareness over time of who would be the best informed leaders in those cases. This *social knowledge* was a key element of its operation (see Ober, 2008, pp 163–4, 179–83). It was based on the capability of each person in the 'mass' of citizenry to learn and on the fact that they each were nodes in extensive networks, able to work out from whom they could take a lead concerning matters on which they were not expert. This was one of the ways in which democracy in Athens was capable of 'sustained and aggregated "institutional learning" over time' (Ober, 2008, p 159). Equally important was the capacity for individual citizens to resist pressure from the powerful to follow their lead when they were trying to exert their interest. For example, the 'individual juror's stubborn unwillingness to follow the lead of even very prominent litigants was an essential epistemic bastion of the Athenian social order' (p 181).

This ancient experience offers clues to the democratisation of network governance. Making networks democratic involves the exercise of responsible social knowledge concerning who, or which organisations, should be accorded influence, building such accumulated knowledge into the institutional learning of networks; it involves encouragement of questioning of power and authority (the advance of monitory democracy may suggest development in this direction is operating in fertile ground); it entails increased lateral accountability and knowing how to do this (experience of networked community governance shows the development of local agencies' accountability to each other, for example); and it demands understanding the different priorities, cultures and values of network participants, and equally being aware of one's self and one's organisation[22]. There are sweeping implications for professional development. Democratisation of networks requires people – especially those at influential points of interaction (nodes) – to develop the awareness, values, capabilities and confidence of critical democratic actors. Or, to put it another way, the aim of leadership development for the future is the nurturing of democratic consciousness.

This chapter has concentrated on what embodied change and fully embodied learning mean, and the role and nature of critical democratic actors who enact the kind of adaptive strategy discussed in Chapter 6. The following two chapters illustrate ideas that have been discussed thus far in the previous chapters. Chapter 8 sets out a way of framing and reflecting on degrees of democracy and engaging in amplification, drawing on three different types of school. Chapter 9 provides further illustrations of approaches and initiatives in the direction of degrees of democracy, within the more democratic, self-organising system that is emerging.

EIGHT

Degrees of democracy[1]

Philip A. Woods and Glenys J. Woods

The path will be known only after walking on it (From 'A Cloud hides the Sun and also Makes it Seen'[2])

Achieving democracy – still more so holistic democracy – is a highly ambitious aim. Democracy, as others have argued before, is best seen as a journey rather than a point of arrival. This chapter puts forward a framework for analysing the idea of 'degrees of democracy', using data from three different kinds of school in England to illustrate and illuminate the framework.

The question of degrees of democracy was brought to the fore in analysis of data from a study of an inner city Academy in England (one of the three schools featured in this chapter). At the time of study one of the key staff development initiatives was an emergent leadership scheme (ELS), initiated, developed and organised by the Academy, which aimed to develop leadership capabilities in teachers early in their career. It appeared to be an example of a phenomenon that is integral to contemporary ideas of effective organisation, including schools – namely, the engagement of organisational members' energy, passion and desire in relationships that build and distribute leadership capacity, blur traditional organisational hierarchies and assumptions and promote innovation and learning within the organisation. It also offered an illuminating illustration of some of the leadership dynamics in the Academy, revealing how it was willing to experiment and attempt to model new forms of leadership practice designed to effect fast-paced change. On field visits, which included interviews and observations[3], the ELS appeared to encapsulate the energy, passion and commitment that could be seen in how many of the staff approached their work and relationships in the Academy and the Academy's aspiration to develop an ideas-generating culture[4]. One possible interpretation of the ELS could be to see it as an instrumental exercise which engages the commitment, enthusiasm and creativity of teaching staff towards achieving performative goals – that is, not about real empowerment, but an example of the way teaching is subjected to policy agendas whilst appearing to be given opportunities for leadership and creativity. After all, the scheme was, at the time of the case study, driven by the goals of the senior leadership and a corporate strategy which (at that time) focused on thinking skills that would increase students' grades in tests and examinations; and decisions on who should join the scheme were in the hands of the senior leadership.

There were, however, other data that prompted pause for further thought. Striking features of the ELS, which communicated itself in visits to the Academy, interviews with emergent leaders and lead teachers (who support the emergent leaders) and observations in the Academy, were the energy and enthusiasm, and the sense of personal achievement and self-belief, it evoked. Numerous comments from participants illustrated the buzz, stimulation and keenness for mutual shared learning that the scheme was perceived as generating. One of the more experienced lead teachers said: 'I mean certainly when we go on our weekends away, it sounds like a cliché but it is actually true, the buzz you get is brilliant. You come away with so many ideas', and another lead teacher gave an example of how it was 'definitely empowering' the emergent leaders, citing one emergent leader in her department who had an agenda slot in departmental meetings and was 'gradually establishing herself as someone with leadership qualities'. This was reinforced by the emergent leaders themselves who generally expressed positive views about the scheme: for example, how they were able to work creatively with fellow newly qualified teachers, as well as senior teachers, across the usual intra-school boundaries (e.g. cross-departmentally) and the numerous opportunities for recognition and leadership during training days that they organised and led, which included DVDs that they designed and made and used to present ideas to the full range of staff. Whilst not everything was rosy about the scheme – certainly not in these early days when there was concern, for example, about lack of transparency about how to get into it – it seemed important to consider that it might also be seen more broadly as a collective expression of change which could have possibilities for an authentic, collegial, democratic professionality.

This sensitivity to the different interpretative possibilities was reinforced by the data being collected about the Academy beyond the ELS during the period of the study. For example, whilst there were evidently some tensions and conflict about the leadership approach and the pace and top-down character of change, a survey of Academy staff found that, although the Academy does not have an articulated democratic vision, just over half of staff nevertheless agreed that 'The academy has a vision of democratic principles and participation'[5]. The question all of this raised – of whether such a scheme constituted an intensification of performative culture or progress in the direction of democratic professional participation – led to development of an analytical framework, bringing in data from other schools, for examining degrees of democracy presented in this chapter.

Methodology

Analysis of the data used to illustrate the framework was undertaken by Glenys Woods and myself, who were involved in the studies of the three schools, and hence 'we' and 'our' in this chapter refer to myself and Glenys. We drafted the analytical framework (based on our analyses of the empirical data analysis and our joint and separate work on leadership, democracy, alternative education and spirituality[6]); and then developed the framework further through an extended recursive process, moving back and forth between theory and data. During this process we selected and examined illustrations from the three schools and, in a series of discussions between ourselves, successively refined the framework. The results are distilled in the following section.

The three schools from which illustrative data are drawn are Sands, Michael Hall and the inner city Academy. For the purposes of reporting the data, the latter is given the fictitious name of Urbanview Academy. These schools were chosen because they configure the variables in the framework in different ways. Sands describes itself as a democratic school. Michael Hall is run by a collegiate of staff in line with the educational philosophy of Rudolf Steiner and, as a Steiner school, is a member of the largest international group of alternative schools. Urbanview Academy is located in one of the most severely deprived inner city areas in England. Its sponsors are two business people and a local university. Key characteristics concerning the schools are given in Table 8.1.

The research on the schools shows them at particular periods of time. Michael Hall is undergoing experimental changes in its leadership structure since the research undertaken there in 2005. Urbanview Academy is especially committed to rapid and continuous change in order to prove itself and tackle fundamental educational problems in its local area: the data on Urbanview Academy refer to its first two years, since which time the school has continued to develop its leadership approach. The insights from the schools at a particular time stand, nevertheless, as empirical cases which illuminate the conceptual framework.

Table 8.1: Characteristics of the three schools

	Sands	Michael Hall	Urbanview Academy
Internal governance	democratically run by staff and students	run by collegiate of teachers	traditional hierarchy with principal and senior leadership team
Funding	private	private	state funded, with private sponsors
Opened	1987	1925	2006
Student age range and gender	11 - 16 co-educational	kindergarten to 19 co-educational	11 - 18 co-educational
Student population	c60	c500	c1200
Social class	mainly middle class	mainly middle class	working class; deprived catchment area with high unemployment
Educational philosophy	democratic	Anthroposophy (the philosophy created by Rudolf Steiner)	creation of a culture of enterprise and enquiry intended to raise educational standards and contribute to local community regeneration
Student admissions	staff and students decide if potential students (and teachers) are right for the school (rarely is anyone turned down)	decided by teachers, who consider if potential student will benefit from Waldorf education	local, non-selective community school; any student has right to enrol if places are available
Uniform	no	no	yes

In summary, our sources of data were as follows:

- Michael Hall: a case study of its distributed leadership structure and practice, undertaken in 2005[7], involving 20 staff and data collection through interviews, focus groups, observed events (including the college meeting), informal conversations, and documentation. This followed a separate study of Waldorf schools in England (including Michael Hall), conducted through survey, school visits and classroom observations[8].
- Urbanview Academy: a case study investigating leadership and entrepreneurialism as distributed phenomena in the organisation (April 2007 to December 2008), with data being collected in seven staged visits through interviews and questionnaire surveys of staff, students, sponsors and others, as well as observations and collection of documentation[9]. Survey data collected from staff included questions that were based on the dimensions of holistic democracy and the responses to these were used to generate questions and issues for further analysis in the case study[10].
- Sands: a day's research visit in 2010 to gain insights into its operation as a democratic school, during which we had conversations with staff and students, observed meetings, took notes and recorded short video clips of students, supplemented by information from its website and writings on the school and democratic education by one of its co-founders.

Preparation for the process of developing and refining the framework involved further analysis of the data sets on leadership from the Urbanview Academy case study, building on our published articles, reports and conference papers reporting Academy data; identifying relevant themes and data from our published work on Michael Hall; and analysis of the data gleaned on and about Sands School.

Degrees of democracy: an analytical framework

The analytical framework (Figure 8.1) comprises a set of contrasting features relating to two organisational ideal types. The left side represents the hierarchical, rationally focused bureaucratic school, with features that represent characteristics in their extreme form that do not all necessarily exist in actual bureaucratic organisations. (Not all the features on the left side are always negative: there are circumstances in which some may be positive and needed.) This is contrasted on the right side with holistic democracy, represented by some of the key organisational practices and priorities associated with an ideal-typical concept of the holistically democratic school. The analysis in this chapter is of what these organisational features appear to encourage and value. (It does not attempt to make claims about individuals – for example concerning their spirituality.)

Figure 8.1: Degrees of democracy: an analytical framework

Variables	Features of rational bureaucratic hierarchy		Features of holistic democracy
			holistic meaning
principal organisational purpose	competitive performance	---->	substantive
knowledge goal	cognitive-technical	---->	holistic
method of teaching & creating knowledge	instruction within boundaries	---->	co-creation across boundaries
modes of learning	cognitive	---->	embodied
			power sharing
authority structure	pyramid	---->	flat
spaces for participation	exclusive	---->	inclusive
scope of participation	minimal	---->	maximal
			transforming dialogue
communication flows	one-way	---->	multiple
key purpose of dialogue	information exchange	---->	transformation of understanding
engagement	transactional	---->	holistic
			holistic well-being
community	instrumental	---->	organic
personal	alienation	---->	connectedness
mindset	compliant mindset	---->	democratic consciousness

We do not conceive the features on each side as binaries, with organisations falling into one or another, but as poles of continua. The framework is an orientating device to holistic democracy as an organisational characteristic. By contrasting the latter with an ideal-typical hierarchical, rational bureaucratic school, it facilitates analysis of degrees of democracy. The continua are not meant to be neat scales, along which schools or other organisations can smoothly move. They make up, rather, a conceptual lens for understanding the complex, often messy range of practices and ideas that constitute real-life schools.

Each pair of contrasting features forms a variable expressed as a continuum. The variables are organised in the framework so that the features of a holistic democratic school are grouped according to which of the four dimensions of holistic democracy they relate to. The dimensions, to repeat them in summary form from Chapter 1, comprise:

- *holistic meaning*: pursuit of truth and meaning through the development of the full range of human capabilities (spiritual, cognitive, aesthetic, affective, ethical, physical);
- *power sharing*: active contribution to the creation of the institutions, culture and relationships people inhabit:
- *transforming dialogue*: exchange and exploration of views, open debate and transcendence of narrow interests:
- *holistic well-being*: social belonging, connectedness and feelings of empowerment embedded in democratic participation.

In this section, each variable and their respective contrasting features are defined and then discussed, drawing on the data from the three schools.

Holistic meaning

> **principal organisational purpose** *This is the predominant kind of aim enshrined in the (explicit or implicit) philosophy that drives the organisation. Where the principal purpose is **competitive performance**, the overriding focus is the narrow metrics of success. Where the principal aspiration is **substantive**, the organisation is led by values. That is, the meaning and purpose of the organisation is amplified so as to make organisational life genuinely and consistently committed to higher-order values beyond profitability and/or success measured in performative goals – specifically (in relation to its internal workings, the focus of this article), holistic democratic principles (freedom, equality, people's holistic development [substantive liberty], organic belonging and social justice – see Figure 3.3 and the related discussion in Chapter 3).*

Both Sands and Michael Hall have explicit substantive aspirations, whilst differing in some important regards. Sands' philosophy is stated as follows: 'We believe that everyone should be treated equally, be happy, and have access to good education ... no-one has more power than anyone else, the teachers and students are equal ... We try to get rid of all the petty rules, making room for everyone to be happy and free to express themselves in whatever way they feel'[11]. As a student at Sands put it, 'In state schools children have to adapt to the system; here ... it's the other way'. Michael Hall follows the philosophy of Rudolf Steiner (anthroposophy[12]). Its aspiration is to create the environment and curriculum that helps the child, as a spiritual being who has become incarnate, on a journey during which his or her full range of faculties unfolds. Teaching is seen as an art, practised in classrooms that are aesthetically pleasing. Urbanview Academy has a specialism in Business and Enterprise, and its stated aims are to increase educational opportunities, instil a culture of enterprise and enquiring minds in students and the community, and contribute to local regeneration. A major goal (on which it is judged nationally) is to drive up attainment in tests and examinations. There are therefore multiple logics – performative (driving up measured attainment) and substantive (such as community regeneration) – with which Urbanview Academy's school leaders have to deal.

> **knowledge goals** *This refers to kinds of knowledge sought in student learning and professional development. Where **cognitive-technical knowledge** is the predominant focus, learning and professional development are concentrated on the acquisition of propositional knowledge, techniques and skills, and progress equated with what can be measured by grades and quantitative criteria. **Holistic knowledge** incorporates cognitive-technical knowledge and other forms, particularly social, emotional, aesthetic, ethical and spiritual understanding concerned with meaning and values and awareness within and beyond the self (Zohar and Marshall, 2000; Woods, G.J., 2007). What counts as knowledge and understanding, especially in relation to areas such as meaning, values and spiritual awareness, is not absolute and is open to debate, challenge and reflection.*

To different degrees the schools are beyond the cognitive-technical end. Michael Hall embraces all the aspects of holistic knowledge, rooted in anthroposophy. Based in detailed texts that examine the pedagogical implications of the philosophy, a broad curriculum is followed for all students right through to school leaving age. The aim is to ensure that each of the child's unfolding faculties – physical, behavioural, cognitive, emotional, social and spiritual – is given balanced attention as interrelated elements of the whole person's development; and that this is in harmony with what are understood to be the phases of young people's development. Equally with staff, their 'inner work' (discussed below) is concerned not only with cognitive knowledge but other areas of understanding, including spiritual awareness. Sands aims to provide the opportunity to foster a breadth of experience – academic, practical, artistic, social and so on – in an environment where students choose their learning programme. Sands is not guided by an explicit spiritual philosophy, but it has been suggested that in practice it shares an implicit concern (consciously articulated in some other democratic schools) with 'planes' of development that include the spiritual, psychic, mental and physical (Gribble, 1998, pp 163, 172). Urbanview Academy, whilst giving attention to other areas such as the ethical and cultural, can be characterised as concentrating chiefly on cognitive-technical-emotional knowledge, i.e. cognitive-technical aims and development of emotional confidence and intelligence in order to enhance learning. For students, there is a very strong focus on advancing their capabilities to achieve grades, making available a much greater range of vocational qualifications and developing entrepreneurial, social and other skills and attitudes (including ethical norms defining good behaviour and development of self-discipline). Teachers' professional development tends to be of a similar kind – instrumentally focused, concerned with cognitive, emotional and practical capabilities.

> **method of teaching and creating knowledge** *This is concerned with pedagogy and modes of professional development.* **Instruction within boundaries** *follows a transmission model in which knowledge is transferred from those with it to those without, often done within separate areas of expertise. At the other end of the scale is* **co-creation across boundaries** *where knowledge develops through more complex and open processes: dialectical movement between transmission of knowledge to learners and critique by learners; sharing of views, expertise and information amongst networks of learners; and constructivist learning.*

Both kinds of approach can be seen in each of the schools. Urbanview Academy is actively developing student voice opportunities, such as peer teaching, student feedback on lessons, and student leadership positions, reducing reliance on instructional pedagogy. Most of these are characteristic of 'new wave student voice activity' of a kind where the effective day-to-day commitment is to high performance and to student voice which concentrates 'primarily on matters that coincide with current preoccupations of staff, on whom there is substantial public pressure to perform' (Fielding, 2006, p 305). Within these and other kinds of student voice, such as the anti-bullying scheme and the student parliament, whilst at the time of the case study there were some opportunities for students to take the lead and set the agenda, it was evident that these could be further developed and students allowed to exercise greater initiative. For staff, there are various fora to facilitate exchanges and staff development, for example staff development groups and the Emergent Leadership Scheme (ELS), mentioned at the beginning of the chapter, in which staff generate innovations and engage in boundary-spanning activities within and across departments. The backdrop to these are Urbanview Academy's priorities (enterprise skills, the vocational curriculum and so on) which set a corporate context that frames and delimits the scope of creativity and innovation.

Sands uses both traditional 'chalk and talk' as well as other pedagogies. Each student designs their own learning programme with the help of an academic tutor, where the underlying philosophy is that children and adults 'honestly deliberating together' make better decisions (Gribble, 1998, p 248); that listening to and respecting children's voices is a fundamental human right; and that students who choose what to study become engaged and active learners[13]. One student explained that she likes 'the fact that we get to take responsibility for our education, and you can make it your own ... Everyone is different, so you can't just put people into the system ... which is going to control everybody. You have to have your own choices in life and that's what Sands is teaching us'.

At Michael Hall, students and staff are seen as having a different position in relation to the model of knowledge generation. Teacher authority in the classroom is important in the sense that teachers are in charge of the curriculum and facilitate learning through principles of shaping and pacing lessons that give a distinctive rhythm and feel to the school's pedagogic environment (Woods et al, 2005); teachers are responsive to students' needs and states, and will alter the focus or timing of what they are doing. As students mature, the relationship changes: from ages 15 to 18, they exchange the 'security' of the 'teacher's "parental" role for a more collegiate approach' with a tutor chosen by the student[14]. With staff there is a strong emphasis on co-creation: working as a learning community through the collegiate of teachers, child study (a collective review of a child) and other staff groups, and interpreting individually and collectively the anthroposophical texts.

> **modes of learning** *This concerns the modes of learning encouraged.* ***Cognitive learning*** *involves placing the main emphasis on left-brain activity (use of reasoning, logical analyses and rationalistic decision making) and abstract learning.* ***Embodied learning****, in its fullest sense, uses spiritual, cognitive, intuitive, aesthetic, affective, ethical and physical*

capabilities (Woods and Woods, 2010). (See Figure 7.1 and the related discussion in Chapter 7.)

Sands' approach is towards embodied learning. It includes, as well as cognitive learning, a strong emphasis on aesthetic and affective learning through art, and on learning socially. Michael Hall's approach embraces all of the capabilities. With students, priorities are decided and pedagogies creatively used in ways intended to nurture and engage these capabilities at appropriate stages of students' development. This is grounded in the detailed body of anthroposophical work alluded to above. A distinctive feature of staff development is the way it integrates the spiritual. Receptiveness to spiritual signs and energies is encouraged, aimed at developing the kind of connectedness which is part of holistic well-being. Staff's 'inner work' includes a variety of activities to support the spiritual dimension of the person, such as meditation, putting questions 'upwards', sleeping on decisions, dialoguing with the guardian angel/higher self of the child, being open to answers emerging in mysterious ways, being 'given' an answer or healing, receiving reassurance through moments of grace and inspiration – all descriptions from staff in their own words (Woods and Woods, 2006a). One staff member described their awareness of their higher self and of an angelic realm beyond the higher self, and of 'working with an evolving consciousness in the school'.

Urbanview Academy's emphasis is predominantly on cognitive-emotional learning. Much attention is given to the application of systematic learning techniques, data-led evaluation of student progress, and systematic evaluation by staff of innovative pedagogies. For students there is a priority on developing thinking and analytical skills, so developing them as learners who engage in 'enquiry-based, research-based, hypothesis-based learning', as one senior leader explained. Equally, the emotional aspect of learning for students and the importance of emotional awareness by staff are recognised. The principal explained how much effort is given to students' self-esteem by paying systematic attention to ways of raising this. One of the ways is to reinforce success. The principal explained, 'if you give them any success whatsoever and say, well there you are, you've done that – see, I told you you were clever ... that's how we manage to get the exam results where they are. It's been blood, sweat and tears of individual children by individual staff'.

Power sharing

> **authority structure** *This concerns the predominating model of authority underlying the organisation. The **pyramid structure** concentrates power in a single source of authority at the head of a hierarchical arrangement, achieving organisational alignment through top-down direction and/or intense socialisation, with upward accountability. **Flat structure** denotes authority equally dispersed amongst an organisational membership, high degrees of self-organisation and lateral accountability (responsibility to one's peers), with intrinsic rights to participation and freedom formally dispersed.*

The schools configure authority and freedom in different ways. Sands exemplifies a flat internal structure, where staff and students have equal authority. The School Meeting, which all staff and students are entitled to attend and vote in, is the sovereign decision-making body. There is no headteacher or principal. There are also student-led groups and a School Council elected by the staff/student body, which discusses and investigates infringements or problems and takes its findings and suggestions to the School Meeting. Members of the school are accountable to the School Meeting if they break a rule. The aim of the school is to create an environment in which individuals exercise discretion and agency, and take responsibility for how they use their freedom.

Michael Hall has a dual structure: staff and students are differently positioned in relation to authority. The staff collegiate is responsible for all educational matters, including staffing and pupil admissions, for maintaining the integrity of the school and/or preserving and deepening the spiritual identity and impulse of the school. The collegiate is mainly made up of teachers, with some non-teaching staff being admitted more recently (more on this below). The collegial structure is intended to encourage collaborative working and an individual and collective sense of responsibility for the school. Decisions concerning the school at the time of our studies were made through a mandate system, through which individuals (collegiate members, parents, administrators and so on) put themselves forward to take responsibility for specific areas of the school – for example, admissions, staffing, curriculum development. A named individual or group (the mandate holder) had the authority and responsibility to carry out consultations and to make and implement decisions within their written remit. In the classroom, teachers are free to be creative and flexible in their pedagogy – working within the anthroposophical framework. Students do not take part in the running of the school. This non-participation is based in how the underlying anthroposophical philosophy is interpreted. A key factor for Steiner education is that all activity (including participation in the school's governance) should be consistent with the principal aim of nurturing students' balanced development and be appropriate to their stage of development.

Urbanview Academy's formal structure is conventionally hierarchical. Its task was explicitly likened to a 'corporate turnaround' by one of the sponsors: under pressure to show improvement, there was a sense of compelling urgency to bring about change. In the early stages after its opening, leadership was modelled on a corporate command–and–control approach, including the senior leadership team as a key engine of leadership. From the beginning there was an intention to develop and distribute leadership capacity, and moves towards this were apparent over the course of our study. Key aims were to develop staff as 'team players' and encourage responsibility-taking, so that the leadership became more like what we describe as *corporate hybrid leadership*, reflecting the emphasis on responsibility, strong central direction and delegation. The intention is to instil an ideas-generating culture engendering energies, enthusiasm and entrepreneurial creativity, and develop new curriculum opportunities as envisaged by the sponsors and senior leadership – through powerful re-socialisation around a vision for purpose, conduct and the self, which included bringing in new staff and 'academisation'. The latter is a term used in Urbanview Academy for a set of strategies to achieve common standards, particularly in teaching – through observation of teachers, on whom detailed notes are made and gradings given based on national criteria, to ensure teaching follows the Academy approach (with the exception of the occasional maverick who is granted their freedom). As one of the senior leaders described it: 'The hard bit is the academisation of humans'.

> **spaces for participation** *This refers to the type of organisational spaces available for participation and how access to these is regulated. Power concentrated in an individual or elite allows only for **exclusive** spaces for decision-making behind a closed boundary. Moving away from this, an organisation creates spaces which open 'boundaries of participation' (Woods, 2004) and, in the most democratic cases, are **inclusive** of all.*

Sands exemplifies a democratic space intended to be inclusive, constituted by the School Meeting, supported by other democratic spaces such as the School Council. At Michael Hall inclusion in its running is confined to membership of the collegiate, and is not all-inclusive. Membership is mainly made up of full-time teachers, as well as managers/administrators (the three cluster managers who then had a coordinating function). The collegiate does not automatically include all staff. For example, teachers new to Waldorf schools have to be at the school for some time before being considered for membership, and part-time teachers and non-teaching staff do not necessarily proceed to membership. Admission to the collegiate requires consensus among existing members of the collegiate, and questions about who ought to be brought into the collegial circle of shared leadership are not always straightforward, with tensions for example over whether administrators compared with teachers are properly valued according to the collegial spirit.

Within Urbanview Academy, there are some spaces for initiative and participation. These have licensed autonomy, because they do not exist as of right and their scope is delimited by the senior leadership. We feature one as an example. The ELS embodies the aspiration to develop an ideas-generating, innovative culture. Members of the ELS, chosen by the senior leadership, comprise selected newly qualified teachers (NQTs), who work with experienced 'lead teachers' in groups. The scheme disperses leadership by opening opportunities to take initiatives, develop leadership experience amongst the NQTs and work across boundaries (across departments for example). The operation of the ELS to some degree inverts the hierarchy as the NQTs, in their areas of innovation, lead professional development for and disseminate to more experienced staff. The agenda of the ELS is prescribed by the senior leadership, and during our case study period was limited to generating innovation and improvement in the teaching of thinking skills and hypothesis testing.(Since completing the research at Urbanview Academy, we understand that it is continuing to work towards developing and embedding leadership through all levels, including the student body, and that, with this end in mind, the majority of staff either have been or are in the process of being trained professionally as coaches.)

scope of participation *This concerns the issues and activities open to independent initiative and participation (Woods, 2004). Participation may cover either or both of two levels of concern: operational and higher-order. The former is to do with the means and techniques to achieve given organisational goals and values. The latter refers to the strategic direction, values and philosophy that underpin the organisation, and opportunities for organisational members to 'reflect on and make meaning of their work together' (Fielding, 2009, p 498). In the most strictly bureaucratic* *organisation, the tendency is to make the scope as **minimal** as possible, restricting it to defined operational matters. In the most democratic organisation, scope is **maximal** and covers both levels.*

At Sands the scope is *maximal*. The arenas for democratic participation are concerned with and make decisions relevant to both levels. This is the case with Michael Hall's collegiate as well. In Urbanview Academy, where licensed autonomy is given, the scope is on operational matters and prescribed by the senior leadership, as with the ELS discussed above.

Transforming dialogue

communication flows *This refers to the freedom and direction of communication.* ***One-way flows*** *involve mainly one-way transmission of thoughts, ideas, advice and instruction, involving restricted exchange of ideas and views.* ***Multiple flows*** *involve openness of debate, free exchange of ideas and the practice of cultural justice (absence of cultural domination, non-recognition and disrespect).*

Sands is characterised by multiple flows of communication, with strong reciprocal norms embedded in participative practice. 'Most new ideas come from the kids' is how one student described life there (Gribble, 1998, p 247). In the School Meeting and School Council we observed, discussion freely flowed amongst students and staff: the structure (an agenda, chair and turn-taking amongst participants) was complemented by a relaxed and informal style (with staff and students sitting on the floor or on chairs, for example). Michael Hall's collegiate and processes of consultation amongst staff also embed strong reciprocal norms of exchange. Consultation is the essential prerequisite of decision making by mandate holders who had, during the period we studied the school, the responsibility to take decisions in the light of consultations they undertake. In Urbanview Academy, at the time of our study there were both marked one-way flows of communication, consistent with top-down leadership which aimed to instil a different culture, and a wish to develop opportunities for listening and responsiveness – a kind of instrumental responsiveness. Struggle and tension in the process of change were apparent, especially in the early stages. For some staff, there was anxiety and, as one put it, a culture of fear existed. A survey of staff showed majorities positive about the Academy in some regards, but a low proportion agreeing that 'Everyone in the academy participates in some way in decision making'[15]. Student leadership was associated by students with 'having a say'. Many students were enthusiastic about the opportunities to lead and express their voice and considered them a positive feature of Urbanview Academy. For others, however, matters were seen much more negatively. Student interviews indicated strong feelings about the way they were disciplined, the pace of change and not being listened to. In the survey of students we undertook, poor perceptions of the overall leadership of Urbanview Academy were strongly associated with feelings that students were not consulted enough[16]. Feelings of being too controlled were a key theme from a number of the student interviews we conducted.

> **key purpose of dialogue** *The focus of this variable is on the purpose of typical exchanges.* **Information exchange** *concerns functional passing of information, such as giving information or feedback, issuing or clarifying instructions. At the extreme end it involves strict hierarchical regulation over who has access to which information.* **Transforming understanding***, as well as involving information exchange, is about bringing different, sometimes conflicting views and perspectives to the surface, diverse sources of information and the fruits of different ways of knowing (including spiritual awareness), and out of these coming to a new understanding that advances collective knowledge and transcends differences. Complementing co-creative learning, this kind of dialogue ensures that the claims to holistic meaning are tested through sharing, dialogue and constructive critique.*

Sands' democracy requires time and effort to share views and information through discussion to reach agreed decisions. This does not mean that the school is without its tensions. The point is that issues and problems are brought to the surface, ultimately in the School Meeting, and the members of the school work together through discussion and debate to deal with these. Dialogue is a key process in Michael Hall, through the collegiate and consultations by mandate holders, where the search is to find the best decision or outcome for the greater good, working through problems drawing on holistic forms of knowing (discussed under 'modes of learning' above). In Urbanview Academy, dialogue, ideas and feedback are encouraged on operational matters. Hence, there are numerous fora for facilitating this, such as the professional development groups and the ELS. Less emphasis is placed on bringing to the surface differences and debates about higher-order matters. Only a minority of staff at the time of our study agreed that 'In the academy we engage in open debate and seek ways of superseding difference through dialogue'[17].

depth of participation *This concerns the kind of investment that people put in and which is valued by the organisation.* **Transactional engagement** *is where the person seeks to maximise his or her own benefits in exchange for the efforts they expend. It is consistent with a hierarchical organisation focused on achieving alignment and staff engagement through material incentives and disciplinary sanctions. At the other end of the scale is* **holistic participation** *which involves the whole person engaging, not just as a role-holder (Woods, 2005), but as a personality with all their faculties and senses, including their spirituality and spiritual awareness.*

Sands is located towards the holistic participation end of the scale. Staff and students participate as members of a close-knit community (which tries to balance mutual respect, the need for some, if minimum, collectively-decided rules, and individual freedom). Staff at Michael Hall go further, engaging explicitly the full range of capabilities (discussed under 'modes of learning' above). Urbanview Academy can be seen as some way along the continuum, as the involvement of staff is not purely transactional. There is a strong, urgent feel to its work, and enthusiasm in activities such as that of the ELS, which means that emotional engagement is often to the fore.

Holistic well-being

community *This refers to the nature of the social relationships in the organisation.* **Instrumental belonging** *is characterised by a set of instrumental associations involving relationships in which ego-centred and instrumental motives are dominant and commitment to collective goals and values is absent or observed only ritualistically.* **Organic belonging** *(Woods, 2005) is characterised by unity through diversity, rich caring relationships and strong affective bonds, in which ethical sensibilities are nurtured and cultural differences respected (i.e. cultural justice is practised).*

Organic belonging is illustrated by Sands. It emphasises a family-type environment (its building has the feel of a nurturing home), and relationships over structure (see Gribble, 1998, p 239). The starting point of Sands School is equality and respect: 'we value people as individuals. Students are free to be themselves ... There are no uniforms, no petty rules resulting in detentions, and everyone is on first name terms'[18]. At Michael Hall this kind of organic belonging is also valued. There is a strong bond between class teacher and children. The collegiate shares a language and discourse based in anthroposophy which underpins its shared aims and values. There is a shared orientation and sensitivity to higher values and aims that are ultimately connected with a spiritual reality and this contributes to the identity of the collegiate group as a community.

In Urbanview Academy, the high-pressure socialisation discussed under 'authority structure' creates a sort of forced community working together to standards and norms cascading from the top. The emotional engagement noted above and the urgency for change encourages 'hyperactive professionalism' (Hargreaves and Shirley, 2009, p 41) and 'greedy work' (Gronn, 2003, p 5). Interpenetrating with this, however, we could see examples of genuine collegiality in the relationships that have formed through the ELS for example, i.e. authentic bonds of professional connection and respect. One of the experienced lead teachers talked of the 'buzz' she got from the scheme and the respect she had for the NQTs: 'You come away with so many ideas ... because I could try that, I could try that, you know, somebody else has done this and why haven't I done this yet. So from my point of view I've learnt loads, just so much from [the Emergent Leaders]'. The beginnings of more organic relationships characterised by multiple information flows were discernible in the ELS, in the sense of its encouraging freer communication amongst all parts of Urbanview Academy and interactions that are 'dynamic, local and evolving rather than static, distant and stable' (Cloke and Goldsmith, 2002, p 141).

> **personal** *This aspect of well-being concerns the personal sense of connection which tends to be encouraged or facilitated by the organisation.* **Alienation** *in its extreme sense, as we have elsewhere defined it, is a state of separateness that 'characterises relationships between people, between the self and the self's capabilities and potential, and between the self and the context (nature, the spiritual realm) in which the self lives' (Woods and Woods, 2010, p 84).* **Connectedness** *refers to the sense of unity with the self, other people, the natural world and, in its fullest sense, what we take to be the ultimate reality.*

Sands' philosophy and curriculum, and its deep concern with community, mean that the emphasis of its connectedness is firmly grounded in the social, the aesthetic and the natural environment. For Michael Hall, its educational philosophy and pedagogies explicitly seek to awaken the full range of human faculties and nurture balanced development of these in a rounded way, as we have seen. An essential part of the professional development of teachers is the 'inner work' they do, and this is the basis for their holistic participation. The predominant aim in Urbanview Academy, through its attention to cognitive-technical-emotional knowledge, discussed above and modelled by staff, and the enterprise theme, is to give students better chances to gain employment, set up their own businesses and to go on to further education. This is the functional aspect of connectedness. At the same time, however, attention is given to other matters – ethical issues and religious education, for example – and most students and staff see enterprise as having an ethical and community dimension (Woods and Woods, 2011). Urbanview Academy is striving to bring about a kind of healing for students and the community by fostering positive self-esteem, celebrating achievement and engaging in community participation.

> **mindset** *Here we are highlighting, for the purposes of the analytical framework, particular aspects of the mindsets encouraged by the respective ideal typical organisations. A* **compliant mindset** *is the ingrained habit of relying on or deferring to authority as a source of direction and purpose and engaging in limited creativity and critical thinking.* **Democratic consciousness** *exercises and values critical, independent thinking, cooperative activity and the nurturing of holistic capabilities to expand awareness in the pursuit of truth and social and cultural justice. (See Figure 7.2 and the related discussion in Chapters 5 and 7.)*

At Sands, the elements of democratic consciousness are fostered through daily living in a (shared staff/student) community of democratic practice. In Michael Hall, reflecting its dual structure, the elements of democratic consciousness are nurtured in different ways for staff and students. For staff in the collegiate, running the school collegially is integral to their practice and is intended to be strengthened by continual 'inner work', evolving their awareness. They are encouraged to be questioning – including of the founding texts of Rudolf Steiner (though there often can be an unwillingness amongst some staff to question these texts – Woods et al, 2005). The strongly framed curriculum and pedagogy are intended to nurture in students over the period of their schooling all the capabilities required to be a truly independent thinker: in other words, a free thinking and independent student is the outcome of schooling.

Whilst being characterised by a strong corporate context which encourages compliance in important ways, Urbanview Academy also pursues key aims, such as developing an entrepreneurial mindset (Woods and Woods, 2011) and raising self-esteem, which include some features important to democratic consciousness – for example, thinking skills and development of self-confidence. As a new institution, it is on a journey, however, and it is possible to envisage further aspects of democratic consciousness being given more explicit attention as the Academy develops.

Concluding remarks

The discussion above shows different degrees of democracy in the three schools and, we suggest, the usefulness of the conceptual lens provided by the 'degrees of democracy' analytical framework. The picture that emerges is more complex than placing each of them in a single position in the framework. Sands and Michael Hall tend to come closest to the right-hand side of the continua in Figure 8.1 (which is to be expected given their founding philosophies and their context – without the pressures to conform to state policies), but in different ways. Urbanview Academy shows many of the features of bureau-enterprise culture (Woods, P.A., 2007) which place it away from the left-hand side in some respects, constituting a distinctive pattern between the poles of the continua. For example, the Academy gives much concentration to cognitive-technical-emotional knowledge and cognitive-emotional learning, is characterised by corporate hybrid leadership and licensed autonomy in its participative spaces, and gives priority to the functional aspects of connectedness.

From the complexity that constitutes the realities of these schools at the times of our studies, we select two overarching themes (Figure 8.2) that we suggest emerge, each important in understanding the degree and nature of holistic democracy.

Figure 8.2: Two key themes: meaning and participation

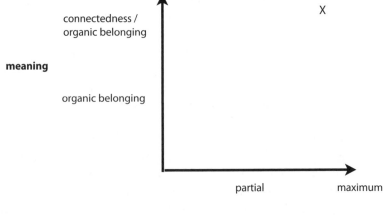

The first theme concerns *meaning*, i.e. how holistic meaning and well-being (the expressive aspect of democracy) are interpreted. One interpretation emphasises *organic belonging*, as defined above. This roots itself in the value of a rich community life and orientates itself principally around social relationships and the importance of the emotional and the aesthetic. Organic belonging is especially apparent at Sands. It is also evident to some degree in Urbanview Academy, which represents many of the main trends in publicly-funded school education. Mainstream education has tended to move along some of the continua in the framework. In Urbanview Academy, for example, whilst there is a strong concentration on cognitive-technical knowledge, there is also increased awareness of the importance of emotional capabilities (hence much of its concentrated effort can be characterised as being on cognitive-technical-emotional knowledge), so nudging in the direction of embodied learning.

The other interpretation emphasises *connectedness*, as defined above, and gives greater rein to the fuller possibilities of holistic meaning and well-being. This incorporates spiritual capabilities and aspirations (which do not have to be set in a religious framework of meaning), as well as the social, emotional and aesthetic. This is explicitly part of the day-to-day life of Michael Hall. This is not to say that spirituality does not exist within and amongst staff and students in Sands and Urbanview Academy. As noted, the analysis in this chapter is not of the degree and type of spirituality of individuals in the schools, but of what their organisational features appear to encourage and value. Whilst there are varying levels of implicit spirituality in all schools, the point is that some contexts, more than others, give explicit recognition to what we refer to here as 'connectedness'.

The second theme concerns *participation* – its breadth and scope. We simplify this into two types. *Partial participation* is the 'curate's egg' model, i.e. limited participation with boundaries of exclusion. This is evident in Michael Hall's dual structure. Urbanview Academy is not untypical of how much has been done in mainstream schooling to develop more active and interactive pedagogies, including student voice, which moves practice in the direction of co-creation of knowledge. These changes, however, have their limitations in terms of degrees of democracy. Authority remains hierarchical and concentrated, priorities are transmitted down, and participation is more operational level than higher-order level. *Maximum participation* facilitates maximum inclusion of the whole community, and is exemplified by Sands.

The ideal-typical form of holistic democracy is where maximal participation and connectedness with organic belonging are found – around point X on Figure 8.2.

Some of the issues that emerge from this analysis which practitioners and policy makers might find useful to address include:

- the value of setting out a school vision of holistic democracy, which articulates a strategy to develop holistic capabilities, increases participation in policy-level matters (both staff and students) and places skills (such as enterprise skills) in a wider educational aim to develop democratic consciousness;
- making explicit in a school ethos not only the value of community and organic belonging, but also of connectedness (the importance of the exploration of deeper meaning and of spiritual perspectives and awareness in human development);
- the importance of setting aside time for inner reflection (to enhance connectedness), especially when fast-paced change is continually expected;
- critically examining boundaries of participation and the rationales for including some community members more than others (which raises the question of distinctions between teaching staff, non-teaching staff and students, for example).

The analytical framework invites people to consider questions of participation and meaning as part of its framework, but then to creatively adapt this so that it reflects the holistic democratic aspirations that they feel will best work in their context and community. Each person (or group or organisation) has different needs at any particular point in time in striving towards holistic democracy. For some, a priority may be to consider how to address spiritual needs and bring deeper awareness to participative dialogues; for others, the priorities may be greater transparency of information and how to disperse decision making. Nonetheless, holistic democracy is greater than the sum of its parts, shown in the right-hand column of the analytical framework. The ultimate aim is to find a configuration of them all which works for the school and its population and community.

The ability to develop degrees of democracy is integral to the possibility of organic meta-governance and to viable adaptive strategies that build upon present conditions in order to create environments more in line with democratic values and holistic development. The analytical framework is, therefore, relevant to other settings and institutions too, such as groups and federations of schools, colleges and other organisations concerned with education as partners or sponsors or in local and central government. The energies for change are dispersed in the emerging system. The framework is offered as a conceptual frame to support practitioner and academic research aimed at gaining a better understanding of the expressive and participative aspects of democracy in diverse settings. Its systematic application will enable it to be tested further, adapted and refined. A democratic, self-organising culture depends upon deep reflection and finding practical ways of improving meaning and participation. The framework is a way of helping to focus and raise awareness of how democracy can be deepened in order to guide effective adaptive strategies for change.

NINE

Practice in the making

Organisational democracy completely fits into schools because if we are taught at a young age that we matter and that somebody cares about what we have to say and we develop that self-esteem muscle, to be able to express our voice and to be able to learn how to contribute to a team, I think that that will incredibly impact the global economy, will incredibly impact the happiness level of people ... (Elannah Cramer[1])

I think democracy needs to be part of the learning environment from the day one, where we are empowering individuals to be part of their future – and that comes through how they are being educated, how they are taught and how they are engaged in their daily lives from a very early age, as opposed to 'hey, do what we tell you, do what we tell you, do what we tell you, and hey by the way now you're old enough, you participate in a democracy'. (Heath Mackay[2])

... a democratic school system is impossible in a capitalist society ... But at the level of the school and the local school system there is the possibility not just of conjunctural campaigns – whether over pay and conditions or over issues such as proposals for Academies – but also of the *institutionalisation* of forms of popular and professional participation in their decision-making processes. In this sense schools and local school systems can be more or less democratic – they are sites of struggle. (Richard Hatcher, 2009, emphasis in original)

In this chapter, examples of practice are featured, drawn mainly from the state sector in England, concluding with insights into examples and perspectives in Latin America, New Zealand, Hawaii and Canada. These illustrate adaptive strategies and amplification, and are characterised to varying extents by aspects of holistic democracy – namely, the expressive elements (holistic meaning and well-being) and the participative elements (power sharing and transforming dialogue). Both elements feature to some degree in all the examples. They are organised within this chapter, in a loose fashion, from those in which the participative elements features more prominently, moving to instances in which expressive democracy and holistic meaning are particularly apparent.

Radical traditions

There is a heritage of democratic innovation in state education in England and elsewhere that we should not forget. Michael Fielding (2009, p 497) especially has been concerned to ensure that the lessons and the inspiration of 'radical traditions of education' illuminate the present and continue to offer 'a fresh and wide-ranging resource'. Examples in the state sector in England include Countesthorpe Community College, a secondary school which in the 1970s and 1980s put in place structures for democratic involvement of staff and students through which policy decisions were made and sought to provide for students a curriculum that was negotiated and individualised. Controversial nationally and locally, it reverted to the normal hierarchical structure in the late 1980s with the coming of the reforms in England that included the national curriculum and began the process of centralisation and local autonomy framed by performative and economistic principles.

According to Fielding, the most adventurous, coherent and successful experiment was a state secondary school pioneered in the East End of London between 1945 and 1955.

This was St George-in-the-East Secondary School in Stepney, whose headteacher, Alex Bloom, led its democratisation and illustrates a critical democratic actor in a position of formal authority. The aim there was to create a school life that actively involved staff and students through its structures (such as staff panels, student panels and committees and meetings of the whole school) and a participative curriculum. There was a strong focus on co-creation across boundaries of learning and knowledge. The majority of the formal curriculum 'was co-constructed within the context of thematic work culminating in a School Conference in which work was celebrated and reviewed in both mixed age and in form groups', whilst 'the remainder of the curriculum was negotiated through mixed age Electives in which "children make up their own timetable" [as Bloom put it]' (Fielding, 2009, p 510). Other aspects of holistic democracy were also evident, such as inclusive spaces for participation, flattening of the hierarchical structure, maximal scope for participation and multiple flows of communication (features of the 'degrees of democracy' analytical framework, Figure 8.1). Fielding gives an insight into the vibrancy of the participation, drawing from E.R. Braithwaite whose book, *To Sir with Love*, was based on his experience at the school. Fielding's account of a school meeting is given in Box 9.1.

Box 9.1: Example of power sharing and transforming dialogue

"'The half yearly report of the Students' Council ... was one of the most important days on the calendar of (the) school" and Braithwaite (1969, p 102) admits to "being as excited as the children as the day approached".The proceedings begin with Bloom speaking "at length, re-iterating the aims and policy of the school and of the important contribution each child could make to the furtherance of those aims" (Braithwaite 1969, p 102). After leaving the stage 'to tremendous applause' Bloom is then followed by the head girl explaining the purpose of the council and its activities prior to each class, through its chosen reps for each subject, reporting on their half-year's work with "the emphasis ... on what they understood rather than what they were expected to learn" (Braithwaite 1969, p 103). Not only was the emphasis on what had been learned, it was also on students' own perspectives and judgement on the value of their experiences. What transpires is a truly remarkable process in which students move into a reciprocally demanding, sometimes critical, dialogue with three randomly chosen members of staff who, with varying degrees of skill and conviction, seek to justify and, in some cases defend, the basis of the school curriculum on which the student body had communally reflected in such detail. In this instance, one of the older boys challenged the nature of PE [physical education]... that the school offered:

> He complained that the [PE] was ill-conceived and pointless, and the routine monotonous; he could see no advantage in doing it; a jolly good game was far better.Apparently, he was voicing the opinion of all the boys, for they cheered him loudly. (Braithwaite 1969, p 105)

There then follows a series of impassioned, thought-provoking exchanges between students and staff about the nature and possible justification of compulsion, the necessity of recognizing differences in need and capacity, the importance of thinking about and helping others, and the relationship between school and wider society, particularly with regard to preparation for adult life. Whilst only a snapshot of one occasion at a particular point in its development, Braithwaite's account nonetheless helps us understand why the School Meeting had such felt significance for both students and staff. Purposes and aspirations, the touchstones of meaning-making, framed the opening and closing of the event; a framework of reflection, dialogue, disagreement and celebration enabled contributions from all ages and identities in ways which challenged traditional hierarchies within the context of an insistent, demanding mutuality. A range of voices were heard, not only through the narratives of learning, but also through the leveller of laughter and the eagerness of exploration. And all through this ran the excitement of the unpredictable and the reassurance of shared responsibility.'

Source: Extract from Fielding, 2009, pp 512–13, reproduced by kind permission of Michael Fielding, Tony Bush – editor of *Educational Management Administration & Leadership* – and the publisher, Sage.

The modern mix: leadership, voice, action and initiative cultures

A point emphasised by Alex Bloom was that this was able to take place, as he put it, 'in the orbit of the State system of education' (Alex Bloom, quoted in Fielding, 2009, p 518). Times are different now, it may be argued – and indeed they are, as is amply demonstrated by the socio-political critique of democratising possibilities encountered in Chapter 5. Nevertheless, the contemporary account in Box 9.2 by a headteacher of a primary school describes a democratic approach which reflects a valuing of student voice and professional participation, particularly aspects of *transforming dialogue* which aims to enhance understanding.

Box 9.2: Example of transforming dialogue

'Our whole approach to teaching and learning is about shared dialogue, decision making and collaboration. Our children are actively involved right from foundation in planning lessons, they contribute to assessment and review what they are doing, and they choose the tasks they do in lessons. So in terms of teaching and learning we are aiming to develop dialogue – genuine listening and responding – between children and adults every step of the way. For teachers too it's about building a culture of participation, about them feeling valued for who they are. Sometimes leadership teams say "right, yeah, now we've got to listen to the kids ..." and then the adults say "well, hang on a moment, it would be quite nice if someone listened to me once in a while". This is much more about a shared responsibility for making learning irresistible. There is a very exciting atmosphere around the place that says anything is possible and everybody feels they can contribute. And because of that you don't get power conflicts. Instead of having a school council, we have a weekly democratic meeting which takes place with all of our children from Year 1 upwards in mixed-age groups with adults as equal members of the groups. These meetings happen every week so there is a regular reliable space where you can formally bring things up that you think might be important ... and that applies to everyone. Through this structure they can get to know each other – and then you get a shared empathy and a shared understanding. When I first came here the children were described by Ofsted [England's national educational inspectorate] as unteachable. Now their behaviour is officially outstanding. A lot of that is to do with tolerance and understanding. We talk about community cohesion, well it needs to begin in the school and there are plenty of schools where it doesn't.'

Source: Account by Alison Peacock, head of the Wroxham School, Potters Bar, Hertfordshire, in Hofkins and Northen (2009, p 11), reproduced by kind permission of the University of Cambridge.

Power sharing – the structural dispersing of authority and freedoms – is less apparent in this example than Alex Bloom's East End school. As well as quality of dialogue, power sharing was a key feature of his school, giving rights to participate (a form of simulated ownership) as far as was possible within the context of a school with a headteacher and accountability within the state system.

In another state school, the workings of which are summarised in Box 9.3, there is a degree of power dispersing and enabling of staff to take and run with initiatives. It displays licensed autonomy and hybrid leadership, but with similarities to the mandate system in Michael Hall School, discussed in the previous chapter, which aims to create an 'initiative culture'. There is also an emphasis on student voice through the Council. The headteacher is very much a critical democratic actor facilitating change and involvement in this case, as was the case with Alex Bloom. The students in key positions – the head boy and others – also play roles as critical democratic actors, being supportive and providing a 'helping hand' to give other students a voice.

Box 9.3: Examples of licensed power sharing and dispersal of initiative, with holistic meaning

Christopher Reynolds is headteacher of Saint Benedict Catholic School and Performing Arts College, Derby. The school is a state–funded voluntary–aided school with students from age 11 to 18. 'The spiritual and academic development of the pupils in school remains in the forefront of what we try to do. We have tried to make our young people aware of others, and through their work for charity to understand the great needs of those less fortunate than themselves.' (www.saintben.derby.sch.uk/Headteacher%27s+Welcome). Christopher explains that the origins of the school's distribution of leadership was learning about the Project Management approach of a locally based multi-national company, explained by a senior trainer who came to the school and spoke about how a flatter hierarchy brought out the good ideas they have in their areas of expertise and knowledge. The school has teams led by junior staff. In addition to the core membership of a team or small group, anyone can join. All associate staff are in teams. Christopher described the system of innovation as being 'I suppose ... in the culture of the school'. The institutional structure consists of:

- Leadership Forum (LF) – this meets every 5 or 6 weeks and comprises everyone who has a leadership responsibility of any sort (including associate staff, e.g. the chaplain, the nurse, and teachers on the lowest of 'teaching and learning responsibilities'). They will often bring ideas from their colleagues. The Forum has an open agenda – about learning and strategic matters. It has run for about 10 years. Christopher explained that the LF is big but efficient.
- Representative Groups (RGs) (now called School Priority Groups). There are 15 to 16 of these. They are cross-departmental groups of ten or so staff, including associate staff. Christopher's view is that they have worked well, but have outlived their usefulness. New ideas are gathered via the LF, so RGs are not so much needed. Allocation to RGs is random, with the aim of crossing boundaries.

A good example of a successful initiative, Christopher explains, is the development of the House system. It was proposed by the assistant headteacher and a classroom teacher, and they were then asked to take the idea away and prepare a proposal for the LF. After six months spent researching it, including bringing in another headteacher to speak and doing focus groups (with staff and students), they put a recommendation to the LF, which was accepted. Another example is the implementation of government changes to the Key Stage 3 (KS3, ages 11 to 14) curriculum. Christopher said to the staff that the school is to have a creative KS3 curriculum (one which had to be imaginative, exciting and connected with skills), but 'in what way it was set up and run is up to you'. Christopher suggested using Personal Learning and Thinking Skills. A project team was set up open to everyone. Membership was mainly junior staff (a dozen in number), chaired by an advanced skills teacher. They got Creative Partnership money, so they could go away for a weekend. The team now runs the curriculum, two of whom now have leadership responsibilities, and it is called the Creative Curriculum.

Christopher also admits that 'There are times when there is a discussion and I become a dictator', but only occasionally. He gave an example of homework. There was parental dissatisfaction about it and quality was very varied (he knew this from his own analysis). So Christopher decided that there was to be no more homework for Years 7 and 8; they will do Independent Learning Assignments (six hours for Year 7, seven hours for Year 8), and it should not be just finishing off. This 'just felt right somehow', he explained.

The Head of the School Council, the Head Boy, Head Girl and the Vice Chair of the School Council explain about student participation through the School Council. It meets once a month, with minutes and action points noted by the Vice Chair. The Head of School Council meets the headteacher each month and delegates issues to Council members. Examples of the impact of the Council volunteered were: a change in the time when form time takes place; uniform (girls allowed to wear trousers as an alternative to skirts); earlier help given with UCAS (university application) forms (before school holidays); appointment of a member of staff as a motivational leader to help students form groups so that there are lunchtime activities (music groups, and so on) – this was in response to student requests to do something. Contentious issues where progress was not being made included: the school jumper rule (if you take your blazer off, you have to take your jumper off too); the scarf rule (can't wear them inside buildings, but as the terrapins are cold teachers tend to use discretion and allow scarves to be worn there); sixth formers not allowed in the library at lunchtime (they are at other times of the day, but other students are allowed in at lunchtime and sixth formers are not allowed in so as to make room). The general view amongst these students was that the School Council system works well – it is 'very effective'. Students come to the representatives with problems (where they don't want to go to a teacher). Asked what student leadership means to them, the student representatives said 'we're not leading them, but giving them a helping hand', giving confidence. 'Leadership is cooperation.' It's about 'being an example'. 'We're not leaders, we're role models.' Asked if the school is run democratically, they say 'Yes', the School Council has influence. 'If you have an idea, it will get taken to the headteacher.' 'What you say can help change how the school is run.' The Head Boy says: 'The smallest person with the quietest voice can make a difference', through the School Council. The Head of School Council gives an example of a quiet lad on the Council – the lad will have a quiet word with him if he doesn't feel able to raise an issue in front of the Council – though the lad is getting better and has developed more confidence over the last year.

Source: Author's visit in 2010 and school website.

Much energy is being given in schools in the state sector to creating opportunities for teacher innovation and initiative, where teachers become critical actors in activating change. An example of an area-wide development to help sustain this is the HertsCam Network. Institutional actors are partners and key players: namely, the University of Cambridge Faculty of Education and Hertfordshire County Council.

The network supports teachers (from all phases of education) who are engaged in 'the leadership of innovation in their own schools and in the building of knowledge about teaching and learning in schools throughout Hertfordshire' (Frost, 2008, p 340). There are over 500 teachers represented in the network and the membership also includes other professionals working in or with schools, with people becoming 'part of the network when they join either the Herts MEd in Leading Teaching and Learning or one of the many school-based Teacher Led Development Work groups'[3]. These teacher-led development work groups are 'jointly led by experienced school staff, usually graduates of the MEd and a tutor appointed by the Faculty of Education. Their purpose is to provide a framework of support for teachers who want to initiate and lead a process of change or improvement in their school'[4].

The HertsCam Network is linked to a larger organisation – 'Leadership for Learning: the Cambridge Network' – and its values are made explicit[5], taking it beyond the confines of performative enterprise:

- Learning and leadership are a shared, as much as an individual, enterprise.
- Leadership should be 'distributed' and exercised at every level.
- Collaborative modes of working strengthen both teams and individuals.
- An independent, critical perspective, informed by research is vital.
- The status quo and received wisdom should be persistently questioned.

In David Frost's account of the HertsCam Network, he is clear that it 'is not so much about teachers sharing administrative responsibility and taking on formal leadership roles; rather it is about the right of teachers to fulfil their human potential, which necessarily entails having influence over their surroundings and each other' (Frost, 2008, p 340). In other words, there is a strong democratic strand to its thinking. The stress on fulfilling human potential is consistent with broader aims of holistic democracy. As well as the energy of teachers and schools, the network provides important resources – in terms of people and symbolic and intellectual resources – including those of the university and the county council, who thus play the role of critical institutional actors. The network illustrates elements of a strategy of adaptation, such as amplification (the explicit statement and commitment to critical and participative values) and mobilisation of resources (by bringing people and institutions into a network that shares support).

Another development linked with the HertsCam Network is the 'Students as Leaders' project. One of the associates of the Network is Amanda Roberts, a former headteacher and then independent consultant who is also an academic at the University of Hertfordshire. As a consultant, she identified a need amongst schools for support to develop students as researchers and leaders. The materials she has co-designed are intended to help schools aiming to encourage the growth of students as leaders through a student/teacher partnership approach and to support students as active participants – leading learning and 'developing and deepening their ability to influence policy and practice' (Roberts and Nash, 2010). The project offers tools, concepts and a practical programme to develop student leadership and to move beyond student voice by helping teachers to facilitate student action. One of its strands is enabling students to be involved in developing the curriculum. With its focus on developing active student/teacher partnership, it can be seen as aiming to move practice in the direction of Fielding's vision of 'radical collegiality', which is characterised by 'students and teachers working and learning together in partnership', based on 'mutual trust, care, autonomy, and respect' and arrangements 'expressive of the spirit of enquiry [and]... key aspirations of a democratic way of life' (Fielding, 2006, pp 308-9). Amanda is an example of a critical actor shaping progressive change in a democratic direction – working with and through others and utilising and extending the impact of a network.

The project has been running for about five years. It works particularly well, Amanda explains, in schools where they already have a HertsCam teacher-led development work group supporting teachers who are accustomed to using enquiry-led change strategies. It benefits from being embedded in a shared, staff-driven enquiry culture which leads to teachers wanting to engage students. The 'students as leaders' materials work less well where they are dependent on the interest of just a single member of staff. The progress of the project illustrates the influence of layers of resources – institutional, personal and the supportive effect of cultures of active networks. The critical actor – in this case Amanda – is able to draw on both personal and shared sources of strength, values and expertise to create a progressive trajectory of change.

The creation of a school system and structure to move from 'student voice' to 'student action' through dispersal of leadership opportunities is the theme of another project – the Learning to Lead project – that originated with the Blue School in Somerset and has spread to others. Its rationale is the recognition 'that it cannot just be the elected few who are involved and that young people not only need to be heard, but also to be actively involved in all aspects of their life and community to improve their education and raise their aspirations and skills for their future' (Piers-Mantell, 2009[6]). This is another example of amplification – explicitly taking student voice beyond an instrumental means of increasing student engagement. A summary of the project and an extract from the project evaluation are given in Box 9.4. Following its inception at the Blue School the model has been adopted by 70 schools in England, including secondary, primary and special schools. At the centre of the model are student project teams. As is clear from the accounts in Box 9.4, it works as a whole-school process that involves the systematic collection of data about concerns in the school and the formation of teams to address the themes that emerge. Community Link Teachers who support the teams are critical democratic actors supporting the development of a participatory approach, working from the background rather than as adults leading from the front. The independent evaluation of the project in 13 pilot schools, carried out by the University of Cambridge, notes that it 'was founded on the belief that students have an incipient capacity for leadership, that they can make a difference to their schools and communities while at the same time contributing to their own personal growth' and concludes that evidence from the project 'justifies the belief that schools flourish as learning communities when young people accept the invitation to participate and schools discover "the treasure within"' (Frost and Macbeath et al, 2010, p 3[7]).

The project exemplifies an adaptive strategy which seeks to change (in part) the structural workings of the school and its culture and to deepen the practical operation of substantive values. The evidence from the evaluation showed that it developed best where there was already a degree of amplification of educational aims beyond performative goals. It 'was able to take root most easily where there was a pre-existing commitment to, or emphasis on, student voice. Linked to this was an interest in education as being wider than the pursuit of academic performance. Learning to Lead seems to flourish where the school's view of education encompasses the goals of citizenship and personal and social education and where it builds on, extends and enhances current practice' (Frost and Macbeath et al, 2010, p 52). The application of Learning to Lead advanced the commitment and practice of democratic learning, 'making a huge contribution to building capacity for learning in its deepest sense' (p 62), with several identified benefits for students (p 41), namely:

- developing a stronger sense of commitment to their own learning;
- experiencing a strengthening of their emerging sense of moral purpose;
- having an enhanced sense of belonging to the community of the school;
- valuing and looking after one another;
- acquiring skills, particularly social, communication and organisational skills;
- developing confidence as learners and members of society;
- enjoying learning and enhancing achievement;
- becoming more aware of their strengths and talents;
- developing a positive approach to challenges;
- being more willing to take risks and try new things;
- experiencing and acting on enhanced agency.

The basic structure is an example of holarchy, with individuals and teams equally valued for their uniqueness, but their identity and purpose also being understood as part of a greater whole (p 2). The project illustrates as well the struggle involved in adaptive strategies:

> There is a tension between the values of Learning to Lead, particularly in relation to the concept of holarchy, and the traditional hierarchical relations that characterise many classrooms, particularly where teachers are under pressure to cover the curriculum and regard time for discussion, exploration and side excursions as a luxury. Students are highly sensitive to these issues and adapt accordingly. Knowing how to play the game is the first important lesson you learn in school. (p 56)

Box 9.4: Example of power sharing through dispersal of student initiative

'Learning to Lead (LtoL) is an approach offering tools, structures and ongoing support for young people to become truly involved in every aspect of their lives in school. In the process, they create positive relationships with those around them, raise their aspirations 'to do' and learn lessons for life.

- LtoL began in 2001 in the Blue School, Wells, Somerset, a comprehensive school with 1,500 students, now the case study school.
- Students 'self-elect' to run teams and lead projects to improve what they have identified as needed.

- LtoL provides a safe inclusive structure, which welcomes the diverse interests, gifts and talents of individuals and gives opportunity for these to develop within a team.
- In the Blue School, around 300 students are involved in all aspects of the school community and currently there are 29 teams: Africa Link, Allotment, Aquarium, Badgers and Spoons (wildlife), Beautiful School, Buddying, Dyslexia Support, Energy, Fair Trade, Finance Support, Fundraising, Garden of the Spirit, Governance Support, Healthy Food & Living, IT Support, Kitchen Garden, Management Support, Mini Beasts & Reptiles, Newspaper, Office Support, Poly-tunnel, Presentations, Pond and Growing, Quiet Team, Science Support, Shelters, Toilets, Transport, Waste and Recycling and Website.
- 2008–2009 Following the development of the approach in 9 other secondary schools the Edge Foundation and The Esmee Fairbairn Foundation have funded a national pilot in a further 12 secondary schools across the country, now being evaluated by the University of Cambridge and the New Economics Foundation.'

Source: Extract from 'A summary paper outlining how Learning to Lead (LtoL) can support the work of HS+ within the primary and secondary school context', by Susan Piers-Mantell, March 2009; available at www.learningtolead.org.uk/docs/healthyschools.pdf (reproduced by kind permission of Susan Piers-Mantell).

'The Learning to Lead model rests on the designation of a member of staff as the Community Link Teacher (CLT), a role that involves coordination and the development of the programme in the school. They also tend to take responsibility for training the student teams and maintaining support for them as they develop their own sense of direction. CLTs are provided with training to familiarise themselves with the structures, processes and materials by the initiators of the programme. The programme in school normally begins with a whole-school, online survey of views about the school and community. The data from this are discussed by all students in a 'This is Our School' planning session usually organised within tutor groups. The outcome of the survey and workshop discussions is the identification of a set of priorities for change and improvement which are then publicised throughout the school. Students of all ages are invited to join project teams focused on the priorities. Examples of teams currently in operation include: 'The Healthy Eating Team', 'The Buddying Team', 'The Transport Team' and 'The Africa Link Team'. Once formed, each team is provided with a training session which is values driven and focuses on team members as individuals. The training aims to launch the teams as self-managing groups in which leadership is shared and reliance on the Community Link Teacher diminishes over time. These training sessions are critical; the CLTs have a significant challenge in that their aim is to enable the team to take control within a very short time span. The training is necessarily intense and very teacher-led, but the desired outcome is for the future activity to be student-led. Team meetings are held at lunchtimes, after school and, in some cases, during scheduled lesson time. The students draw on the tools provided as part of their training to structure their team meetings which might feature the design of a project action plan or a project review. Agendas are drawn up and minutes recorded, and the meetings are led by student facilitators. The task of facilitating the discussion is not tied to particular individuals but is a shared responsibility with the leadership of the meeting often taken up by the younger students within the team. The decisions taken lead to practical action of all kinds including such things as painting murals on the walls of the sports changing rooms, distributing recycling bins around the school, tending a vegetable patch, raising funds to support the work of other teams or producing a podcast to tell the rest of the school what is happening within the LtoL teams. These activities are entirely led by the students themselves with a teacher coordinator – the 'Community Link Teacher' – in the background ready to help if called upon.'

Source: Extract from Frost et al, 'Learning to Lead: an evaluation', Leadership for Learning, University of Cambridge Faculty of Education, March 2010, p 2 (reproduced by kind permission of the University of Cambridge).

The presence of different, and not necessarily compatible, rationalities is an inherent feature of adaptive strategies. The account in Box 9.5 illustrates some of the differing strands that can flow into student voice and participation and the educational philosophy of schooling. For example, there is business entrepreneurialism (the 'ultra competitive' cafe) as well as the imaginative creation of a democratic town council and participation of students in curriculum design; and the account closes by emphasising that 'what is significant' is the impact on results, suggesting a rootedness in performative success. The hybridised concepts of 'entreployee' and 'edupreneur', mentioned in Chapter 3, are symptomatic of the coming together of different cultures. The question of compatibilities and incompatibilities in all of this begs critical reflection by practitioners as critical actors. For example, is the principal goal, in instances like that illustrated in Box 9.5, to create 'entre-students' – that is, learners who are to become adult entreployees – or is it to enable students to be citizens of the school, in preparation for democratic citizenship – and what are the tensions between these aims?

Box 9.5: Example of multiple rationalities

'Grange is a fairly large primary school (430 children including a nursery) on the borders of Derbyshire and Nottinghamshire. It is an urban primary school housed in the 1940s purpose-built accommodation. The catchment is an interesting socio-economic mix ranging from professional to socially deprived families. It does not have a high ethnic mix. "As educators", says Richard Gerver [headteacher], "we need to rethink approaches to teaching, realise that we have important 'products', and find ways to convince our pupils that they need them. If they want to learn, they will, but we have to make it personal to each of them. Part of that is letting them help design their curriculum". "Teachers need to be like advertising executives", he goes on. "We have to sell learning to pupils". So Richard and his staff decided to create an environment, a town. "Grangetown" was born in 2002. The town inside the school is entirely run by children and includes a school council that acts in the way a town council does. There is an elected mayor who carries out ceremonial, as well as democratic, responsibilities. From the council stems the town's enterprises: there is a cafe and the team who run it are trained in food hygiene, marketing and customer relations. The language in use is French; children wanting to use the cafe must order food in French. The school shop is ultra-competitive and runs at a profit. The museum has the school's archives, and the media centre has a radio station, television studio and a journalism group. The writers have complete editorial control. Initially, Grangetown was a Friday afternoon project but then it extended to run 5 days a week and became part of the fabric of the school. Teaching children to learn and live is the priority, and the nature of the project means that they can use their learning in a context. Pupils have roles in the town and they have to negotiate with their teachers to gain time to do some of the town work. What is significant is that this change of focus has enabled the school to raise attainment and achievement. Since introducing this new, personalized curriculum, Grange Primary School results have doubled in achievement, and the school has gone from below average to "outstanding" within 3 years.'

Source: Excerpt from Groves et al, 2008, pp 14–15, reproduced by kind permission of Continuum International Publishing Group.

Co–operativism

Emblematic of the opportunity to embed structures nurturing an alternative ethos in the education system is the growth in recent years of cooperative schools within the state system in England. They institutionalise values and ways of working which express cooperative ideals of self-help, self-responsibility, democracy, equality, equity and solidarity. They also illustrate success in terms of conventional measures: their improvement in attainment of the benchmark 5 or more GCSEs (including maths and English) at grade A*–C level is well above average, which included a rise at the Co-operative Academy in Manchester from 17% in 2009 to 42% in 2010. The Co-operative College and Co-operative Group have worked together to develop a distinct cooperative trust model and to support the creation of cooperative schools, and are further examples of institutional critical democratic actors[8]. By January 2011, 117 cooperative trust schools and two cooperative academies were running within the state system, with work under way to develop a cooperative model for the new–type Academies (i.e. Academies created under the programme as envisaged by the Coalition Government) with a projected estimate of a minimum of 200 cooperative schools in place by the end of 2011[9]. These include individual schools and groups of schools organised as clusters or federations.

As well as fostering a cooperative ethos, the governing structure of a cooperative trust school facilitates participation and accountability:

> Anyone with an interest in the school including students, teachers, parents, and the local community will be encouraged to become members of the Trust, making the Trust a community based mutual. The members will elect representatives to a Trust stakeholder forum, which will meet on a regular basis, in order to ensure that those in positions of responsibility remain sensitive to the needs, views and aspirations of the different groups.[10]

The creation of cooperative schools is a radical innovation within the state system which opens power and responsibility for the school to everyone. Sir Thomas Boughey School is an example (Box 9.6), and how it interprets cooperative principles is shown in Figure 9.1.

Box 9.6: Example of cooperatively shared power and holistic meaning orientated around organic belonging

Sir Thomas Boughey Co-operative Business School, Staffordshire, is a state school taking students between 11 and 16 years of age. It was a specialist school with a cooperative business specialism sponsored by the Cooperative Group until 2010 when it took the radical step, whilst remaining in the state sector, of becoming a cooperative trust school. David Boston has been headteacher of Sir Thomas Boughey School since 1994. When he took over it was a 'tired school', with inadequate buildings, a mix of outstanding and poor departments and a climate where 'people worked as individuals'. The surrounding community had lost its traditional source of work – coalmining, with the closure of mines since the 1960s, and there was a lack of aspiration in the community. Now the school is oversubscribed and more successful in terms of its national examination results (the proportion achieving the standard 5 GCSE A*–Cs increasing from less than 30% to 80%). 'You may say I've branded the school', says David. 'My main driver was to get kids right.' How he has done that is rooted in his background in the cooperative movement. His grandmother – a fervent cooperator – for example had given him a book that explained that cooperativism 'helps your self to lead your own life' – not a party, or a company or any other organisation. The school adopted cooperative values and became a specialist school, choosing Business as a specialism (because it could be a cross-curriculum theme), sponsored by the Cooperative Group. It was a set of values intended to lead self-improvement. 'We have cooperative over the door; we're cooperative in our being', David explains. 'We're not a flatarchy', however. The school is managed cooperatively, meaning that heads of department and staff are involved in discussions, including an annual staff conference, and know where the school is going. Strong management is combined with initiatives being typically led by staff, including newly qualified teachers. The definition of being cooperative is making sure 'we work with each other' to create things. It is a philosophy of supporting each other. Staff areas have been created to facilitate talk and collegial activity. The school constantly asks if things will help our values. An example had been refusing a free 'enterprise day' from a private provider because it taught students how to take advantage of others. The school measured it against the school's clear values. Another example is running the young enterprise group as a workers' cooperative, because running a company means that you should be into ethics. The school has connections with workers' cooperatives making jewellery started by 'war vets' against apartheid in South Africa. After returning from a visit to the cooperative, students sold jewellery it had produced and took profits back to the cooperative. Subsequently, students have joined a fair trade organisation through which to make sales. Students study examples of cooperativism overseas that have had a positive impact on their community, such as Trentino in northern Italy. With the demise of non-conformist churches that were once so important in the community, cooperativism projects values that churches did in the past. David describes the school's locale as still 'residually a religious community'. We still have full assemblies, David explains, because we start the day together and face problems together. This is about community. Cooperativism provides a set of rules and values that, as David describes it, are not scary, but internationally agreed priorities, checks and balances. From July 2010, the school became a cooperative trust school. The delay in taking this step was because the staff 'own' the school and it was important to give staff the time and opportunity to discuss the option in some depth. Being a cooperative trust school means that it is run by trustees, made up of individuals in any interested group – which includes students – who choose to join and pay the £1 joining fee. 'One of the essential differences between a cooperative type business and a PLC one is that each member of the cooperative only gets one vote regardless of how many shares they hold. This is also true in our cooperative. Additionally every type of member is equal regardless of the category of their membership' (www.cooperative.stb.coop/). In other words, power and responsibility are equally shared amongst the trustees and membership is completely open.

Source: Author's visit in 2010 and school website.

Figure 9.1: Sir Thomas Boughey School – Our Values and Principles

The co-operative principles are guidelines by which co-operatives put their values into practice. For us these are the ways we will develop our school, its members, its pupils and its staff.

1st Principle: Voluntary and Open Membership

Co-operatives are voluntary organisations, open to all persons able to use their services and willing to accept the responsibilities of membership, without gender, social, racial, political or religious discrimination. In our case membership is voluntary and open to pupils, parents and members of the community. As a school we guarantee to offer places to all pupils regardless of aspects such as background or ability. We aim to develop all our pupils!

2nd Principle: Democratic Member Control

Our membership is open to staff, learners, parents and members of the community. They all have an equal say, through membership, in the school's future.

3rd Principle: Member Economic Participation

In many co-operatives this is about what they will do with their profits. In our case we do not intend to 'make a profit' - any surplus will be kept within the school and used to further develop what we can offer to our pupils.

4th Principle: Autonomy and Independence

Co-operatives are autonomous, self-help organisations controlled by their members. As a cooperative in our own rights we will aim to keep our school locally owned and supportive of its community. We will aim to work with co-operatives particularly educational co-ops to help us develop.

5th Principle: Education, Training and Information

A very important aspect of any co-operative and vital for us.

6th Principle: Co-operation Among Co-operatives

Co-operatives serve their members most effectively and strengthen the co-operative movement by working together through local, national, regional, and international structures. Although we are independent as a co-operative we are part of an international movement of co-operators with a membership greater than the population of Europe!

7th Principle: Concern for Community

Co-operatives work for the sustainable development of their communities through policies approved by their members. For school, which should be part of its local community this principle is very important for all in the school, especially learners!

Source: School website (www.co-operative.stb.coop/)

All Hallows, a faith-based cooperative school, is an example of an explicitly spiritually orientated school based on cooperative democratic principles, expressive of holistic meaning (see Box 9.7). In response to a requirement to raise the achievement levels of its above-average ability intake, the decision to focus on culture, identity, belonging and values illustrates amplification in an adaptive strategy that is not principally driven by performative targets.

Box 9.7: Example of holistic meaning and cooperative dialogue

Tony Billings is the headteacher of All Hallows Catholic College, Macclesfield, a state school which describes itself as a faith school specialising in business, ethical enterprise and languages. It is a 'co-educational and inclusive 11–19 school, welcoming children from our voluntary aided partner Church schools, the wider community, and also other schools where parents are choosing our distinctive ethos for their children. All parents agree to support our Catholic Learning Community, its culture and values' (www.allhallows.org.uk/). Prior to Tony's arrival, four years ago, the school was given the remit, by the national inspection agency, OfSTED, to address its teaching and learning in order to help its above average ability intake achieve better. There has been an exponential rise in results and the school has secured a place as a high performing school with over 86% of students gaining five or more A*–Cs and an average point score at A level that usually places the school in the top 30 comprehensives at national level. Tony explains that the leadership team took a bold decision, however, not to concentrate just on teaching and learning. It took the view that what they needed to focus on was culture, identity, belonging and values, because these are 'more powerful than anything else' in creating an ethos of high expectations. One of the initiatives undertaken was to renew the mission statement, core values and key principles of the Church school. Groups of parents, staff and students were invited to discuss the values of the college and state how they would be seen in action. The aim was 'to contemporise the gospels' and the process resulted in the identification of five summative or core values: honourable purpose; respect; compassion; cooperation; and stewardship. These values are 'signposted' around the school and through 'corporate signals', such as: a teacher's raised hand in a classroom is a recognised signal to stop all talking; if the headteacher holds up and points to the five fingers of his hand, this is an invitation to students to say what the school's five values are. These values underpin an ethical approach which pervades the life and curriculum of the school. A booklet on the school's subjects demonstrates how both enterprise and ethics are embedded in each one. Spending time looking at ethical issues at the school was also related to the collapse of the banks and financial crisis starting in 2008, which led to further 'discourse around values' and a renewed recognition that individualism destroys the common

---

good. Tony describes the leadership as a 'collaborative style of leadership'. There is strong consultation of students, which includes a college council of student representatives, but the school is not run by students. Tony explains that this involves seeking 'win-win' outcomes 'around consensus', operating an 'open-door' philosophy, joining students for lunch, and so on. One longstanding teacher and Head of Maths speaking warmly of the changes at the school summed it up as: 'it's the culture and how we feel about each other'. As a faith school, the school's approach is to make the concepts and language of religion accessible to all by using contemporary words and explanations. There is a belief that good religion comes out of and articulates ordinary human experience. The inclusive nature of the Catholic tradition in the Christian faith is apparent in the use of the language of values and in the school's symbolic environment (iconography). A statue of Christ with outstretched arms of welcome greets visitors in the foyer and related images and phrases, such as inspirational quotes, are frequent in the visual environment – 'aspire not to have more but to be more' (Archbishop Oscar Romero, who came to be an outspoken critic of poverty, social injustice, assassinations and torture in San Salvador, and was assassinated in 1980) and '... for nothing is impossible with God' (words of Mary in response to news of her conception). There are also numerous posters, phrases, photographs and so on throughout the school emphasising the importance of taking an ethical stance in life, such as images of Fair Trading philosophy and posters on the 3 Ps of social enterprise ('People, Planet, Profit, a different way to do business'). The school emphasises a philosophy called 'Pay it Forward' and 'Random Acts of Kindness' whereby good deeds are passed on at random in the proportion of three to one! The partners and business supporters of the school are also chosen because of their ethical emphasis; All Hallows is a 'Cooperative School' with close links to the cooperative movement because, as Tony says, there is a huge synergy of values, and many of the early cooperative ventures were started by Christians who had an interest in promoting the common good. One of the senior staff who is seconded from the Specialist Schools and Academies Trust says the values run through the school like the words 'in a stick of rock'.

Source: Author's visit in 2010 and school website.

Further expressive examples

It extends our sense of possibilities to look at examples in different cultures, so I conclude the illustrations by giving a brief insight into examples from non-UK jurisdictions in which expressive democracy (encompassing holistic meaning and well-being) is to the fore. The first example refers to initiatives – part of Convivencia Democrática y Cultura de Paz en América Latina (Democratic Collaboration and Culture of Peace in Latin America) – sponsored by UNESCO-Santiago), being studied by a Latin American network of university-affiliated researchers. The other examples illustrate mobilisation of resources, including cultural and spiritual identities, in order to increase self-worth and participation, involving struggles in creating counter-hegemonic educational spaces for disadvantaged peoples and cultures to overcome social injustices.

The Latin American study is investigating seven case studies of primary (elementary) schools in Mexico, Costa Rica and Chile, which are developing innovative practices in inclusive, citizen education and the development of social, emotional and ethical capabilities[11]. Its central focus is *convivencia*, which literally means 'living together' and is understood as meaning for schools 'the construction of school practices based on the principles of equality, solidarity, peace, and democracy'. The researchers' analysis found not only students, teachers and parents developing capabilities such as active listening, dialogue, empathy, self-control, critical thinking, deliberation, and decision making, but also activity that the researchers term 'practices that build *response-ability*'. The latter involve sustained processes of participation that become 'spaces of collective learning for *convivencia*', i.e. promoting daily experience in caring for oneself, others and the world around them. In particular, the research identifies four practices conducive to this:

- joint construction of school standards by the school community;
- dialogical reflection and evaluation as part of pedagogy;
- collective social action ('the entire systematic effort of the students of making sense of the learning process in a global and local context as well as of understanding the systematic support activities needed by the local community ... [and the importance of] solidarity, empathy and support for communities or regions in other parts of the world plagued by war, poverty, natural catastrophes or any other situation affecting their development');
- conflict resolution (through processes of 'deliberation and dialogue to which everyone contributes their points of view').

The initiatives, as presented through the research findings, illustrate a form of holistic democracy. There is participative involvement aimed at maximising inclusive involvement and contributions to dialogue and decision making, and organic belonging expressed through attention to respect and care for others and the development of ethical sensibilities. Integral to these democratic practices is school members' growing ability to construct '*meaning* with respect to moral action' and 'to think and act thoughtfully in the present moment ... living in the here and now turned into practice'. The researchers conclude that this creates a different 'moral order', i.e. a continual process of 'construction and renegotiation at a local level, of the agents' understanding of their rights and responsibilities', enhancing their 'socio-moral development' and promoting a culture which values and practises mutual care.

In Aotearoa New Zealand, Māori education has been at the centre of efforts to sustain and enhance the identity of Māori peoples (Waitere and Court, 2009). Successes have been gained in moving educational policy towards a bicultural frame of reference in which Māori education is seen, not as an alternative but as a norm, central to the mainstream, alongside Pākeha (Western) state education provision. Achieving equal status means that Māori self-determination in education is 'not a gesture of charity or provision of an alternative option but an act of justice that realizes a democratic ideal that centrally locates Māori within the mainstream' (Woods and Woods, 2009d, p 11). The story of promoting Māori education is not one of projecting a single 'Māori' way, but one of expressing the diversity celebrated amongst the Māori people. Hine Waitere and Marian Court examined Ngā Manu Kōrero (national and local speech competitions) as a renewed cultural form of Māori life and education – an honoured cultural format encompassing competition, debate and varied traditions, which constitutes a format and practice symbolic 'of what might seem to some to be a paradoxical unity of Māori peoples within their diverse realities' (Waitere and Court, 2009, p 161). They argue that 'locating Māori education in its rightful place ... will benefit all in our country. Already we can see how some of the diversely textured strands of Māori initiatives woven into the borders have bled into the centre, impacting on mainstream education and educators' (pp 163-4). Examples include (pp 163-4):

- Māori academics and postgraduate students investigating strategies for school cultural self-review and producing guidelines for change;
- descriptions of Māori women's experiences in leadership positions in education;
- critiques of Pākeha teachers' varied understanding and limited implementation of the partnership principle in their everyday mainstream school practices;
- Pākeha academics' and postgraduate students' investigations of the experiences of Māori parents, board members, and teachers in a unique three-stranded school;

- research into Māori Board of Trustee members' experiences in and recommendations to their mainstream schools;
- gathering parents' views (the majority of whom were Māori) of how a mainstream school could better provide a bicultural learning community in which all students were valued and successful;
- researching the place of emotion in critical pedagogy using the methodology of Māori language immersion schools.

The Māori experience is an example of the kind of cultural activism taking place in different parts of the world in which education features strongly. In the US, charter schools attract the same kind of controversy as Academies and other sponsored and trust-based schools in England. There are about 3,000 charter schools, which are state-funded schools run by non-governmental people and organisations, such as private companies, universities or other groupings. Research suggests that they do not necessarily all do better than conventional schools, and they are open to the criticism – as with Academies – that they fragment and privatise public education. Some, however, are approaching the charter school option strategically – to protect and promote marginalised cultures and to advance democratic practices. In Hawaii, charter schools form part of an adaptive strategy to address deep-seated cultural and material inequalities. Community organisers have taken the opportunity provided by the charter school programme to develop schools intended to act as centres in reinvigorating Hawaiian culture and language as a part of community life (Shatkin and Gershberg, 2007[12]). A White Paper of the Native Hawaiian Charter School Alliance expresses its aims:

> A Hawaiian-focused 21st century pedagogy, known as *Education with Aloha*, is offering viable solutions to the quandary in education Hawaii's native public school students have experienced for decades. Finally there is hope for Hawaii's native public school students. An innovative, culturally-driven educational approach, that is at once ancient and modern presents unprecedented potential to address the distinctive needs of Hawaii's largest, most undereducated major ethnic group. *Education with Aloha* balances culturally driven methods with the latest 21st century educational paradigms. Collaboratively developed by a group of native Hawaiian educators, visionaries and community leaders, with support from various agencies and organizations, *Education with Aloha* has been successfully incubated over the past six years by nearly a dozen Hawaiian

communities located in some of Hawaii's most destitute areas. These communities collectively make up NĀ LEI NA'AUAO – Native Hawaiian Charter School Alliance, which currently serves more than 1,500 native public school students on three islands.[13]

The importance of sensing and remembering place, history and culture is woven into First Nations education in Canada too. Myth – in the sense of a remembered story denoting profound truths, which resonates with the right brain and embodied learning – is integral. This is exemplified in how two researchers – one Western, one First Nations – begin their account of recent developments in aboriginal education in Canada:

> Let us begin by acknowledging that this chapter has been written on the traditional lands of the Mississauga people of the great Anishinaabe Nation, those of the Huron, the Neutral, and the Petun, and the lands of the Hotinonshó:ni, of the Six Nations located in what some now call the province of Ontario in Canada. (Haig-Brown and Hodson, 2009, p 167)

This act of honouring amplifies meaning. Healing is an important theme as First Nations education establishes its identity and presence in equal relation to colonially sourced discourses: 'many Aboriginal peoples in Canada are heavily invested in healing and wellness as a process of extracting individuals, families, communities, and nations from the contemporary outcomes of the colonial era and reengaging with traditional cultures, values, beliefs, and languages' (p 180). As with the Hawaiian and Aotearoa New Zealand examples, the movement is not about restoring the old or ancient ways, but about restoring dignity and renewing aboriginal cultures in a reflective and spirited relationship with modern, Western culture. These approaches are adaptive strategies in which holistic meaning and well-being are the dynamics and ultimate goal of power sharing and transforming dialogue. They are instances of democratic entrepreneurialism in the augmented sense of participative change that nurtures aspirations to meaning and the discovery and rediscovery of profound truths.

TEN

Energies for change

[D]emocracy often comes camouflaged ... democratic
inventions happen under other names. (John Keane, 2009,
p 131)

Our democracy has to become militant if it is to survive.
Of course, there is a fundamental difference between the
fighting spirit of the dictators on the one hand, who aim at
imposing a total system of values and a strait-jacket social
organization upon their citizens, and a militant democracy
on the other, which becomes militant only in the defence
of the agreed right procedure of social change and those
basic virtues and values – such as brotherly love, mutual
help, decency, social justice, freedom, respect for the person,
etc. – which are the basis of the peaceful functioning of a
social order. (Karl Mannheim, 1943, p 7)

Karl Mannheim's proposition about militant democracy (the second of
the quotes above), although written during the Second World War, still
has meaning for today. Democracy is not an accomplished fact of our
way of life. Nor is it free from dangers. It is under immense pressure –
from inequalities of power immersed in and spread across the economic
system, and cascading through to education; from political threats
that restrict freedoms in response to conflicts and perceived threats to
security; and from the low standing often accorded to elected politicians
and the system that they are at the heart of. If it is understood in its
richest sense – as holistic democracy concerned with meaning, sharing
power, dialogue that transforms and transcends narrow interests, and
holistic well-being – there is much to do to make it a reality.

The discussion in this book has highlighted trends that point to
positive possibilities. The third way policies of marketising meta-
governance have generated a dynamic from which a democratic
self-organising system is able to emerge: from the spaces and tensions
within plural controlled schooling, bureau-enterprise culture,
entrepreneurialism, network-focused working, student voice and co-
constructive approaches to learning. In these are sown the seeds of

organic meta-governance – that is, governance which steers rather than prescribes and which nurtures democratic ways of working, encourages deep reflection and facilitates diversity in service of the development of people's 'substantive liberty'[1] (the flourishing of all their capabilities as human beings). The development of organic meta-governance faces profound challenges, however. If it is not to be a self-organising system that is scarred by deep-seated social inequalities or in thrall to narrow measures of educational attainment (i.e. the metrics of marketising meta-governance), deliberate initiatives and strategies need to be pursued. If it is to be a paradigm shift, a transformation of the 'constellation' (Kuhn, 1970, p 175) of features shared by the educational community is involved – changes in shared awareness (beliefs, values, and so on) and shared action (institutional arrangements, behaviour). The changes necessary are not the preserve of the central state. Rather, everyone in the system – state, local government, professional bodies, teachers, students, parents, communities, sponsors and partners – has a contribution to make. Figure 10.1 summarises (interlinking) implications for shared awareness and shared action which are discussed in this chapter. They offer an 'actionable framework' (Chaltain, 2010, p 11), or what might be better described as features of a plausible scenario that subverts passive acceptance of a more limiting reality (see Booth et al, 2009 on scenarios).

Seeing things differently is fundamental. A system subject to forces of diversification requires a different approach. It remains in the socialised sphere of relationships but forces encouraging a larger view of education are contending with economistic perspectives on the

Figure 10.1: Constellation of change

shared awareness

see the system at every level as a democratic self-organising system
set the system's 'large-scale' aims and substantive values
nurture democratic consciousness

shared action

embrace opportunities for the dispersed and diverse parts of the system to energise change
imbue these dispersed changes with holistic democratic principles
promote organic steering
work towards degrees of democracy
construct adaptive strategies
turn accountability upside down
cultivate critical democratic actors
create bridging environments

purpose of schooling. The narrative of change advocated by the analysis in this book is one that envisages a trajectory from traditional welfare bureaucracy, through marketising meta-governance to a democratic self-organising system (organic meta-governance).

Two central implications emerge from this. One is the importance of seeing and shaping the system at every level as an emerging democratic self-organising system. The second is to recognise that the energies for its leadership are dispersed and diverse. The holarchic character of a democratic self-organising system means that the parts have within them generative capacities and resilience. They as much create the energy for change and progress as the features of the system as whole. As one headteacher recently put it, 'practice is overtaking policy'[2]: in the fast–changing schools system in England with all its uncertainties, decisions are having to be made daily by headteachers, school governors and others that effectively create what the national policy comes to mean in practice. These decisions are, of course, made within a policy context that produces constraints and pressures as well as opportunities. This is the context that requires adaptive strategies which look to larger and ideal purposes. The implication is that if we want a more democratic, fair and people-centred system of education, those dispersed points of leadership need to strive to embody those very principles.

The spirit of this idea of dispersed energy sources for change is encapsulated in the approach articulated by the Cambridge Primary Review[3] to its own policy recommendations. The Review is an example of what it means to see the system differently. Its recommendations will be advanced, the Review states,

> only if teachers, and the communities they serve, seize the opportunity and the evidence provided by initiatives such as the Cambridge Primary Review, and use them to debate the central educational questions which too often go by default: what primary education is for; what constitutes an enabling and balanced curriculum; how research on learning and teaching can be translated into effective classroom practice that engages every child; in what kinds of decisions about their lives and learning young children can or should be involved; how educational quality and standards should be defined and assessed; and how – individually and in partnership – schools should be organised. (Cambridge Primary Review, 2010, p 2)

The Review goes on: 'political transformation will not happen voluntarily or overnight. It requires those in the educational front line to take hold of the agenda and make it their own; and it requires sustained effort and, for some, professional re-education' (p 2). As an example, one of its recommendations is to 'Make children's agency and rights a reality in policy, schools and classrooms', by applying 'the UN Convention on the Rights of the Child in ways which reinforce what we now know about how children most effectively learn, but do so with common sense and an understanding of context so that "pupil voice" does not degenerate into tokenism or fad'. Crucially, it is urged that 'action on this priority is as much the responsibility of schools as of government' (Alexander, 2010b, p 11).

A defining characteristic of self-organising systems is that they have strong guiding values and norms, but a minimum of detailed rules and directions. It is important, therefore, that the governance of the emerging system is explicit about its 'large-scale aims and values of transcendent importance' (Mannheim and Stewart, 1962, p 44). As a democratic system it has to be open to difference, diversity and uncomfortable challenges, from a variety of persuasions. But its overarching purpose and substantive values – which protect minority and dissident views, as well as promoting democratic awareness and capabilities, and are open to interpretation through practice in diverse settings – can and should be articulated succinctly. For example, a democratic self-organising system in education could be guided by the overarching 'large-scale' aims of:

- nurturing freedom, democracy and compassion;
- striving for a fairer, cooperative and sustainable society and world order that resolve differences by peaceful means; and
- helping the growth of people as whole persons able to draw on all their capabilities in their practical lives.

Within the system there is scope for debate and difference about the interpretation and means of achieving these guiding aims. Central prescription, however detailed, cannot eliminate the difficult questions entailed in education; whilst marketising meta-governance tends to attenuate these questions by fostering attention to material and economistic ends. Succinct guiding aims of the kind suggested above are important in creating a culture that encourages the extension and creation of opportunities for young people and adults to participate, to seek and create meaning, to nurture and practice their holistic capabilities, and to develop as flourishing, independent–thinking individuals who strive to balance collective and personal wishes and who are vigilant against political and economic oppression.

Absolutely key is not to see such a set of ideal overarching aims as turning their back on the pressing and difficult demands of day-to-day living – the pressures of seeking and holding a job, of family life and negotiating one's way in a complex, fast-moving world. Rather, these aims encourage the transcendence of the binary between education for practical life and employment and education for academic and larger aims of spiritual, ethical and cultural development. The term 'holistic' at its simplest reinforces the necessity of recognising 'the connections between all aspects of life' (Bloom, 2011, p 2). These 'large-scale' aims envisage a practical life which is imbued with, not separated from, the higher sensibilities and ethical concerns that everyone is capable of developing. Education is about helping people to be active in the everyday world as fully human beings enjoying the richness of all their ethical, aesthetic and other sensibilities and nurturing their inner spirit as a connected part of the 'great moving spirit of things'[4].

The policy activity that frames the system has crucial effects. It can do a number of things to help develop a democratic self-organising system, through steering which is founded in an organic metaphor of human development. This kind of steering (organic steering) can set the aims and substantive values in broad terms as suggested above. It can – through discussion documents, policy statements, speeches and debates – reconstruct the policy discourse so it expresses the values, principles and ways of working involved in such a system. This is to do what has been done for the neo-liberal agenda (see Ball, 2008a, pp 14-18), but for a very different purpose and vision. The discourse reconstruction over time involves creating a lexicon, identifying 'heroes and villains', and including alternatives and challenging voices (such as cooperativism and holistic approaches to education) which are all conducive to democratic change. It creates the narrative that shapes the system. Organic steering sows seeds that take root elsewhere: for example, promoting a supportive professional base through the permeation of the ideas and challenges of a democratic self-organising system into professional development, including initial teacher education and leadership preparation. It encourages new growth – opening opportunities for new players valuing the substantive purpose and values of the system to come in. It creates open policy spaces where discussion, ideas and debates can cross over new and traditional boundaries – across the public/private boundary, across the new sectors (conventional and 'quasi-independent schools', Academies, Free and Trust Schools and so on), and across faith and non-faith boundaries.

Being a democratic self-organising system, or a democratic part of that system as an organisation or inter-organisational network, is not a monolithic state which is either achieved or not. It is helpful to recognise that there are degrees of democracy. Understanding it in this way shows that differential progress can be made in the dimensions of democracy (holistic meaning, power sharing, transforming dialogue and holistic well-being) which some settings will be more engaged in than others. Recognising degrees and dimensions of democracy is important for constructing adaptive strategies which grapple with the deep challenges facing paradigmatic democratic change and progress towards social justice and which involve:

- *amplification.* This is the explicit and systematic articulation of substantive values of holistic democracy and their meaning in the local context of a particular organisational or inter-organisational setting, placing performative goals and the constraints of an economistically dominated culture in a wider set of priorities. It involves deepening reflective practice by exploring present and possible frames, such as those provided by alternative education and the 'degrees of democracy' analytical framework in Chapter 8, in order to creatively visualise the future and transform current perspectives (see Redmond, 2006; Woods and Woods, 2009d). Now is an opportune time for schools to 'explore their aims and values and to assess how these are enacted in school and classroom life' (Alexander, 2010b, p 11[5]), because the dynamics of the system are in flux and the potential exists for a paradigmatic shift.
- *building on instrumental artefacts.* Products of the instrumental drive to change – such as flexibilisation of roles, team working, teacher leadership, student voice and student leadership, ands concern with 'soft' virtues such as sensitivity, reciprocity and emotional intelligence – offer opportunities for deepening reflection and practice in democratic directions.
- *giving particular attention to freedom as capability.* Freedom is not simply an individualistic notion of 'direct control' (Sen, 2009, p 302), but is more typically co-constructed through the support and cooperation of others. This cooperative view of 'freedom as capability' is fundamental to education which is about enabling people to feel and think for themselves and to be active agents in the co-creation of their lives.
- *mobilising symbolic and material resources.* Mobilisation includes bringing together the energies and resources of players with the same or overlapping aims and values in order to maximise opportunities

for progressive change – whether it be faith groups, trades unions, cooperatives or alternative education movements. The potential from working together is greater than their separate capacities. Already synergies are being found – as between Catholic and cooperative principles in All Hallows School, for example, described in Chapter 9, Box 9.7.

Accountability is a key issue, especially since hierarchies of authority continue to characterise in some form most organisations and some significant systemic relationships (with government, for example, where some degree of controls and checks follows public funding). Whilst the emergent system does not lend itself to neat answers, this does not preclude multiple modes and directions of accountability. Different models are available. The cooperative model grounds accountability for an organisation, such as a school, in the trustees, and any interested person may join and become a trustee. Hierarchical organisations are experimenting with different kinds of accountability: HCL Technologies, a large international company, has set upon a policy of 'inverting the organisational pyramid' by making management accountable to the people (the mass of employees) who 'create value' – for example, by opening up and making transparent managers' 360-degree reviews, so that anyone whom a manager might affect can comment on him or her, and the results of the reviews are available to everyone in the company (Nayar, 2010, p 13 and Chapter 3). Such reciprocal accountability has also been advocated in education – the idea that if 'the formal authority of my role requires that I hold you accountable for some action or outcome, then I have an equal and complementary responsibility to assure that you have the capacity to do what I am asking you to do' (Elmore, 2000, p 21). Ways of formally recognising and encouraging this have been tried and evaluated. One interesting case is peer-assisted review which evolves hierarchy by beginning to replace the hierarchy of individual administrators with the hierarchy of a joint panel of teachers and administrators that gives teachers a majority voice, and weighs the input of teacher leaders most heavily (Goldstein, 2009). There is much scope for further experimentation and practice of these kinds of multiple and reciprocal accountabilities, both in schools and colleges and in the national and local educational policy system, trying out different and radical ways of making senior decision makers open and accountable. These are practical ways of shifting the centre of gravity of governance towards the democratic point of the governance diamond in Chapter 5, Figure 5.3.

The mindset of leadership competencies and skills, so dominant in much of professional development in education, is the product of a limited marketising meta-governance mode of thinking. The nurturing of democratic consciousness – essential to a system that encourages democratised self-organisation at all levels – is an altogether more ambitious goal which requires diverse forms of holistic professional development. The notion of system leaders in education, tied to performative goals, is one of the seeds of change in the evolving system, challenging narrow, individualistic assumptions of education. It too, however, needs to be broadened and to be substituted by the more ambitious conception of critical democratic actors who work out of democratic consciousness. Critical democratic actors creatively – or, more precisely, co-creatively (working with others) – take advantage of the possibilities in the system by means of various practical actions, which include:

- *being entrepreneurial in a democratic way* – integrating enterprising capabilities for energy, resource-mobilisation and creative visualisation for change within a bigger context that promotes participation and meaning (in short, they reshape enterprise as democratic entrepreneurialism);
- *increasing degrees of democracy* (not necessarily looking to make 'one big leap') by devising *adaptive strategies*;
- *advancing the re-embodiment of education*, helping to make it the norm that education is about helping everyone to live a full practical life as people who enjoy the richness of all their capabilities;
- *working to spread a democratic culture in networks and inter-organisational relationships* – for example, by developing democratic consciousness as a network norm or aspiration and creating ways of encouraging multiple and reciprocal accountabilities.

The importance of *institutional* critical democratic actors should not be underestimated. Examples were recognised in Chapter 9. The New DEEL (Democratic Ethical Educational Leadership) network is a further example, based in the US[6]. Established in 2004, it is an illustration of critical democratic actors working together to influence policy, scholarship and the development of educational leaders. Its overall purpose is to change the course of the field of educational leadership around the world away from narrow accountability regimes towards democratic, ethical community-building that transcends the school walls. The network identifies itself as an 'action-oriented partnership, dedicated to inquiry into the nature and practice of democratic, ethical educational leadership through sustained processes of open dialogue, right to voice, community inclusion, and responsible participation toward the common good'[7]. Its activities include its own conference, having a presence and meetings at other educational conferences, lobbying to influence government policy on educational administration, adding new scholarship and new curriculum in educational leadership programmes, and bringing together scholars and practitioners concerned to advance the aims of democratic ethical leadership. The kind of initiative that the New DEEL represents illustrates the capacity to bring together key actors' diverse and dispersed generative capacities: rather than being run hierarchically, its members have a holarchic relationship within the network as equal identities.

Change comes not all at once. The emergent democratic self-organising system is made up of people in thousands of organisational settings and networks in recurrent processes of change – all at varying stages. This applies to schools, colleges, collaboratives of schools, teacher and student networks, communities, and so on. Where people and their organisational settings and networks are seeking to advance progressive change, they are engaged in creating and successively renewing a narrative over a long period of time: these organisational settings and networks are, therefore, forever provisional in their character – a feature of cooperative organisations (Rothschild and Whitt, 1986/2009). They are, to put it another way, 'bridging environments', at any one time being in a phase that will generate changes that lead to another phase. This can be described ideal-typically as follows: purpose and aims are set, amplifying and transcending narrower instrumental goals; closely associated with this are processes of deep reflection, using alternative frames to challenge current awareness, which result in reframing of thinking, action and plans for further action, and at the profoundest level transformations of identity (moving towards democratic consciousness); challenges, problems and setbacks inevitably occur, which – together with personal and professional development that brings new awareness and new goals (like teacher development groups looking to move forward to teacher/student participation) – are drivers for further change, creating movement to another bridging stage. Thus a dynamic of change is built into the system.

This dynamic, however, involves change-agents working not so much by devising neat, linear plans, which attempt to apply a mechanical or engineering model to the complexities of organisations, networks and the emerging education system, but by 'facilitating emergence' (Seel, 2000, p 6) through the co-creation of new ideas, opportunities and conditions that connect and interact with other initiatives and help build momentum for transformative change. The metaphor of the organisation or system as a 'brain' comes to mind here: order is not imposed but emerges from process, diffused leadership and networks of interaction (Morgan, 1998, pp 71, 107-8). Critical actors make a difference through their diverse initiatives and 'parallel activities' which make 'complementary and competing contributions' from which coherent patterns emerge (p 73). The more those critical actors introduce the ideals and practices of holistic democracy into adaptive strategies, the more the emergent patterns will give the system a democratic character in which the human spirit flourishes.

The lesson of the time we are in is that the ways in which things were done in the past can be changed to bring more meaning and participation to the everyday environment. The old education system of marketisation and micro-management is breaking down. Whilst some were enthusiastic about it, too many were trapped and dispirited in an imposed, narrow philosophy of education. The drivers for democracy, however, provide an impetus for changes that signal a new direction. The chains of the old way may not yet be lost. But democrats, unite! They are loosening. And the more the dispersed sources of change within the system are inspirited by a larger vision of democratic and holistic education and linked together in a bigger picture, the more the hold of these chains will be loosened and undone.

Notes

Chapter 1: New openings

[1] Originally published in 1986.

[2] On the steering role of government, the competition state and trends in governance, see for example Ball (2006b, 2008a, 2008b), Osborne (2010), Woods, P.A. (2003).

[3] I have drawn upon and adapted the discussion in Callinicos (2010, p 134).

[4] Interview with Roxanne Erdahl, June 2010. Now a leadership coach, she explained: 'I was a coach in the corporate world for ten years and what I realised is that giving people their voice, being able at the end of the day that people left knowing that they had a sense of significance was what I really saw that brought people passion, success, a feeling of worth and so the last two years I've really explored this whole idea of organisational democracy. When I left my job my goal was to really to go two paths, one in coaching and further get training in that area but also look at spirituality because I believe [...] there is a kind of sense of spiritual bankruptcy within the corporate world. I saw wonderfully good people make decisions based on what they felt they should do rather than who they really were and so that became my passion.'

[5] www.worldblu.com/ (There is more about WorldBlu in Chapter 2.)

[6] The concept of critical democratic actor is outlined in Chapter 7.

[7] Parliamentary Debate, House of Commons Deb, 11 November 1947, vol 444, 203–321 (http://hansard.millbanksystems.com/commons/1947/nov/11/parliament-bill).

[8] HRH The Prince of Wales (2007, p 2). The garden was Highgrove at the Prince of Wales's home in Gloucestershire, which I visited in 2009.

[9] Talk by Sir Ken Robinson, 'Bring on the learning revolution!', posted May 2010, www.ted.com/talks/sir_ken_robinson_bring_on_the_revolution.html

[10] In previous work (such as Woods, 2004, 2005, 2006; Woods, G.J. and Woods, P.A., 2008) I have used the term 'developmental democracy' and termed its four dimensions 'ethical rationality', 'decisional rationality', 'discursive rationality' and 'therapeutic rationality'. In recent work, I have adopted a different, more accessible terminology, namely: 'holistic democracy', with the four rationalities labelled respectively 'holistic meaning', 'power sharing', 'transforming dialogue' and 'holistic well-being'.

[11] See, for example, Cloke and Goldsmith (2002); Manville and Ober (2003); Kensler et al (2009); O'Hair et al (2009); Chaltain (2010); Kensler (2010).

[12] Accordingly, the conception of holistic democracy complements and extends the identification of democratic principles, such as the 10 democratic principles presented in the WorldBlu Democratic Design System (WBDDS) (Fenton, 2002; Kensler et al, 2005). (The advocacy work of WorldBlu for organisational democracy is cited in Chapter 2.) These have been tested in research on democracy in schools by Lisa Kensler (2008, 2010) and found to possess a significant degree of correlation with each other as indicators of 'democratic community' (Kensler, 2008, lxi). The ten principles can be related to the holistic democracy dimensions: they are listed in the table below against the dimension they particularly relate to:

Holistic democracy dimensions	WBDDS democratic principles
holistic meaning	*purpose & vision* (when an organisation and the individual know their reason for existing and have a sense of intentional direction); *integrity* (when each person steadfastly adheres to high moral principles); *individual & collective* (when individuals understand the unique contribution they make towards achieving collective goals).
power sharing	*accountability* (when each person and the organisation as a whole is responsible to each other and their community for their actions); *decentralisation* (when power is appropriately shared among people at all levels of the organisation); *choice* (when each person is encouraged to exercise their right to choose between a diversity of possibilities).
transforming dialogue	*dialogue & listening* (when we listen and engage in conversation in a way that brings out new levels of meaning and connection); *transparency* (when ideas flow freely and information is openly and responsibly shared); *fairness & dignity** (when each person is treated justly and regarded impartially); *reflection & evaluation*** (when there is careful and thorough consideration and feedback; ditto regarding previous actions, events, or decisions). * runs through the practice of power sharing as well. ** part of the practice of holistic meaning (aspiring to advance understanding and truth) as well.
holistic well-being (The concept of holistic democracy additionally and explicitly includes the idea of holistic well-being as a dimension.)	(Although not a democratic principle, WorldBlu includes as one of its core values 'Inspire Healing & Transformation': 'Sustainable change can only occur when the heart, not just the head, has been touched. WorldBlu is committed to working in such a way that inspires deep transformation in individuals and organizations, ultimately having a profound healing effect on the world.' (http://www.worldblu.com/studio/values.php [accessed 29 November 2009])

[13] See note 10 above.

[14] The first three are drawn from Kooiman (2009). Democratic governance is added and made integral to the 'diamond governance' schema devised for this book.

Chapter 2: Driving democracy

[1] www.worldblu.com/democratic-design/

[2] See especially pp xxx–xxxi, 690, 695, 731, 743, 738-9.

[3] Organisations which applied and met the criteria as democratic organisations were given awards at WorldBlu's annual award event, held in June 2010 in Las Vegas. I attended the event and the quotes from awardees and other participants are drawn from short video interviews that I conducted during the event. Awardees comprised 44 organisations (in aerospace, technology, manufacturing, healthcare, telecommunications, retail, services, energy, and so on), located in the US, Canada, Mexico, the UK, the Netherlands, Malaysia and India and ranging in size from five to 60,000 employees. For more information, access www.worldblu.com/

[4] www.namastesolar.com/cmsPages/view/page:who_we_are/section:our_story.

[5] Heath McKay (interviewed, WorldBlu 2010).

[6] Now at Equis Staffing.

[7] These will be discussed in Chapter 5.

[8] See Marsden and Cañibano's (2009) meta-survey of research on the effects of participation.

[9] Marsden and Cañibano (2009) provide an interesting review, on which the summary in this sentence is based. They highlight the influence of voice theories, for example: 'Most organisations work well below their peak level of efficiency because of "x- inefficiency" or "organisational slack" (Liebenstein, 1966). Often, managers have difficulty obtaining the necessary information to improve efficiency levels because of information asymmetries between themselves and their subordinates' (p 4). On the term 'frontier of control', they observe that this 'has a long radical history, as is shown by Hyman's (1975) foreword to the reprinting of Goodrich's (1920) classic study of British workshop politics in the years up to 1920, and in similar studies such as that by Cole (1923). Nevertheless, it has its roots in the open-ended nature of the employment relationship and how the respective obligations of employee and employer are regulated. At its core lies management of the 'zone of acceptance',

the range of tasks across which employees consent to management directing their labour, a concept that has played a key part for theorists ranging from Simon's (1951) formal theory of the employment relationship, to Rousseau's (1995) psychological contract theory.' (p 6).

[10] 'To stay ahead of the curve, you have to work with more energy, more enthusiasm, and most important of all, more innovation' (Gratton, 2009, p 2), with innovation 'fast becoming the core capability for organizational success' (Gratton, 2007, p 5).

[11] Cathcart concludes that through this partners are constituted 'as materially self-interested subjects ... prioritising economic rewards above everything else' and, the potential for resistance weakened: 'Rather than seeing the model of co-ownership as the freedom to determine priorities or challenge dominant business orthodoxy, co-ownership was used instead to constrain and limit democratic engagement. Partners were asked to demonstrate their commitment by privileging the financial success of the organisation over their own personal beliefs and desires' (Cathcart, 2009, p 275).

[12] See Haig-Brown and Hodson (2009); Waitere and Court (2009).

[13] Spiritual awareness is discussed further in Chapter 7.

[14] See Casey (2002, 2004), Benefiel (2003, 2005), Kinjerski and Skrypnek (2004), Dent et al (2005), Tischler et al (2007), Malloch (2008), Poole (2009).

[15] See McKenna et al (2009), Poole (2009).

[16] Malloch defines spiritual capital as the 'fund of belief, examples and commitments that are transmitted from generation to generation through a religious tradition, and which attach people to the transcendental source of human happiness'. I have adapted this to broaden it from too great a focus on faith traditions.

[17] I have recognised elsewhere (Woods, 2010a) that as well as being capable of authentic expression, the most personal and demanding questions of meaning are at times are embedded in and dominated and appropriated by the single-minded focus of bureaucratic capitalism on marshalling the best means to serve the ends of organisational performance and maximisation of income. As Casey (2004, p 70) observes, 'programmes currently extolled by organization culturalists and management motivators – among the most influential organizational consultants promoting bureaucratic reform – now overtly encompass the utilization of religio-affective, desecularized impulses'.

[18] It also contrasts with the Marxian approach. (See Rothschild and Whitt, 2009, pp 12-18.)

[19] Alan Rusbridger, Editor, *The Guardian*, 'The Hugh Cudlipp lecture: does journalism exist?', 25 January 2010 (available at www.guardian.co.uk/media/2010/jan/25/cudlipp-lecture-alan-rusbridger).

[20] The first 'Settlement in Trust' sold the business of John Lewis and Company and of Peter Jones Ltd to the workers 'present and prospective' (Cathcart 2009, p 103).

[21] AxiomNews advocate, June 2010, p 4. (Available at www.axiomnews.ca/2010/PDF/ AxiomNewsAdvocateWorldBluJune2010web.pdf)

[22] John Shaw, senior consultant, Future Considerations (AxiomNews advocate, June 2010, p 4, available at www.axiomnews.ca).

Chapter 3: Radicalising entrepreneurialism

[1] See Hess (2010), for example.

[2] See du Gay (2004), Courpasson and Clegg (2006), Gleeson and Knights (2006), Woods et al (2007a).

[3] 'Entrepreneurship' is the term used in much of the business literature.

[4] www.co-operative.coop/enterprisehub/what-is-a-co-operative/

[5] www.school.coop/

[6] Postmodern theories implicitly extend and respond to Weber's account of modernity. Their strength, according to Gane (2002), is their exposition of the limits of radical critique and the experimental search by postmodernism for forms that challenge the order of modern rationalism. They, *contra* Weber, 'affirm the possibility of *transcending* the confines of modern culture, and hence of undoing or even escaping the rationalization process' (p 154; emphasis in original).

[7] Ecoescape, for example, aims to change people's attitudes to environmental sustainability through UK tourism activities (Emberton, 2010). See Burnett (2009) on the Steiner Hereford Academy. Cultural entrepreneurialism can be controversial. One of the sponsors of Academies is the Emmanuel Schools Foundation which runs schools with standard corporate identities and provides education with a Bible-based Christian ethos, and which has been a source of controversy because of its association with creationism (Green, E., 2009; Pike, 2009).

[8] Leadbeater and Goss (1998) writing about what they term 'civic entrepreneurship' include amongst its distinctive features organisations asking

fundamental and far-reaching questions about their aims and purpose and see it as being as much about political renewal as managerial change.

[9] The findings summarised in the rest of this paragraph are from Woods and Woods (2011). More data from the Academy are reported in Chapter 8.

[10] Reproduced from Woods and Woods (2011), by kind permission of the editors of the journal *International Journal of Technology and Educational Marketing* (Purnendu Tripathi and Siran Mukerji) and the publisher IGI Global.

[11] Elannah Cramer, interviewed at WorldBlu Awards, June 2010, and also quoted in Chapter 2.

Chapter 4: The rise of plural control

[1] This chapter is based on an article published in French (Woods and Broadfoot, 2008) which I have re-worked, expanded and updated for this book. Text (in English) which remains from the original French language article is used with the kind permission of Patricia Broadfoot and the editors of the journal *Revue Internationale d'éducation de Sèvres* (Alain Bouvier and Marie-José Sanselme).

[2] Although there is much to criticise about subsequent developments, the pre-1988 system was not without its tensions or critics. There was a 'fragility' to the 'myth of public sector values' (Brereton and Temple, 1999, p 457). Critiques of the post-War welfare state argued that professions could be 'deeply paternalistic' and that their 'construction of "the client" was often discriminatory and oppressive' (Hoggett, 2000, p 197).

[3] www.education.gov.uk/schools/leadership/typesofschools/academies/sponsoring/a0067863/academysponsorship

[4] www.education.gov.uk/news/press-notices-new/academy-status

[5] www.education.gov.uk/inthenews/pressnotices/a0071852/more-than-one-in-ten-secondary-schools-nowacademies-with-many-more-in-the-pipeline

[6] www.education.gov.uk/news/speeches/mg-westminsteracademy ;www.education.gov.uk/schools/leadership/typesofschools/freeschools/a0066077/free-school-proposals-approved-to business-case-and-plan-stage%7D. A new network, independent of government and founded by Rachel Wolf (a former education adviser to the Conservative Party), has been started to increase 'the number of independent, innovative schools within the state sector' (http://newschoolsnetwork.org/).

[7] Source: 'All trust schools inc NC @ 06 Aug 2010', downloaded from www.trustandfoundationschools.org.uk/ schools/trust_schools.aspx

[8] Michael Gove, Secretary of State for Education, Speech to National College Annual Conference, Birmingham, 17 June 2010.

[9] www.education.gov.uk/schools/teachingandlearning/curriculum/ a0061705/changes-to-the-national-curriculum. The proposed curriculum refers to the proposals of the previous, Labour, government.

[10] See, for example, Clegg et al (2006, p 217) on mobilising resources and meanings.

[11] As Vernon Bogdanor observes, 'New Labour was a matter of substance as well as style' (*Times Higher Education*, 19-25 August 2010, Book review, p 44).

[12] This was Michael Gove speaking before the election which led to his becoming Secretary of State for Education. Source: 'Michael Gove admits that Tony Blair inspired his education policies', *The Times*, 24 August 2009 (www.timesonline.co.uk/tol/news/politics/article6807174.ece). Tony Blair is quoted approvingly in the Coalition Government's White Paper on education (Department for Education, 2010, p 56).

[13] Gordon Brown (2010), former UK Prime Minister and Chancellor of the Exchequer, affirms in his reflections on the financial crisis that he and Tony Blair spent 'twenty years building New Labour on the foundation of market competition, private enterprise, and economic stability' (p 23), but has also to admit that a lesson of the first decade of the 21st century is that markets 'can be shaped by vested interests, that economic players are not always rational, that markets are not self-correcting' (p 12).

[14] See for example the Cambridge Primary Review (2009), Balatin et al (2009), Westland (2009), as well as Alexander (2010a, p 1), who highlights the fact that 'there's now a highly critical counter-culture' against tests in England and the US, which includes the 'dramatic reversal' of Diane Ravitch, the former assistant education secretary to President George Bush. See Ranson (forthcoming) for a recent critical discussion of trends in school governance.

[15] David Carter, executive principal of the John Cabot Learning Federation in Bristol, A school for the 21st century, in Leading System Redesign (www. sec-ed.co.uk/downloads/ssat_supp.pdf).

Chapter 5: A different view: organic meta-governance

[1] As suggested by the diversification thesis discussed in Chapter 6.

[2] Paul Ormerod's argument is that in order to induce mass behaviour change, which will be needed on matters such as climate change, public policy needs

to rely less on incentives than on understanding and utilising the power of social networks. Whilst offering valuable insights, this analysis does not put to the fore enhancing democratic participation and consciousness.

[3] A further twist to the use of the term 'localism' is that it can be associated with strengthening of the central state's agenda-setting power, as some view New Localism in the US. Val Storey comments: 'Grounding support in response to the need to provide local solutions to national complex problems is characterized by "New Localism" [...]. This agenda is not restricted to education. Crowson and Goldring [...] identify four impacting forces: (1) an updated approach to devolution, amid a framework of national standards; (2) a strengthened back–to–the–neighbourhoods movement with school–community partnerships in learning much in mind; (3) a new appreciation of interest in family choice and expressions of lifestyle in education; and, finally, (4) a societal expression of some increasing concerns and/or fears regarding American education, expressed most frequently at the levels of school-site community (p 5). Characterizing the movement as new is the continued primacy of the central government in setting the agenda surrounding local autonomy and action ... At the core of the New Localism is an emerging paradox – while the state and federal mandates in education strengthen centrally, the nation's prime attention under these mandates is determined locally ... Not surprisingly, this brings with it enormous dilemmas as stakeholders wrestle with translating state-level policy into localized practices' (Storey, 2010, p 5).

[4] Prime Minister David Cameron speaking at the launch of the 'Big Society' programme, 18 May 2010 (source: www.number10.gov.uk/news/latest-news/2010/05/big-society-50248).

[5] HM Government, 2010, p 29.

[6] Tessa Jowell, MP, *Mutual moment*, www.progressonline.org.uk/Magazine/article.asp?a=5121

[7] In the US, this builds on developments in earlier years such as Jo Murphy's call for educational leadership as a profession to be recultured around social justice, school improvement and democratic community (Murphy, 2002) and the founding of a movement to promote democracy and social justice in educational leadership – the New DEEL (Democratic Ethical Educational Leadership) network. See www.temple.edu/education/newdeel/index.html and Chapter 10.

[8] I have discussed ideas relevant to this argument in Woods (2010b).

[9] These issues are discussed in more detail in Chapter 7.

[10] From 'The German Ideology' in Feuer (1971, p 288).

[11] *Oxford Companion to Philosophy*, Oxford University Press, 1995 (from website, www.xrefer.com/entry/552724).

[12] See Woods and Woods (2009c) on mindful practice.

[13] See Chapter 6, note 11.

[14] See also Woods, P.A. (2003) for a discussion of democratic legitimation as an addition (and challenge) to Weber's typology of legitimation.

[15] The study also found that headteachers are perceived as the main source of leadership by staff, governors and parents and concluded that 'greater attention [is needed in policy and training] to the process of distributing leadership and the practicalities of ensuring effective patterns of distribution' (Day et al, 2009, p 4).

[16] These are the 10 WorldBlu Democratic Design System (WBDDS) principles, listed in Chapter 1, note 12.

[17] See, for example, Chaltain (2010), Day et al (2009), Harris (2009), Leithwood and Mascall (2008).

[18] The pervasiveness and power of the economistic culture is a well-noted international phenomenon, which continues in current US policy, for example: 'Providing a high-quality education for all children is critical to America's economic future. Our nation's economic competitiveness and the path to the American Dream depend on providing every child with an education that will enable them to succeed in a global economy that is predicated on knowledge and innovation. President Obama is committed to providing every child access to a complete and competitive education, from cradle through career' (Guiding principles on President Obama's White House website, www. whitehouse.gov/issues/ education/). The opening sentences of the Obama administration's 2010 educational technology plan declares, for example: 'Education is the key to America's economic growth and prosperity and to our ability to compete in the global economy. It is the path to good jobs and higher earning power for Americans' (National Education Technology Plan, 2010, www.ed.gov/technology/netp-2010/executive-summary). Policies such as these are framed with an acute sense of being in an economic race in which the contestants are powered by education: 'the countries that out-educate us today will out-compete us tomorrow' (*A Blueprint for Reform*, Washington: US Department for Education, March 2010, www2.ed.gov/policy/elsec/ leg/blueprint/ blueprint.pdf).

Chapter 6: The concept of adaptive strategies

[1] In the same place, Sørensen quotes Sørensen et al (2001, p 455): 'every human creation (idea, relationship, action), which on the surface seems simply to be a mundane response to the vicissitudes of every day life, is in fact a bold proclamation and announcement of a desired future, a living testimony to the generative power of hope' (citation in Sørensen (2009) as: Sørensen, P.F., Yaeger, T.F., Whitney, D. and Cooperrider, D.L. (2001) *Appreciative Inquiry: An Emerging Direction for Organization Development*, Champaign, IL: Stipes Pub).

[2] This is the term I use for '"new openings" theories' (Antonio, 1998, p 46), as developed by theorists such as Tony Giddens and Alberto Melluci, to emphasise an essential focus on the capacity and potential in contemporary society for agency, innovation and difference. See Woods (2010b).

[3] David Spangler, *A Vision of Holarchy*, 2008 (www.sevenpillarshouse.org/index.php/article/a_vision_of_holarchy1, accessed). The concept of holarchy is also developed and used by writers such as Arthur Koestler and Ken Wilbur.

[4] For example, analysis of self-improvement systems is not embedded in reflection on and articulation of substantive values. As a result the goal of 'rounded persons' is invoked but not elaborated and is placed in secondary position to measured results in this description of the 'most critical core competences' for school leaders: 'the relentless focus on learning and teaching, and the conviction that the best teaching and learning yield high examination and test results and rounded persons with the right qualities for a successful life in the 21st century' plus 'ensuring order, attendance and good behaviour as a precondition of improvement in learning and teaching' (Hargreaves 2010, p 15).

[5] 'The open-ended nature of the employment relationship places the "zone of acceptance" at its core, and participation can be understood as one of the processes by which the right to direct labour, the "right to manage", is altered, and by which the zone itself may be adjusted from time to time' (Marsden and Cañibano, 2009, p 15). See also Woods and Gronn (2009).

[6] *The Fundamental Question for Strategic CSR*, by Gus Romano (available at www.quantacitizenship.com/fundamental-question-for-strategic-citizenship.html).

[7] The levels are: (1) passive unintended moral agency; (2) passive, intended moral agency; (3) active, intended moral agency and the creation of ethical capital; (4) active, intended blended value ('While the first three views of ethical behaviour pertain to the accumulation of "profitability' in terms of economic capital, it is only at level 4 that it is reconceptualised as a way of building ethical capital grounded in both social and economic rationality"). (5) Beyond the

fourth level, 'we might postulate a fifth position that embraces the concept of "charity". In its purest form, there is an attempt to remove economic thinking completely from decisions regarding social action. When acting from a sense of charity – literally translated as "love" in early texts – the giver receives no economic benefit from the act of giving' (Bull et al, 2008, pp 6-7).

[8] For example, see Kensler (2008). Further references are in Chapter 1, note 12.

[9] Interview with Lisa Kensler, 7 January 2011.

[10] Reporting research with policy and managerial actors, Janet Newman (2005, pp 728-9) found that they 'enlarge the space for agency around "social" agendas'; 'They did so in part by selectively amplifying elements of Labour's narrative: those concerned with social exclusion, public involvement, community capacity building, preventing ill health, restorative justice and so on.'

[11] Effective freedom and freedom as capability are discussed in Sen (2009, pp 301-9). Sen makes the point that freedom is not a singular concept but has different conceptions which are not necessarily in tension. I have discussed notions of freedom, drawing on Isaiah Berlin amongst others, and have argued the case for the idea of substantive liberty. Substantive liberty is the notion that certain potentialities are inherent in the make-up of people as human beings and that freedom involves the holistic development of persons (physically, psychologically, spiritually) so that they are able to enjoy their full capabilities. See Woods, P.A. (2003, 2005).

[12] Basil Bernstein (1996, pp 76, 78, 79) writes of the weakening of ascribed and achieved identities with the possibility of new constructions. These new identities are constructed from different resources, which he terms *decentred* (those which derive from local resources), *retrospective* (from grand narratives, cultural or religious, i.e. past narratives), and *prospective* (from narrative resources which create a recentring of the identity, i.e. a new collective base which is future orientated). I have distinguished between four types of identity orientation – introjected, exogenous, externalised and categorical (Woods, P.A., 2003) – which are significant in contemporary society and which social actors draw upon to differing degrees: *exogenous* orientation refers to enduring points beyond the individual and the social. Examples include ideas and concepts such as logic and truth as absolute points of reference, as well as ultimate ideals and divine entities. *Externalised* orientation refers to a phenomenon increasingly characteristic of modernity whereby the self is defined by external features, such as consumer fashion items, that tend to be of relatively short–term or passing value, or whose value is principally instrumental. *Introjected* orientation concerns Bernstein's (1996) notion of introjected identities which are focused on regulating and developing the self though the manipulation of psychological

and physical capacities. *Categorical* identity (Taylor, 1998) encompasses social identities which give a sense of 'definiteness' and have a deep impact on the sense of self. An enduring public professional identity is an example.

[13] In their study of cooperative organisations, Rothschild and Whitt (1986/2009) found that a strong internal identity and sense of difference with conventional hierarchical organisations was significant for the viability of an alternative democratic order.

[14] www.namastesolar.com/cmsPages/view/page:who_we_are/section:our_story

[15] These are an elaboration and embellishment of Rothschild and Whitt's (1986/2009) findings on cooperative organisations.

Chapter 7: Embodying change

[1] D.H. Lawrence, from 'Democracy', an essay, part of which is printed in Dyson and Lovelock (1975, p 285).

[2] See Cushman (1996), for example. The 'empty self' of consumerism is not the same concept as the Buddhist notion of the empty self (see www.americanscientist.org/bookshelf/pub/daniel-goleman). The concept of externalised identities is defined in Chapter 6, note 12.

[3] Brain Gym is an example. It offers a programme 'based on physical techniques that have the aim of preparing brain and body for learning – and daily life' (www.braingym.org.uk/about/about.htm). This is not to delve into the effectiveness or otherwise of Brain Gym, but to observe that its rationale is a linear model of cause-and-effect change typical of the left-brain approach. This in itself is not problematic. What it typifies, however, is the dominant approach which eschews deeper expressions of meaning as an integral part of educational activity.

[4] 'The best school systems generate rich quantities of data which enable us all to make meaningful comparisons, learn from the best, identify techniques which work and quickly abandon ideologies which don't. In America President Obama, the Gates Foundation, the top charter schools and the principal education reformers all recognise the need for richer, timelier, more in-depth data about performance. That is why we need to keep rigorous external assessment. Improve and refine our tests, yes, but there can be no going back to the secret garden when public and professionals were in ignorance about where success had taken root and where investment had fallen on stony ground. Indeed I want to see more data generated by the profession to show what works, clearer information about teaching techniques that get results,

more rigorous, scientifically robust research about pedagogies which succeed and proper independent evaluations of interventions which have run their course. We need more evidence-based policy making, and for that to work we need more evidence' (Michael Gove, Secretary of State for Education, Speech to National College Annual Conference, Birmingham, 17 June 2010).

[5] Elsewhere the review urges people to forget 'right-brain versus left-brain functions' and other dichotomies about child development (Hofkins and Northen, 2009, p 13). The review's approach, nevertheless, in effect seeks to roll back many of the manifestations of left-brain dominated approach as understood by McGilchrist's examination of understandings of the brain.

[6] William Wordsworth, a letter to John Wilson, June 1802. ('The Romantic Poets: William Wordsworth', *Guardian*, undated, p 26, www.guardian.co.uk).

[7] Milton, *Paradise Lost*, lines 100-1.

[8] Figure 7.1 was originally published in Woods, P.A. and Woods, G.J. (2010) 'The geography of reflective leadership: the inner life of democratic learning communities', *Philosophy of Management*, vol 9, no 2, pp 81-97, and is reproduced with the kind permission of the journal and with due acknowledgement that the work is: (c) Copyright Reason in Practice Ltd, 2010.

[9] This is discussed in more detail in Woods and Woods (2010, p 92). The argument there concludes: 'the claim that there is a capacity, in-built to the human body, to sense a transcendent spiritual reality, and that this is what is involved in the reflective activity which constitutes spirituality, is three-fold:

• Spirituality is at root an activity which leads to a relationship with and an appreciation of that which is transcendent, and as such must logically entail a human capability to sense and experience the object of the activity. A sensing capability is implied (different and additional to emotional and aesthetic feelings) for which "opening the heart" is a metaphor.

• Acceptance of the proposition that there is a transcendent spiritual reality, knowable to a greater or lesser degree through experiential awareness by means of this human capability, is epistemically responsible.

• Accounts of experiential awareness of spirituality can be taken, as a group, to be valid (that is, to be epistemically trustworthy).'

[10] Tony Hsie explains how the experience elicited a 'response from my entire being' (Hsie, 2010, p 78). His company (Zappos) was one of the organisations chosen by WorldBlu to be awarded in 2010 as a democratic workplace (see www.worldblu.com/awardee-profiles/).

[11] Bettany Hughes (2010, p 102) writes of the beautiful banks of the River Ilissos frequented by Athenians, including Socrates, and how this must have been 'a rich experience: typical of life in Athens, where a sensuous spirituality and a brisk belief in the sacred importance of the new democratic *polis* collided ... where deep thought and a vigorous engagement in day-to-day life sit happily side by side'. She also makes clear that in many other ways democratic Athens was by no means idyllic, but that is a discussion beyond the focus of this book.

[12] Mitchell (2005, p 17) argues that the development of rational and spiritual capabilities 'gave the citizen the apperceptive tools that ... allowed the citizen to defend himself against becoming an abject subject of the law'. It made each citizen 'a reasoning judge'. 'Entrusting the individual citizen with sacred knowledge is the fundamental metaphysical characteristic of a democratic consciousness' (p 17). By the end of the 4th century BC this balance was lost and it was tilted towards the rational.

[13] Socrates' view, as recounted in Xenophon, *Recollections of Socrates*, quoted in Bowden (2005, pp 65–6).

[14] In feminist action, for example, critical actors 'are those who initiate policy proposals on their own, even when women form a small minority, and embolden others to take steps to promote policies for women, regardless of the proportion of female representatives' (Childs and Krook, 2006, p 529).

[15] Authenticity is discussed in more detail in Woods, P.A. (2007).

[16] Wenger (2000, p 231) draws attention to the role of 'community co-ordinator' as a leader in communities of practice, and to the need for 'multiple forms of leadership: thought leaders, networkers, people who document the practice, pioneers etc'.

[17] David Galenson observes that research to date identifies two types of creativity – conceptual and experimental. See *Understanding Creativity*, NBER Working Paper No. 16024, May 2010, The National Bureau of Economic Research (available at www.nber.org/papers/w16024).

[18] See, for example, Chaltain (2010), Shields (2010).

[19] I gained some insight into holarchy and what it entails from research I undertook with Glenys Woods at Meadow Steiner School in England and discussions with Jonathan Wolf-Phillips, an external consultant for the school and founder of New Leadership Ltd. See Woods and Woods (2006b), especially page 7.

[20] The text in Box 7.1 is from: Weiskopf, R. and Steyaert, C. (2009) 'Metamorphoses in entrepreneurship studies: towards an affirmative politics of entrepreneuring', in D. Hjorth and C. Steyaert (eds) *The Politics and Aesthetics of Entrepreneurship*,

Cheltenham: Edward Elgar; and is reproduced with kind permission of the authors (Chris Steyaert and Richard Weiskopf), the editors of the book in which it was originally published (Chris Steyaert and Daniel Hjorth) and the publisher Edward Elgar.

[21] Avaaz.org is one such web-based network. It describes itself as follows: 'Avaaz.org is a 5.5-million-person global campaign network that works to ensure that the views and values of the world's people shape global decision-making. ("Avaaz" means "voice" or "song" in many languages.) Avaaz members live in every nation of the world; our team is spread across 13 countries on 4 continents and operates in 14 languages.'

[22] On public services and networks, see Martin (2010, pp 344-5).

Chapter 8: Degrees of democracy

[1] This chapter is based on an article jointly authored with Glenys Woods (Woods and Woods, forthcoming). Reproduction of text from the article in this chapter and in Chapter 1 (pp 9-10) is with the kind permission of the editor of the *Journal of School Leadership* (Jeff Brooks) and its publisher Rowman & Littlefield Education.

[2] 'A Cloud hides the Sun and also Makes it Seen' – Explaining the Unreal in a Letter of Infinite Love, posted 2009 (www.free-meditation.ca/archives/801).

[3] These visits and data collection, and the analysis of the data for this chapter, involved myself and Glenys Woods, who was a member of the research team for the Academy study.

[4] For some other staff the change to Academy status led to disaffection and concerns about the leadership approach from the top.

[5] The proportion was 53%. (base: 107). See note 10 below for further information about the staff survey.

[6] Woods, P.A. 2005, 2006, 2008; Woods, G.J., 2003, 2007; Woods and Woods, 2006a, 2008, 2009a, 2009c, 2010; Woods et al, 2005.

[7] Funded by the British Academy, Award SG-40233.

[8] Commissioned by the UK Government. See Woods et al (2005).

[9] Funded by the British Academy (Award LRG-45018), conducted by a research team comprising Philip Woods (award holder), Glenys Woods and Helen Gunter. The Academy is anonymised. Accordingly, details concerning location are not provided and background information is kept to a minimum.

[10] Woods (2008). One hundred and seven staff completed a questionnaire in January 2008 – a 57% response rate out of 187 staff (99 teaching and 88 non-teaching staff).

[11] www.sands-school.co.uk/?page_id=34

[12] The fundamental proposition grounding Steiner education is that 'each human being comprises body, soul and spirit' (Rawson and Richter, 2000, p 14), and its curriculum and pedagogy aim to awaken the range of human faculties according to the anthroposophical model of human development. Integral to Steiner school education is encouragement of balanced growth towards 'physical, behavioural, emotional, cognitive, social and spiritual maturation' (p 7). As these faculties open up, 'the spiritual core of the person [strives] to come ever more fully to expression' (p 7). Each child needs to come to their own individual expression. The stated aim of Steiner education is not to create adherents of anthroposophy. Rather, it is to awaken young people to the spiritual and ethical dimensions of human life and to enable them to be free and independent thinkers and to make decisions for themselves.

[13] www.sands-school.co.uk/?page_id=41,20thjuly2010

[14] www.michaelhall.co.uk/a-childs-journey/upper-school/default.aspx

[15] The proportion was 36%. More positively, 78% of staff considered the Academy well led and most (53%) agreed that it 'has a vision of democratic principles and participation'. (The base for each of these percentages is 107.)

[16] Students who considered the Academy not to be well led were much more likely to feel that students were not consulted enough: of students who disagreed it was well led, 65% (base: 185) also disagreed that 'Students are asked their views before a major change takes place in the school', compared with 28% (base: 267) of those who considered the Academy was well led. (A self-completion student survey was conducted in February 2008, completed by 606 students across all years, a response rate of 52%.)

[17] 39% of 107 staff. See note 10 above for further details of the survey.

[18] www.sands-school.co.uk/?page_id=6

Chapter 9: Practice in the making

[1] Interviewed at the WorldBlu Awards 2010. See Chapter 2.

[2] Interviewed at the WorldBlu Awards 2010. See Chapter 2.

[3] www.leadershipforlearning.org.uk/teacher-networks

[4] www.leadershipforlearning.org.uk/teacher-networks

[5] www.leadershipforlearning.org.uk/component/content/article/86-our-values

[6] The project website is: www.learningtolead.org.uk

[7] The phrase 'the treasure within' is from Delors (1996).

[8] See www.co-op.ac.uk/schools-and-young-people/co-operative-schools/. The Co-operative College, based in Manchester, 'works with all the major co-operative societies in the UK and delivers programmes of training and education around the world to help individuals and groups achieve the level of skill, knowledge and understanding required to translate ideals into effective practice' (www.co-op.ac.uk/about/). The Co-operative Group is the UK's largest mutual retailer – providing food, banking, travel, pharmacy and funeral care services (www.co-operative.coop/corporate/aboutus/).

[9] Figures in this paragraph are from a paper produced by Mervyn Wilson, Principal and Chief Executive, The Co–operative College, Manchester – 'Co-operative Schools', 2010; and 'Schools boosted by launch of new Co-operative Schools Network' (www.co-op.ac.uk/schools_conference_Nov09.htm), updated by a personal communication, dated 11 January 2011.

[10] www.beecoop.co.uk/Co-operative%20trusts%20schools%20%20April%20revised.pdf

[11] The source for and quotes in this paragraph and the one that follows is an English paper prepared and sent to me by María Cecilia Fierro, a member of the network of researchers studying the initiatives (Red Latinoamericana de Convivencia Escolar, Universidad Iberoamericana León, Mexico). The paper is a synthesis of an article by Fierro (2008).

[12] There are controversies surrounding charter schools in Hawaii. Shatkin and Gershberg note that some people 'are concerned that graduates will be ill equipped for future education and employment'. They go on to observe that this tension 'between the role of schools in producing productive citizens and their role in building stronger communities is common to discussions of parent participation. Although the debate is important, it is also necessary to remember that the two goals are not necessarily in conflict' (Shatkin and Gershberg, 2007, p 605).

[13] *Education with Aloha*, White Paper, 2006, http://kuaokala.org/downloads/whitepaper.pdf

Chapter 10: Energies for change

[1] See Chapter 6, note 11.

[2] Sue Robinson, Headteacher, Cherry Orchard Primary School and Children's Centre, Birmingham.

[3] The Cambridge Primary Review, conducted between 2006 and 2009, was a major, independently funded enquiry into primary education in England. Its scope and the range of evidence collected made it the most comprehensive enquiry into English primary education since the Plowden report of 1967. The Review is being followed up by a programme of professional networking and policy engagement from 2010 to 2012. For more information, see www. primaryreview.org.uk/cpr/overview.php

[4] William Wordsworth, a letter to John Wilson, June 1802. ('The Romantic Poets: William Wordsworth', *Guardian*, undated, p 26, www.guardian.co.uk).

[5] On the Cambridge Primary Review's policy recommendation to address the perennially neglected question of what primary education is for, Robin Alexander (Director of the Review) urges 'schools themselves to take hold of this one and use the opportunity created by the dropping of the Rose framework [the previous Labour Government's curriculum review] to explore their aims and values and to assess how these are enacted in school and classroom life' (Alexander, 2010b, p 11).

[6] For more information, see www.temple.edu/education/newdeel/index. html, and Gross and Shapiro (2009).

[7] www.temple.edu/education/newdeel/docs/NewDEELnewsletterSept%20 06.pdf

References

Adler, P.S., Forbes, L.C. and Wilmott, H. (2007) Critical Management Studies (http://dialspace.dial.pipex.com/town/close/hr22/hcwhome/CMS-AAM.pdf).

Albrow, M. (2001) 'Society as social diversity: the challenge for governance in the global age', in OECD, *Governance in the 21st century: Future studies*, Paris: OECD, pp 149-82.

Alexander, R. (2010a) 'The perils of policy: success, amnesia and collateral damage in systemic educational reform', public lecture, Melbourne Graduate School of Education, University of Melbourne, 10 March 2010.

Alexander, R. (2010b) 'Legacies, policies and prospects: one year on from the Cambridge Review', The 2010 Brian Simon Memorial Lecture, Institute of Education, University of London, 6 November 2010.

Antonio, R.J.(1998) 'Mapping postmodern social theory', in A. Sica (ed) *What is social theory? The philosophical debates*, Oxford: Blackwell, pp 23-75.

Apple, M. and Beane, J. (2007) *Democratic schools: Lessons in powerful education* (2nd edn), Portsmouth, NH: Heinemann.

Balatin, M., Brammer, S., James, C. and McCormack, M. (2009) *The school governance study*, London: Business in the Community.

Ball, S.J. (2006a) 'The teacher's soul and the terrors of performativity', in S.J. Ball, *Education policy and social class: The selected works of Stephen J. Ball*, London: Routledge.

Ball, S.J. (2006b) *Education policy and social class: The selected works of Stephen J. Ball*, London: Routledge.

Ball, S.J. (2007) *Education plc: Understanding private sector participation in public sector education*, London: Routledge.

Ball, S.J. (2008a) *The education debate*, Bristol: The Policy Press.

Ball, S.J. (2008b) 'The legacy of ERA, privatization and the policy ratchet', *Educational Management Administration and Leadership*, vol 36, no 2, pp 185-99.

Ball, S.J. (2009) 'Privatising education, privatising education policy, privatising educational research: network governance and the "competition state"', *Journal of Education Policy*, vol 24, no1, pp 83-99.

Ball, S.J. and Exley, S. (2010) 'Making policy with "good ideas": policy networks and the "intellectuals" of New Labour', *Journal of Education Policy*, vol 25, no 2, pp 151-69.

Bartlett, D. and Dibben, P. (2002) 'Public sector innovation and entrepreneurship: case studies from local government', *Local Government Studies*, vol 28, no 4, pp 107–21.

Beattie, N. (1985) *Professional parents: Parent participation in four Western European countries*, Lewes, East Sussex: The Falmer Press.

Benefiel, M. (2003) 'Mapping the terrain of spirituality in organizations research', *Journal of Organizational Change Management*, vol 16, no 4, pp 367-77.

Benefiel, M. (2005) 'The second half of the journey: spiritual leadership for organizational transformation', *Leadership Quarterly*, vol 16, no 5, pp 723–47.

Bernstein, B. (1996) *Pedagogy, symbolic control and identity: Theory, research, critique*, London: Taylor & Francis.

Beyes, T. (2009) 'Spaces of intensity – urban entrepreneurship as redistribution of the sensible', in D. Hjorth and C. Steyaert (eds) *The politics and aesthetics of entrepreneurship*, Cheltenham: Edward Elgar, pp 92-112.

Blair, T. (1998) *The third way: New politics for the new century*, London: The Fabian Society.

Bloom, W. (2011) 'Finding our unified voice', *Cygnus Review*, vol 2, pp 2-3.

Booth, C., Rowlinson, M., Clark, P., Delahaye, A. and Proctor, S. (2009) 'Scenarios and counterfactuals as modal narratives', *Futures*, vol 41, pp 87-95.

Bottery, M. (2004) *The challenges of educational leadership*, London: Paul Chapman Publishing.

Bowden, H. (2005) *Classical Athens and the Delphic Oracle: Divination and democracy*, Cambridge: Cambridge University Press.

Braithwaite, E.R. (1969[1959]) *To Sir with love*, London: New English Library.

Branson, R. (2007) *Screw it, let's do it*, London: Virgin Books.

Breakspear, S., Sheahan, P. and Thurbon, D. (2008) *Talent magnets: Attracting and retaining young teachers through courageous leadership and inspiring cultures*, Camperdown, New South Wales: Centre for Skills Development.

Brereton, M. and Temple, M. (1999) 'The new public service ethos: an ethical environment for governance', *Public Administration*, vol 77, no 3, pp 455–74.

Broadfoot, P., Osborn, M., Planel, C. and Sharpe, K. (2000) *Promoting quality in learning: Does England have the answer?*, London: Cassell.

Brown, G. (2010) *Beyond the crash: Overcoming the first crisis of globalisation*, London: Simon & Schuster.

Bull, M., Ridley-Duff, R., Foster, D. and Seanor, P. (2008) 'Seeing social enterprise through the theoretical conceptualisation of ethical capital'. Available from Sheffield Hallam University Research Archive (SHURA) at: http://shura.shu.ac.uk/758/

Bunt, L. and Harris, M. (2010) *Mass localism: A way to help small communities solve big social challenges*, London: NESTA.

Burnett, J. (2009) 'Authentic assessment in the first Steiner Academy', *Management in Education*, vol 23, no 3, pp 130-4.

Burrall, S. (2010) 'From ballot box to dictatorship? Engaging in the struggle for dDemocracy', in *Twenty for twenty* (20 essays exploring the future of the public and not-forprofit sectors over the next ten years), www.dhacommunications.co.uk/resourcecentre/twenty-for-twenty/

Caldwell, B.J. (2006) *Re-imagining educational leadership*, London: Sage.

Callinicos, A. (2010) *Bonfire of illusions: The twin crises of the liberal world*, Cambridge: Polity Press.

Cambridge Primary Review (2009) *Towards a new primary curriculum*, Cambridge: University of Cambridge.

Cambridge Primary Review (2010) *After the election: Policy priorities for primary education*, Cambridge: University of Cambridge Faculty of Education.

Cameron, D. (2010) 'Transforming the British economy', Speech by Prime Minister, 28 May, www.conservatives.com/News/Speeches/2010/05/David_Cameron_Transforming_the_British_economy.aspx

Casey, C. (2002) *Critical analysis of organizations: Theory, practice, revitalization*, London: Sage.

Casey, C. (2004) 'Bureaucracy re-enchanted? Spirit, experts and authority in organizations', *Organization,* vol 11, no 1, pp 59-79.

Cathcart, A. (2009) 'Directing democracy: the case of the John Lewis Partnership', PhD Thesis, University of Leicester.

Chaltain, S. (2010) *American schools: The art of creating a democratic community*, Lanham, MA: Rowman & Littlefield.

Chell, E. (2009) *The identification and measurement of innovative characteristics of young people*, London: NESTA.

Childs, S. and Krook, M.L. (2006) 'Should feminists give up on critical mass? A contingent yes', *Politics & Gender*, vol 2, no 4, pp 491–530.

Clapton, E. (2007) *Eric Clapton: The autobiography*, London: Random House.

Clarke, J. and Newman, J. (1997) *The managerial state*, London: Sage.

Clegg, S.R., Courpasson, D. and Phillips, N. (2006) *Power and organizations, power and organization*, London: Sage.

Cloke, K. and Goldsmith, J. (2002) *The end of management*, San Francisco, CA: Jossey-Bass.

Conservative Party (2009) *Control shift: Returning power to local communities*, London: Conservative Party.

Cooperrider, D.L. and Whitney, D.K. (2005) *Appreciative inquiry: A positive revolution in change*, San Francisco, CA: Berrett-Koehler.

Cottingham, J. (2005) *The spiritual dimension: Religion, philosophy and human value*, Cambridge: Cambridge University Press.

Courpasson, D. and Clegg, S. (2006) 'Dissolving the iron cages? Tocqueville, Michels, bureaucracy and the perpetuation of elite power', *Organization*, vol 13, no 3, pp 319-43.

Craig, J., Horne, M. and Mongon, D. (2009) *The engagement ethic: The potential of cooperative and mutual governance for public services*, London: The Innovation Unit.

Cushman, P. (1996) *Constructing the self, constructing America: A cultural history of psychotherapy*, Cambridge, MA: The Perseus Books Group.

Dahrendorf, R. (1999) Whatever happened to liberty? *New Statesman*, 6 September.

Davies, B. with Macaulay, H. (2006) *Leading academies*, London: Specialist Schools and Academies Trust.

Davies, G. (2006) 'The sacred and the profane: biotechnology, rationality and public debate', *Environment and Planning A,* vol 38, no 3, pp 423-44.

Day, C., Sammons, P., Hopkins, D., Harris A., Leithwood, K., Gu, Q., Brown, E., Ahtaridou, E., and Kington, A. (2009) *The impact of school leadership on pupil outcomes: Final report*, Research Report DCSF-RR108, London: Department for Children, Schools and Families.

Dees, J.G. (2001) *The meaning of 'social entrepreneurship'*, www.fuqua. duke.edu/centers/case/documents/dees_SE.pdf

Delors, J. (1996) *Learning: The treasure within*, Report to UNESCO of the International Commission on Education for the Twenty-first Century, Paris: UNESCO.

Dent, E.B., Higgins, M.E. and Wharff, D.M. (2005) 'Spirituality and leadership: an empirical review of definitions, distinctions, and embedded assumptions', *The Leadership Quarterly* , vol 16, pp 625–53.

Department for Education (2010) *The importance of teaching: The schools White Paper 2010*, London: Her Majesty's Stationery Office.

Deuchar, R. (2006) ' "Not only this, but also that!" Translating the social and political motivations underpinning enterprise and citizenship education into Scottish schools', *Cambridge Journal of Education*, vol 36, no 4, pp 533–47.

Deuchar, R. (2007) *Citizenship, enterprise and learning: Harmonising competing educational agendas*, Stoke-on-Trent: Trentham.

Drucker, P. (1985) *Innovation and entrepreneurship*, London: William Heinemann.

Dryzek, J.S. (1996) *Democracy in capitalist times,* Oxford: Oxford University Press.

Du Gay, P. (2000) *In praise of bureaucracy*, London: Sage.

Du Gay, P. (2004) 'Against 'Enterprise' (but not against "enterprise", for that would make no sense)', *Organization*, vol 11, no 1, pp 37–57.

Dyson, A.E. and Lovelock, J. (eds) (1975) *Education and democracy*, London: Routledge & Kegan Paul.

Elmore, R. (2000) *Building a new structure for school leadership*, Washington, DC: The Albert Shanker Institute.

Emberton, J. (2010) 'Beyond public services, beyond active citizens', in *Twenty for twenty* (20 essays exploring the future of the public and not-for-profit sectors over the next ten years), www.dhacommunications.co.uk/resource-centre/twenty-for-twenty/

Fenton, T. (2002) *The democratic company*, Washington, DC: WorldBlu, Inc.

Feuer, L.S. (ed) (1971) *Marx and Engels: Basic writings on politics and philosophy*, London: Collins-Fontana.

Fielding, M. (2006) 'Leadership, radical student engagement and the necessity of person-centred education', *International Journal of Leadership in Education*, vol 9, no 4: pp 299–313.

Fielding, M. (2009) 'Public space and educational leadership: reclaiming and renewing our radical traditions', in P.A. Woods and M.J. O'Hair (eds), special issue on Democracy and School Leadership, *Educational Management Administration & Leadership*, vol 37, no 4, pp 497-521.

Fierro, C. (2008) 'Educational community, a training process towards response-ability', in C. Hirmas and D. Eroles (eds) *Democratic coexistence, inclusion and a culture of peace. Lessons learned from educational practice in Latin America*, Santiago, Chile: UNESCO Innovations Network, pp 255-80.

Flowers, P. (2008) 'A systematic review of Enterprise2.0 and its relationship with organisational democracy', MsC by Research, Cranfield: Cranfield University.

Frost, D. (2008) 'Teacher leadership: values and voice', *School Leadership & Management*, vol 28, no 4, pp 337-52.

Frost, D. and MacBeath, J., with Stenton, S., Frost, R., Roberts, A. and Wearing, V. (2010) *Learning to lead: An evaluation*, Cambridge: Leadership for Learning, University of Cambridge Faculty of Education.

Fullan, M. (2001) *Leading in a culture of change*, San Francisco, CA: Jossey-Bass.

Fullan, M. (2008) *The six secrets of change,* San Francisco, CA: Jossey-Bass.

Gane, N. (2002) *Max Weber and postmodern theory: Rationalization versus re-enchantment*, New York and Basingstoke: Palgrave.

Gardiner, M. (2004) 'Wild publics and grotesque symposiums: Habermas and Bahktin on dialogue, everyday life and the public sphere', in N. Crossley and J.M. Roberts (eds) *After Habermas: New perspectives on the public sphere*, Oxford: Blackwell Publishing, pp 28-48.

Gardner, H. (1999) *Intelligence reframed: Multiple intelligences for the 21st century*, New York: Basic Books.

Gewirtz, S. (1999) 'Education Action Zones: emblems of the Third Way', in H. Dean and R. Woods (eds), *Social Policy Review 11*, Luton: University of Luton, Social Policy Association, pp 145-65.

Giddens, A. (1994) *Beyond left and right: The future of radical politics*, Cambridge: Polity.

Glatter, R. (2003) 'Governance and educational innovation', in B. Davies and J. West-Burnham (eds) *Handbook of Educational Leadership and Management*, London: Pearson.

Glatter, R. and Woods, P.A. (1995) 'Parental choice and school decision making: operating in a market-like environment', in K-C Wong and K-M Cheung (eds) *Educational leadership and change: An international perspective*, Hong Kong: Hong Kong University Press, pp 155-72.

Gleeson, D. and Knights, D. (2006) 'Challenging dualism: public professionalism in "troubled" times', *Sociology*, vol 40, no 2, pp 277–95.

Goldstein, J. (2009) 'Designing transparent teacher evaluation: the role of oversight panels for professional accountability', *Teachers College Record*, vol 111, no 4, pp 893-33.

Goleman, D. (2005) *Emotional intelligence*, New York: Bantam Books.

Goodrich, C. L. (1920) *The frontier of control: A study in British workshop politics*, London: Bell and Sons.

Goodson, I. (2003) *Professional knowledge, professional lives*, Maidenhead: Open University Press.

Gratton, L. (2004) *The democratic enterprise*, London: FT Prentice Hall/ Financial Times.

Gratton, L. (2007) *Hot spots*, Harlow: Pearson Education.

Gratton, L. (2009) *Glow*, Harlow: FT/Prentice Hall.

Green, E. (2009) 'Corporate features and faith based Academies', *Management in Education*, vol 23, no 3, pp 135-8.

Green, H. (2002) *Ten questions for school leaders*, Nottingham: National College for Leadership of Schools and Children's Services,www.ncsl. org.uk/media/2C9/A6/tenquestions-for-school-leaders.pdf

Green, S. (2009) 'Seeking salvation', *New Statesman*, 2 July, www. newstatesman.com/business/2009/07/world-economic-market-china

Gribble, D. (1998) *Real education: Varieties of freedom*, Bristol: Libertarian Education.

Gronn, P. (2003) *The new work of educational leaders*, London: Sage.

Gross, S. and Shapiro, J. (2009) 'Fear versus possibility: why we need a new DEEL for our children's future', in H. Svi Shapiro (ed) *Education and hope in troubled times*, New York: Routledge.

Groves, M., with Baumber, J. and Leigh, G., Pullen, D., Temple, B. and Yates, S. (2008) *Regenerating schools: Leading transformation of standards and services through community engagement,* London: Network Continuum.

Gunter, H. (2010) 'A comment on Karsten et al', *Public Administration,* vol 88, no 1, pp 113–17.

Habermas, J. (1974) *Theory and practice*, London: Heinemann.

Haig-Brown, C. and Hodson, J. (2009) 'Starting with the land: toward indigenous thought in Canadian education', in P.A. Woods and G.J. Woods (eds) *Alternative education for the 21st century*, New York: Palgrave.

Hargreaves, D.H. (2007) *System redesign – 1: The road to transformation in education*, London: Specialist Schools and Academies Trust.

Hargreaves, D.H. (2008) *Leading system redesign – 1*, London: Specialist Schools and Academies Trust.

Hargreaves, D.H. (2010) *Creating a self-improving school system*, Nottingham: National College for Leadership of Schools and Children's Services.

Hargreaves, A. and Shirley, D. (2008) 'The Fourth Way', *Educational Leadership*, October, pp 56-61.

Hargreaves, A. and Shirley, D. (2009) *The Fourth Way*, Thousand Oaks, CA: Corwin Press.

Harrington, P. and Karol Burks, B. (eds) (2009) *What next for Labour?,* London: Demos.

Harris, A. (ed) (2009) *Distributed leadership: Different perspectives*, Dordrecht, The Netherlands: Springer.

Hatcher, R. (2009) *Participation and democratisation in the local school system*, 23 November, http://socialismandeducation.wordpress. com/2009/11/23/participation-anddemocratisation-in-the-local-school-system/

Heelas, P. (2008) *Spiritualities of life*, Oxford: Blackwell.

Hess, F.M. (2010) *Education unbound:The promise and practice of Greenfield Schooling*, Alexandria, VA: ASCD.

Hjorth, D. and Bjerke B. (2006) 'Public entrepreneurship: moving from social/consumer to public/citizen', in C. Steyaert and D. Hjorth (eds) *Entrepreneurship as social change*, Cheltenham: Edward Elgar.

Hjorth, D. and Steyaert, C. (eds) (2009) *The politics and aesthetics of entrepreneurship*. Cheltenham: Edward Elgar.

HM Government (2010) *The Coalition: Our programme for government*, London: Cabinet Office.

HM Treasury (2004) *Creating an enterprise culture*, London: HM Treasury.

HM Treasury (2008) *Enterprise: Unlocking the UK's talent*, London: HM Treasury.

Hofkins, D. and Northen, S. (2009) *Introducing the Cambridge Primary Review*, University of Cambridge Faculty of Education (www.primaryreview.org.uk).

Hoggett, P. (2000) *Emotional life and the people and the politics of welfare*, Basingstoke: Macmillan.

Holland, D., Lachicotte, W., Skinner, D. and Cain, C. (1998) *Identity and agency in cultural worlds*, Cambridge, MA and London: Harvard University Press.

Hopkins, D. (2007) *Every school a great school: Realizing the potential of system leadership*, Maidenhead: Open University Press.

Hotho, S. and Pollard, D. (2007) 'Management as negotiation at the interface: moving beyond the critical-practice impasse', *Organization*, vol 14, pp 583-603.

HRH The Prince of Wales (2007) 'Introduction', *The Gardens at Highgrove,* Highgrove, Gloucestershire.

Hsie, T. (2010) *Delivering happiness: A path to profits, passion and purpose*, New York: Business Plus.

Hughes, B. (2010) *The hemlock cup: Socrates, Athens and the search for the good life*, London: Jonathan Cape.

Johnson, J. and Hess, M. (2010) 'Cultivating space for democratic education and democratic leadership, connexions content commons', National Council of Professors of Education, http://cnx.org/content/m34193/latest/

Jones, C. and Spicer, A. (2009) 'Is the Marquis de Sade an entrepreneur?', in D. Hjorth and C. Steyaert (eds) *The politics and aesthetics of entrepreneurship*, Cheltenham: Edward Elgar, pp 131-47.

Judge, P. (2005) 'Brave new world?', *RSA Journal*, December, pp 50-4.

Jue, A.L. (2007) 'The demise and reawakening of spirituality in Western entrepreneurship', *Journal of Human Values*, vol 13, pp 1-11.

Keane, J. (2009) *The life and death of democracy*, London: Simon and Schuster.

Kensler, L.A.W. (2008) 'The ecology of democratic learning communities', unpublished PhD thesis, Bethlehem, PA, US: Lehigh University.

Kensler, L.A.W. (2010) 'Designing democratic community for social justice', *International Journal of Urban Educational Leadership*, vol 4, no 1, pp 1-21.

Kensler, L.A.W. (forthcoming) 'Ecological sustainability: shining a light on the blind spot in K-12 educational leadership theory and practice', *Journal of School Leadership*.

Kensler, L.A.W., White, G.P., Caskie, G.I.L. and Fenton, T. (2005) 'A study of democratic principles at both the district and school level', Annual meeting of the University Council for Educational Administration, Nashville, TN, 10–13 November.

Kensler, L.A.W., Caskie, G.I.L., Barber, M.E. and White, G.P. (2009) 'The ecology of democratic learning communities: faculty trust and continuous learning in public middle schools', *Journal of School Leadership*, vol 19, no 6, pp 697-734.

Kinjerski, V.M. and Skrypnek, B.J. (2004) 'Defining spirit at work: finding common ground', *Journal of Organizational Change Management*, vol 17, no 1, pp 26-42.

Kooiman, J. (2009) *Governing as governance*, London: Sage.

Kuhn, T. (1970) *The structure of scientific evolutions*, Chicago: University of Chicago Press.

Lawrence, E. (1970) *The origins and growth of modern education*, Harmondsworth: Penguin.

Leadbeater, C. (2006) 'The socially entrepreneurial city', in A. Nicholls (ed) *Social entrepreneurship: New models of sustainable social change*, Oxford: Oxford University Press.

Leadbeater, C. and Goss, S. (1998) *Civic entrepreneurship*, London: Demos.

Leithwood, K. and Mascall, B. (2008) 'Collective leadership effects on student achievement', *Educational Administration Quarterly*, vol 44, no 4, pp 529-61.

Levačič, R. (2008) 'Financing schools: evolving patterns of autonomy and control', *Educational Management Administration and Leadership*, vol 36, no 2, pp 221-34.

Liebenstein, H. (1966) "Allocative Efficiency vs. 'X-Efficiency'", *American Economic Review*, vol 56, no 3, June, pp 392-415.

Lindgren, M. and Packendorff, J. (2006) 'Entrepreneurship as boundary work: deviating from and belonging to community', in C. Steyaert and D. Hjorth (eds) *Entrepreneurship as social change*, Cheltenham: Edward Elgar, pp 210-30.

Lowith, K. (1993) *Max Weber and Karl Marx*, London: Routledge.

Malloch, T.R. (2008) *Spiritual enterprise*, New York and London: Encounter Books.

Mannheim, K. (1943) *Diagnosis of our time: Wartime essays of a sociologist*, London: Kegan Paul, Trench, Trubner & Co.

Mannheim, K. and Stewart, W.A.C. (1962) *An introduction to the sociology of education*, London: Routledge & Kegan Paul.

Manville, B. and Ober, J. (2003) *A company of citizens*, Boston, MA: Harvard Business School Press.

Maravelias, C. (2009) 'Freedom, opportunism and entrepreneurialism in post-bureaucratic organizations', in D. Hjorth and C. Steyaert (eds) *The politics and aesthetics of entrepreneurship*, Cheltenham: Edward Elgar, pp 13-30.

Marsden, D. and Cañibano, A. (2009) *CEP discussion paper no 945. Participation in organisations: Economic approaches*, London: London School of Economics.

Martin, S. (2010) 'From new public management to networked community governance? Strategic local public service networks in England', in S.P. Osborne (ed) *The new public governance?*, London: Routledge.

Marx, K. and Engels, F. (1967) *The communist manifesto*, Harmondsworth: Penguin.

McCombs, B.L. and Miller, L. (2008) *The school leader's guide to learner-centered education: From complexity to simplicity*, London: Sage.

McGilchrist, I. (2009) *The master and his emissary: The divided brain and the making of the western world*, New Haven, CT and London: Yale University Press.

McKenna, B., Rooney, D. and Boal, K.B. (2009) 'Wisdom principles as a meta-theoretical basis for evaluating leadership', *Leadership Quarterly*, vol 20, no 2, pp 177-90.

McLaughlin, T. (1996) 'Education of the whole child?', in R. Best (ed) *Education, spirituality and the whole child*, London: Cassell.

Michalski, W., Miller R. and Stevens, B. (2001) 'Governance in the 21st century: power in the global knowledge economy and society', in OECD, *Governance in the 21st century*, Paris: OECD.

Mitchell, R. (2005) *Nurturing the souls of our children: Education and the culture of democracy*, Bloomington, IN: AuthorHouse.

Morgan, G. (1998) *Images of organization: The executive edition* (jointly published), San Francisco, CA: Berrett-Khoeler.

Mulgan, G. (2010) 'The birth of the relational state', in *Twenty for twenty* (20 essays exploring the future of the public and not-for-profit sectors over the next ten years), www.dhacommunications.co.uk/resource-centre/twenty-for-twenty/

Murchú, D.O. (2000) *Religion in exile: A spiritual homecoming*, Chestnut Ridge, NY: The Crossroad Publishing Company.

Murphy, J. (2002) 'Reculturing the profession of educational leadership: new blueprints', *Educational Administration Quarterly*, vol 38, no 2, pp 176-91.

Nayar, V. (2010) *Employees first, customers second*, Boston, MA: Harvard Business Press.

Newman, J. (2005) 'Enter the transformational leader: network governance and the micro-politics of modernization', *Sociology*, vol 39, no 4, pp 717–34.

Ober, J. (2008) *Democracy and knowledge: Innovation and learning in classical Athens*, Princeton and Oxford: Princeton University Press.

Ofsted (2002) *Local education authorities and school improvement 1996–2001*, London: Ofsted.

O'Hair, M.J., Williams, L.A., Wilson, S. and Applegate, P.J. (2009) 'The K20 model for systemic educational change and sustainability: addressing social justice in rural schools and implications for educators in all contexts', in P.A. Woods and G.J. Woods (eds) *Alternative education for the 21st century: Philosophies, approaches, visions*, New York: Palgrave, pp 15-30.

Ormerod, P. (2010) *N squared: Public policy and the power of networks*, London: RSA.

Osborne, D. and Gaebler, T. (1992) *Reinventing government*, New York, Penguin.

Osborne, S.P. (ed) (2010) *The new public governance?*, London: Routledge.

Ozga, J. (2009) 'Governing education through data in England: from regulation to self-evaluation', *Journal of Education Policy*, vol 24, no 2, pp 149-62.

Paredes Scribner, S.M. and Bradley-Levine, J. (2010) 'The meaning(s) of teacher leadership in an urban high school reform', *Educational Administration Quarterly*, vol 46, pp 491-522.

Peters, B. G. (2010) 'Meta-governance and public management', in S.P. Osborne (ed) *The new public governance?*, London: Routledge, pp 36-51.

Piers-Mantell, S. (2009) *A summary paper outlining how Learning to Lead (LtoL) can support the work of HS+ within the primary and secondary school context*, Shepton Mallet: Learning to Lead.

Pike, M.A. (2009) 'The Emmanuel Schools Foundation: Sponsoring and leading transformation at England's most improved Academy', *Management in Education*, vol 23, no 3, pp 139-44.

Poole, E. (2009) 'Organisational spirituality – a literature review', *Journal of Business Ethics*, vol 84, pp 577-88.

Popper, K.R. (1971) *The open society and its enemies (volume 1)*, Princeton, NJ: Princeton University Press.

Ranson, S. (2008) 'The changing governance of education', *Educational Management Administration and Leadership*, vol 36, no 2, pp 201-19.

Ranson, S. (forthcoming) 'The governance of schools mediating civil society', *Journal of Education Policy*.

Rathunde, K. (2009) 'Montessori and embodied education', in P.A. Woods and G.J. Woods (eds) *Alternative education for the 21st century: Philosophies, approaches, visions*, New York: Palgrave, pp 189-208.

Rawson, M. and Richter, T. (2000) *The educational tasks and content of the Steiner Waldorf curriculum*, Forest Row, Sussex: Steiner Waldorf Schools Fellowship.

Redmond, B. (2006) *Reflection in action: Developing reflective practice in health and social*, Aldershot: Ashgate.

Roberts, A. and Nash, J. (2010) *Supporting the growth of students as leaders: A student/teacher partnership approach*, Cambridge: Leadership for Learning, The Cambridge Network, University of Cambridge Faculty of Education.

Roper, J. and Cheney, G. (2005) 'The meanings of social entrepreneurship today, corporate governance', *International Journal of Business in Society*, vol 5, no 3, pp 95–104.

Ross, A. (2009) *CEO flow: Turn your employees into mini-CEOs*, Hollywood: PebbleStorm.

Rothschild, J. and Whitt, J.A. (1986/2009) *The cooperative workplace*, Cambridge: Cambridge University.

Rowe, A. (1973) 'Human beings, class and education', in D. Rubenstein and C. Stoneman (eds) *Education for democracy* (2nd edn), Harmondsworth: Penguin, pp 18-25.

Russell, J. (2009) 'Politics as if people mattered', in *What next for Labour: A collection of essays*, London: Demos.

Sahlberg, P. (2006) 'Education reform for raising economic competitiveness', *Journal of Educational Change*, vol 7, no 4, pp 259–87, www.pasisahlberg.com/downloads/Education%20reform%20for%20economic%20competitiveness%20JEC.pdf

Schneider, A. and Ingram, H. (2007) 'Ways of knowing: implications for public policy', presented at the annual meeting of the American Political Science Association, Chicago, 29 August–2 September.

Seel, R. (2000) 'Culture and complexity: new insights on organisational change', *Organisations & People*, vol 7, no 2, pp 2–9.

Sen, A. (2009) *The idea of justice*, London: Allen Lane,

Sennett, R. (2006) *The culture of the new capitalism*, New Haven, CT and London: Yale University Press.

Shatkin, G. and Gershberg, A.I. (2007) 'Empowering parents and building communities: the role of school-based councils in educational governance and accountability', *Urban Education*, vol 42, no 6, pp 582–615.

Shields, C. (2010) 'Transformative leadership: working for equity in diverse contexts', *Educational Administration Quarterly*, vol 46, pp 558–90.

Simon, H.A. (1951) 'A formal theory of the employment relationship', *Econometrica,* vol 19, no 3, July, pp 293-305.

Slater, C.L. (2010) 'The formation of educational entrepreneurs through doctoral programs in Mexico and California', Paper presented at the British Educational Leadership, Management & Administration Society (BELMAS) Annual International Conference, 9-11 July.

Sørensen, B.M. (2009) 'The entrepreneurial utopia. Miss Black Rose and the holy communion', in D. Hjorth and C. Steyaert (eds) *The politics and aesthetics of entrepreneurship*. Cheltenham: Edward Elgar, pp 202-20.

Spreitzer, G.M. and Doneson, D. (2005) 'Musings on the past and future of employee empowerment', in T. Cummings (ed) *Handbook of organizational development*, Thousand Oaks, CA: Sage.

Steyaert, C. and Katz, J. (2004) 'Reclaiming the space of entrepreneurship in society: geographical, discursive and social dimensions', *Entrepreneurship & Regional Development*, vol 16, no 3, pp 179–96.

Steyaert, C. and Hjorth, D. (eds) (2006) *Entrepreneurship as social change*, Cheltenham: Edward Elgar.

Storey, V.A. (2010) 'New localism vs. centralism: The New DEEL', paper presented at the British Educational Leadership, Management & Administration Society (BELMAS) Annual International Conference, 9-11 July.

Taylor, C. (2007) *A secular age*, Cambridge, MA: The Belknap Press of Harvard University Press.

Taylor, D. (1998) 'Social identity and social policy: engagements with postmodern theory', *Journal of Social Policy*, vol 27, no 3, pp 329–50.

Tischler, L., Biberman, J., Altman, Y. (2007) 'A model for researching about spirituality in organizations', *Business Renaissance Quarterly*, Summer, http://findarticles.com/p/articles/ mi_qa5430/is_200707/ ai_n21294688/

Touraine, A. (1997) *What is democracy?,* Boulder, CO and Oxford: Westview Press.

Tutu, D. (2005) *God has a dream,* New York: Doubleday.

Vacher, K. (2008) *Leading system redesign – 3: The students,* London: Specialist Schools and Academies Trust.

Waitere, H. and Court, M. (2009) '"Alternative" Māori education? Talking back/talking through hegemonic sites of power', in P.A. Woods and G.J. Woods (eds) *Alternative education for the 21st century: Philosophies, approaches, visions,* New York: Palgrave.

Warren, L. and Anderson, A. (2009) 'Playing the fool? An aesthetic performance of an entrepreneurial identity', in D. Hjorth and C. Steyaert (eds) *The politics and aesthetics of entrepreneurship.* Cheltenham: Edward Elgar, pp 148-61.

Weber, M. (1956/1978) *Economy and Society, vols I & II,* Berkeley, CA: University of California Press.

Weber, M. (1970a) 'Science as a vocation', in H.H. Gerth and C. Wright Mills (eds), *From Max Weber,* London: Routledge & Kegan Paul, pp 129-56.

Weber, M. (1970b) 'The meaning of discipline', in H.H. Gerth and C. Wright Mills (eds), *From Max Weber,* London: Routledge & Kegan Paul, pp 253-64.

Weiskopf, R. and Steyaert, C. (2009) 'Metamorphoses in entrepreneurship studies: towards an affirmative politics of entrepreneuring', in D. Hjorth and C. Steyaert (eds) *The politics and aesthetics of entrepreneurship,* Cheltenham: Edward Elgar, pp 183-201.

Wenger, E. (2000) 'Communities of practice and social learning systems', *Organization,* vol 7, no 2, pp 225–46.

Western, S. (2008) *Leadership: A critical text,* London: Sage.

Westland, N. (2009) 'We want the wow factor', *Guardian,* 26 May.

Whitehead, J. (2008) 'Using a living theory methodology in improving practice and generating educational knowledge in living theories', *Educational Journal of Living Theories,* vol 1, no 1, pp 103–26, http://ejolts.net/node/80

Woodin, T., Crook, D. and Carpentier, V. (2010) *Community and mutual ownership: A historical review,* York: Joseph Rowntree Foundation.

Woods, G.J. (2003) 'Spirituality, educational policy and leadership: a study of headteachers', PhD thesis, The Open University.

Woods, G.J. (2007) 'The "bigger feeling": the importance of spiritual experience in educational leadership', *Educational Management Administration & Leadership,* vol 35, no 1, pp 135–55.

Woods, G.J. and Woods, P.A. (2002) 'Creativity in educational policy: sociological and spiritual perspectives', Paper presented at a seminar of the Open University's Creativity Research Group, Milton Keynes, 8 January.

Woods, G.J. and Woods, P.A. (2008) 'Democracy and spiritual awareness: interconnections and implications for educational leadership', *International Journal of Children's Spirituality*, vol 13, no 2, pp 101–16.

Woods, P.A. (2003) 'Building on Weber to understand governance: exploring the links between identity, democracy and "inner distance"', *Sociology*, vol 37, no 1, pp 143–63.

Woods, P.A. (2004) 'Democratic leadership: drawing distinctions with distributed leadership', *International Journal of Leadership in Education: Theory and Practice*, vol 7, no 1, pp 3–26.

Woods, P.A. (2005) *Democratic leadership in education*, London: Sage.

Woods, P.A. (2006) 'A democracy of all learners: ethical rationality and the affective roots of democratic leadership', *School Leadership and Management*, vol 26, no 4, pp 321–37.

Woods, P.A. (2007) 'Authenticity in the bureau-enterprise culture: the struggle for authentic meaning', *Educational Management Administration and Leadership*, vol 35, no 2, pp 297–322.

Woods, P.A. (2008) 'Investigating developmental democracy: early data from an academy in England', Paper presented at the New DEEL Conference, Temple University, Philadelphia, US, 21–23 February.

Woods, P.A. (2010a) 'Rationalisation, disenchantment and re-enchantment: engaging with Weber's sociology of modernity', in M. Apple, S.J. Ball and L.A. Gandin (eds) *International handbook of the sociology of education*, London: Routledge, pp 121-31.

Woods, P.A. (2010b) 'Academies: alienation, economism and contending forces for change', in T. Green (ed) *Blair's educational legacy: Thirteen years of New Labour*, Basingstoke: Palgrave.

Woods, P.A. and Broadfoot, P. (2008) 'Vers le contrôle pluriel de l'Ecole? La nature changeante du pouvoir dans le système educatif anglais' ['Towards plural controlled schooling? The shifting nature of power in the English education system'], *Revue Internationale de Sévres*, vol 48, pp 83–95.

Woods, P.A. and Gronn, P. (2009) 'Nurturing democracy: the contribution of distributed leadership to a democratic organisational landscape', in P.A. Woods and M.J. O'Hair (eds) Special issue on democracy and school leadership, *Educational Management Administration & Leadership*, vol 37, no 4, pp 430–51.

Woods, P.A. and Woods, G.J. (2004) 'Modernizing leadership through private participation: a marriage of inconvenience with public ethos?', *Journal of Education Policy*, vol 19, no 6, pp 643–72.

Woods, P.A., and G.J. Woods (2006a) Feedback report (Michael Hall Steiner School): collegial leadership in action, Aberdeen: School of Education, University of Aberdeen.

Woods, P.A. and Woods, G.J. (2006b) Feedback report (Meadow Steiner School): collegial leadership in action, Aberdeen: School of Education, University of Aberdeen.

Woods, P.A. and Woods, G.J. (2009a) 'Testing a typology of entrepreneurialism: emerging findings from an academy with an enterprise specialism', *Management in Education*, vol 23, no 3, pp 125–9.

Woods, P.A. and Woods, G.J. (eds) (2009b) *Alternative education for the 21st century: Philosophies, approaches, visions*, New York: Palgrave.

Woods, P.A. and Woods, G.J. (2009c) 'Pathways to learning: deepening reflective practice to explore democracy, connectedness and spirituality', in P.A. Woods and G.J. Woods (eds) *Alternative education for the 21st century: Philosophies, approaches, visions*, New York: Palgrave.

Woods, P.A. and Woods, G.J. (2009d) 'Introduction', in P.A. Woods and G.J. Woods (eds) *Alternative education for the 21st century: Philosophies, approaches, visions*, New York: Palgrave, pp 1-13.

Woods, P.A. and Woods, G.J. (2010) 'The geography of reflective leadership: the inner life of democratic learning communities', *Philosophy of Management*, vol 9, no 2, pp 81–97.

Woods, P.A. and Woods, G.J. (2011) 'Lighting the fires of entrepreneurialism? Constructions of meaning in an English inner city Academy', *International Journal of Technology and Educational Marketing*, vol 1, no 1, pp 1-24.

Woods, P.A. and Woods, G.J. (forthcoming) 'Degrees of school democracy: A holistic framework', *Journal of School Leadership*.

Woods, P.A., Ashley, M. and Woods, G.J. (2005) *Steiner Schools in England*, London: Department for Education and Skills. Ref No: RR645, www. dfes.go.uk/research

Woods, P.A., Woods, G.J., and Gunter, H. (2007a) 'Academy schools and entrepreneurialism in education', *Journal of Education Policy*, vol 22, no 2, pp 263–85.

Woods, P.A., Levačič, R., Evans, J., Castle, F., Glatter, R. and Cooper, D. (2007b) *Diversity and collaboration? Diversity pathfinders evaluation: Final report*, London: Department for Education and Skills. Ref No: RR826, www.dfes.gov.uk/research

Woods, P.A., Woods, G.J. and Cowie, M. (2009) '"Tears, laughter, camaraderie": professional development for headteachers', *School Leadership & Management*, vol 29, no 3, pp 83–104.

Zerbinati, S. and Souitaris, V. (2005) 'Entrepreneurship in the public sector: a framework of analysis in European local governments', *Entrepreneurship and Regional Development*, vol 17, no 1, pp 43–64.

Žižek, S. (2008) 'Use your illusions', *London Review of Books*, 14 November (www.lrb.co.uk/2008/11/14/slavoj-zizek/use-your-illusions).

Zohar, D. and Marshall, I. (2000) *Spiritual intelligence: The ultimate intelligence*, London: Bloomsbury.

Index

Note: Page numbers followed by *fig* or *n* refer to information in a figure or a note respectively.

A

aboriginal education in Canada 153
Academies programme 37, 46-7, 49, 53, 72, 79
  cooperative schools 145
  and emergent leadership scheme 107-9, 116, 120, 124
  Urbanview Academy case study 109-11, 113-28
'academisation' 119
accountability 15, 32, 54
  and authority structures 118, 161
  monitory democracy 27-8, 58, 105
  and networks 104, 105
  and organic meta-governance 64
adaptive rationality 81-7, 90
adaptive strategies 77-87, 96, 102, 128, 129, 160-1, 162
affect *see* emotional aspect
agency 1, 7, 11
  and adaptive strategies 77, 79, 80
  and democratic paradigm shift 63, 89
  and entrepreneurialism 30, 35
  and flat authority structure 118, 132
  and governance 51
  organic meta-governance 64-5, 66
  and new openings theory 79
  see also autonomy and control
Albrow, Martin 45
Alexander, R. 54-5, 158, 160
alienation and degrees of democracy 112*fig*, 124-5
All Hallows Catholic College, Macclesfield 148-9, 161

amplification as adaptive strategy 82-4, 87, 102, 104, 140, 160
anthroposophy and Steiner schools 114, 117, 118-19, 123-4
Apple, M. 87
architectonic principles and entrepreneurialism 39-40
  and holistic democracy 41-2, 113
Athenian democracy model 98, 99-100, 104-5
authority structure variable 112*fig*, 118-19, 127, 132
autonomy and control 48-51
  cooperative schools 147
  'quasi-autonomous schools' 47, 48, 49
  and self-governance 68
  see also agency

B

Ball, Stephen J. 49-50, 57, 71, 72, 74, 78, 81-2
Beane, J. 87
belief and spiritual capital 25
Berliner, David 93
Bernstein, Basil 175-6*n*
Beyes, T. 35
'Big Society' 59-60
Billings, Tony 148-9
Blair, Tony 52-3, 171
Bloom, Alex 132, 133, 134, 135
Blue School, Wells, Somerset 139-40, 141-3
Bolan, Richard 81
Boston, David 145-7

Bottery, M. 54
boundaries *see* co-creation across
    boundaries
boundary organisations 92
Bowden, Hugh 99–100
Brain Gym 176*n*
brain research and rationalised
    approach 90–1
Braithwaite, E.R. 133–4
Branson, Richard 31
Breakspear, S. 32
'bridging environments' and change
    163
Broadfoot, P. 49, 170*n*
Brown, Gordon 3, 171*n*
Bull, M. 73, 83
Bunt, L. 63
bureau-entrepreneurial culture 32–3,
    34, 44, 67, 79, 126
business entrepreneurialism 35, 36
    and education 39, 80
business view of entrepreneurialism
    39

C

Caldwell, B.J. 33, 51
Callinicos, A. 2–3, 60, 70–1
Cambridge Primary Review 50, 54,
    93, 157–8, 182*n*
Cameron, David 31, 172*n*
Canada and First Nations education
    153
Cañibano, A. 167–8*n*
capabilities for holistic democracy 89–
    100, 102, 128
    freedom as capability 85–6, 160
capacity
    democratic capacity 69, 74
    and new openings theory 79
capitalism
    demand for change in 3–4, 60
    dominance of economistic and
        performative culture critique 70–3,
        74, 77–8, 132
    see also private business/markets
        model
Casey, Catherine 21, 25, 81, 168*n*
categorical identity orientation 176*n*

Cathcart, A. 22
central control
    association with localism in US
        172*n*
    Coalition drive to decentralisation
        59–60
    and education 45, 48–50, 53, 54, 55,
        69, 78, 158
    student views 122
    see also decentralisation
change
    and capitalism 3–4, 60
    and embodied actors 89–106
    as emergent process 163–4
    energies for 11–12, 25, 129, 155–64
    localism and spirit of change 59–62
    personal change 21
    system redesign 53, 55, 57–8, 62
    see also organic change; structural
        change
Charles, Prince of Wales 7
charter schools in US 152–3
citizenship
    corporate citizenship 83
    in school curriculum 49
civic capacity 69
'civic entrepreneurship' 169–70*n*
Clapton, Eric 95
clash of rationalities critique 70, 74
Cloke, K. 16, 22, 26, 29, 124
Coalition Government
    and central control of education 45,
        46–7, 48
    decentralisation and localism 59–60,
        71
    and plural controlled schooling 53,
        78
co-construction 55, 62, 80, 132, 160
co-creation across boundaries 112*fig*,
    115–16, 127, 132, 162
cognitive learning 112*fig*, 116, 117,
    126, 127
cognitive-technical knowledge 112*fig*,
    114, 115, 124–5, 126, 127
co-governance 67, 68
collaborative teacher groups 85
collective action and new openings
    theory 79
collegiate systems 61, 108

D

Dahrendorf, Ralf 60
data-driven decision making 90
Davies, Gail 80-1, 97
Day, C. 69-70
decentralisation
  and localism 59-60, 62, 71
  and organisational democracy 9-10
degrees of democracy analytical
  framework 23, 29, 80, 84, 107-29
  and change to democratic self-
    organising system 160-1, 162
  and democratic entrepreneurialism
    42, 162
  ideal-types and framework analysis
    111-28, 163
  methodology 109-11
  and radical traditions in schools
    132-3
democratic capacity 69, 74
Democratic Collaboration and
  Culture of Peace in Latin America
  149-51
democratic consciousness 64-6, 67,
  89, 98
  and critical democratic actors 102-4,
    105, 162
  as degrees of democracy variable
    112*fig*, 125-6
democratic education 65, 87
  change to democratic self-
    organising system 157-64
  as paradigm shift 1, 6-7
  practical examples 131-53
  see also holistic democracy
democratic entrepreneurialism 35,
  40-4, 66, 67, 74-5, 162
democratic governance 67, 68
democratic leadership in education
  65-6, 69-70, 101-2, 132-44
democratic paradigm shift 57-75
  and adaptive strategies 77-87, 96,
    102, 128, 129, 160-1, 162
  challenges to 69-75
    operational problems 69-70
    socio-political critiques 70-5,
      77-8, 80
  and education 1, 6-7, 57, 62-75, 160
  embodiment of change 89-106

energies for change in education
  155-64
evolutionary nature of democracy
  58-9
localism as spirit of change 59-62
requirements for 62-8
  democratic consciousness 64-6, 89,
    98, 102-4, 105, 162
  organic meta-governance 62-75
  trend towards democratic times 1,
    2-6, 15-30
democratic school case study 109
democratic self-organising system 8,
  13, 64, 106, 155-60
democratising networks 104-6, 162
depth of participation variable 112*fig*,
  123
Deuchar, Ross 34
developmental democracy *see* holistic
  democracy
dialogue *see* key purpose of dialogue
  variable; transforming dialogue
  and holistic democracy model
difference *see* diversity
disadvantaged communities and
  curriculum 74
disembodied learning 94, 95*fig*
disenchantment and organisational
  life 23, 73, 91
dispersal of power *see* power sharing
distributed leadership 61, 111
diversification hypothesis 78-9, 156
diversity
  community and educational change
    57-8
  and eco-leadership discourse 26-7
  and holistic democracy 158
  and new openings theory 79
divination and Greek gods 99-100
Drucker, P. 36

E

eco-leadership discourse 26-7
ecological awareness 37
economic crisis *see* financial and
  economic crisis
economistic and performative culture
  70-3, 74, 77-8, 90, 132, 160

Michael Hall school 109, 116, 118–19, 119–20, 125
'radical collegiality' 139
communication flows variable 112*fig*, 121–2, 132
community
  and cooperative schools 145–6, 147
  as degrees of democracy variable 112*fig*, 123–4, 128
  education and cultural activism 151–3
  local authorities as community leaders 100
  localism as empowerment of 63
  and organisational democracy 5, 26
  and governance of schools 51–2
  operational problems 69
community link teachers (CLTs) 142–3
community organising and educational change 57–8
'company circle' 30
compassion 66, 94, 102, 158
competitive market governance in education 50
competitive performance as principal purpose 112*fig*, 113, 114
complexity of work 20–1
compliance culture in education 61
compliant mindset variable 112*fig*, 125–6
conceptual innovations and critical democratic actors 101
connectedness 23–4, 27, 58, 94, 95
  as degrees of democracy variable 112*fig*, 124–5, 126, 127, 128
Conservative Party
  and localism 59–60
  see also Coalition Government
content change and central control 48–9
control 45–55
  and adaptive strategies 81–2
  cooperative schools 147
  see also central control; plural controlled schooling
convergence thesis and education 72–3, 78–9, 86
Convivencia Democrática y Cultura de Paz en América Latina 149–51

Co-operative Academy in Manchester 145
Co-operative College here, p 181*n*
Co-operative Group 145, 146, 179*n*
cooperativism
  cooperative organisations 5, 18–19, 29
  provisional character 163
  cooperative schools 34, 69, 144–9, 161
  and freedom as capability 85–6, 160
  and localism 59, 60–1
Cooperrider, D.L. 89
co-ownership model 18, 22, 29–30, 86
corporate citizenship 83
corporate hybrid leadership 119, 126
Cottingham, J. 95
Countesthorpe Community College 132
Court, Marian 151–2
Craig, J. 3, 61
Cramer, Elannah 19, 43, 131
creativity
  and expressive drivers 25–6
  as holistic capability 89–90
  visualisation of change 33, 102, 103, 160, 162
  see also innovation
critical democratic actors 5, 100–4, 164
  and democratic consciousness 102–4, 105, 162
  and educational practice 132, 135, 139, 143
  institutional critical democratic actors 162–3
cultural diversity
  and educational practice 151–3
  and new openings theory 79
cultural entrepreneurialism 35, 36, 37, 41
cultural renewal and disenchantment 23
curriculum
  and central control 48, 49
  disadvantaged communities and selective change 74
  narrowing and standards 54–5

education *see* democratic education; educational policy
Education Reform Act (ERA) (1988) 45
Education with Aloha programme 152-3
educational policy
  and central control and governance 45-51, 53, 54, 69
    and spirit of change 61-2, 78, 161-2
    and energies for change 157-8, 161-2
  and entrepreneurialism 32, 33-4, 38-9, 53, 80
  instrumentalist approach 90, 92
  and organic change 6-7, 63-75, 157
  radical tradition in England 132-4
  and right-brain approaches 92-3
  see also schools; teachers
educational practice and holistic democracy 131-53
  practice as energy for change 157
Elmore, R. 161
Emberton, J. 36, 37
embodied actors and change 89-106
embodied learning 44, 94-8, 101, 105, 162
  and degrees of democracy framework 112*fig*, 116-17, 127
emergent leadership scheme (ELS) in Academy school 107-9, 116, 120, 124
Emmanuel Schools Foundation 169*n*
emotional aspect
  amplification and holistic democracy 82-3, 104
  and bureau-enterprise culture 32-3
  and education 93, 94
    cognitive-emotional learning 117, 126, 127
empathy and corporate citizenship 83
employees
  and entrepreneurialism 31-2, 67, 73, 143
  organisational democracy and empowerment 15-16, 17-19, 20-1
  and ownership of organisation 18, 22, 29-30, 86
  and participation 81

empowerment and organisational democracy 15-16, 17-19, 20-1, 63
  autonomy and education 50-1, 52, 61, 79
  teachers and emergent leadership scheme 108, 116
'empty self' of consumerism 89
endemic inequality critique 73-4
energy
  and change 11-12, 25, 129, 155-64
  and entrepreneurialism 33
  spiritual awareness and educational practice 96-7
engagement and depth of participation variable 112*fig*, 123
engineering model of education 7-8, 53
entrepreneurial leadership 21, 53
entrepreneurialism 30, 31-44
  and Academy approach 125
  and critical democratic actors 101, 162
  democratic entrepreneurialism 35, 40-4, 66, 74-5, 162
  and educational policy 32, 33-4, 38-9, 53, 80
  and employees 31-2, 67, 73, 143
  generic view 33-4, 39, 40
  mobilising resources and holistic democracy 33, 86-7, 90
  and plural controlled schooling 53
  substantive meanings of 34-40
  typology 35-8
entrepreneurship, *see* entrepreneurialism
equality and democracy 42
  endemic inequality critique 73-4
Erdahl, Roxanne 5
ethics
  cooperative schools 148-9
  and entrepreneurial approach 34, 83
  ethical educational leadership 162-3
  ethical sensibilities 25
  see also values
exclusive spaces for participation 112*fig*, 119-20
Exley, S. 74
exogenous identity orientation 175*n*
experimental innovations and critical democratic actors 101, 132

expressive dimensions of holistic democracy 10, 74, 127
and democratic entrepreneurialism 41-2
as drivers for change 19, 23-7, 30, 58
and practice in education 131-2
non-UK examples 149-53
see also holistic meaning and holistic democracy model; holistic well-being and holistic democracy model
externalised identity orientation 175*n*

F

faith schools 46, 148-9
faith and spiritual capital 25
feminist critical actors 178*n*
Fenton, Traci 16, 19, 166*n*
Fielding, Michael 72, 115, 132-4, 139
Fierro, María Cecilia 181*n*
financial and economic crisis 2, 3-4, 6, 71
First Nations education in Canada 153
flat structure of authority 112*fig*, 118-19, 132, 136
flexible organisations 20-1, 32, 84-5, 160
flow
communication flows variable 112*fig*, 121-2, 132
education and theories of 92
Flowers, P. 20, 30
Free Schools model 47
free-thinking mindset 102
freedom
as capability as adaptive strategy 85-6, 160
and democracy 42, 158
ignored by third way 60
and organic meta-governance 64-5, 66
'frontiers of control' 167-8*n*
Frost, David 138, 140-1
Fullan, Michael 34, 54
fully embodied learning 94, 95*fig*, 98, 101, 105
Future Considerations 30

G

Gaebler, T. 32
Galenson, David 178*n*
Gane, N. 169*n*
gardening metaphor for education 7-8, 64
Gardiner, M. 90
generic entrepreneurialism 33-4, 39, 40
Gershberg, A.I. 181*n*
Gerver, Richard 144
Giddens, Anthony 27-8, 58, 174*n*
Goldsmith, J. 16, 22, 26, 29, 124
Goodson, I. 93
Goss, S. 169-70*n*
Gove, Michael 48, 171*n*, 176-7*n*
governance
and democratic paradigm shift 57-75, 78
and education 45-55, 78, 161-2
localism as spirit of change 59-62
new public governance 28-9, 58, 62, 64, 100
overviews 66-8
see also control; marketising meta-governance; organic meta-governance
governance diamond 67-8, 161
governance frame 66-7
government
Coalition Government and spirit of change 59-60
emphasis on enterprise 31
'relational state' concept 28-9
self-government and holistic democracy 15, 22
steering role 2, 45
see also central control; Coalition Government; Labour Government
'Grangetown' project 144
Gratton, Lynda 5, 21, 23, 25-6, 31, 71
Greek gods and divination 99-100
Green, H. 93
Green, Stephen 3
Green, T.H. 9
Gronn, P. 70, 124
Gunter, H. 64

H

Habermas, J. 72, 90, 97
Haig-Brown, C. 153
Hargreaves, Andy 5-6, 33, 53, 57-8, 61-2, 73, 90, 124
Hargreaves, David 57, 61, 62
Harris, M. 63
Hatcher, Richard 58, 131
Hawaiian culture and charter schools 152-3
HCL Technologies 17, 161
Heelas, Paul 24-5, 77, 92
HertsCam Network 137-8
Hess, F.M. 31, 32, 35
Hess, M. 101
heterarchical system and education 78
hierarchy
  and accountability 161
  and bureau-enterprise culture 32
  and educational practice 136, 141
  hierarchical governance 67, 68, 161
  as ideal type in degrees of democracy analytical framework 111-28
    and pyramid structure of authority 12*fig*, 118, 119, 161
    and transactional engagement 123
  new openings theory and alternatives to 79
  and participation 30
higher order values 34, 72, 84, 87
  and degrees of democracy 113-14, 120
Hjorth, D. 41
Hodson, J. 153
holarchy 79, 103, 141, 157
holistic democracy 9-12
  and adaptive strategies 82-7, 96, 102, 128, 129, 160-1, 162
  and democratic entrepreneurialism 41-4, 74-5, 162
  energies for change 155-64
  holistic capabilities 89-106, 128, 160
  as ideal type in degrees of democracy analytical framework 111-28, 163
  and organic meta-governance 67, 68
  practical examples in education 131-53

see also degrees of democracy analytical framework; democratic education
holistic knowledge 112*fig*, 114-15
holistic meaning and holistic democracy model 10, 23, 42, 160, 166*n*
  and degrees of democracy variables 113-18, 126, 127
  and practice in education 132, 135-7, 145-9, 153
holistic participation variable 112*fig*, 123
holistic well-being and holistic democracy model 10, 11, 23, 42, 160, 166*n*
  and degrees of democracy variables 113, 123-6, 127
  and practice in education 132, 149, 153
Hotho, Sabine 81
Hsie, Tony 95
Hughes, Bettany 178*n*
human capital and 'market servitism' 71
humility and democracy 99

I

Idealism and holistic democracy 9
identity construction and new openings theory 79, 86
imagination
  and democratic paradigm shift 89
  see also creativity
immanent utopias 89-90
inclusive spaces for participation 112*fig*, 119-20, 132
individual characteristics and organisational democracy 9
individualistic entrepreneurial motivation 39, 40, 72
'Industrial Age' paradigm of education 7, 8
inefficiency critique of democracy 69
inequality: endemic inequality critique 73-4
information exchange as purpose of dialogue 112*fig*, 122
Ingram, H. 92

'initiative culture' in schools 135-7
innovation and organisational
    democracy 17
    and critical democratic actors 101,
        132, 135, 139, 162-3
    and educational practice 134-44
    and expressive drivers 25-6
    and new openings theory 79
    and organic meta-governance 67
    profession-led culture of innovation
        in education 61-2
    and public sector 32
    teacher-led innovation 80, 120, 138,
        139
    see also entrepreneurialism
Innovation Unit 61
institutional critical democratic actors
    162-3
institutional learning in Athens 105
instruction within boundaries 112*fig*,
    115-16
instrumental belonging 112*fig*, 123
instrumentalism
    and adaptive strategies 80-7, 96, 160
    and bureau-enterprise culture 32
    dominance of rational approaches
        90-2
    as driver for greater meaning and
        participation 19-22, 30, 58
        building on instrumental artefacts
            84-5, 160
    and economistic and performative
        culture 71-3, 74, 90, 132, 160
    and expressive drivers 25
    see also rationality
intelligences: expanding range 93
introjected identity orientation 175-
    6*n*

J

John Lewis Partnership 22, 29
Johnson, J. 101
Jones, Campbell 34
Judge, P. 33
Jue, Arthur 26

K

Katz, Jerry 31, 40
Keane, John 15, 27-8, 29, 65, 155

Kensler, Lisa 83-4, 166*n*
key purpose of dialogue variable
    112*fig*, 122
knowledge
    and degrees of democracy
        framework 112*fig*, 114-16, 124-5
    social knowledge and networks 105
knowledge economy and
    organisational democracy 21
knowledge goals variable 112*fig*, 114-
    15, 124-5
Kooiman, Jan 67-8, 167*n*
Kuhn, T. 6

L

Labour Government
    and central control of education 45-
        6, 47, 53, 54
    and radical view of localism 60-1
    third way and partnerships in
        education 52-3
Labour Party 23
Lawrence, D.H. 89
Lawrence, E. 7
Leadbeater, C. 169-70*n*
leadership
    corporate hybrid leadership in
        schools 119, 126
    democratic leadership in education
        65-6, 69-70, 101-2, 132-44
    cooperative schools 149
    New DEEL network 162-3
    student leadership projects 139-43
    teacher leadership and new
        openings theory 79-80
    and democratic turn in
        organisations 5, 62
    emergent leadership scheme in
        Academy school 107-9, 116, 120,
        124
    entrepreneurial leadership 21, 53
    and expressive dimension to
        organisational change 26-7
    reflective leadership and embodied
        learning 94
    spiritual awareness of headteachers
        96
    system leaders in education 100, 162

tranformational leadership and critical actors 101-2, 132
learning modes variable 116-17
Learning to Lead project 139-43
left-brain dominance and rationality 90, 91-2
cognitive learning 116, 117
Liberal Democrats *see* Coalition Government
liberty
substantive liberty 42, 67, 156, 175*n*
see also freedom
Libson, Sylvia 38-9
'life spiritualities' 24-5, 65, 92
local authorities
as community leaders 100
diminished role in education policy 69
local empowerment model and education 50, 52
localism 47, 51, 58-63, 74, 80, 172*n*
drawbacks of poor implementation 62-3, 80
and instrumental drive 58
operational problems 69
as spirit of change 59-62
and sponsorship of schools 51, 79

M

Macbeath, J. 140-1
McCombs, B.L. 7
McGilchrist, Iain 8, 91, 92
Mackay, Heath 18, 131
McLaughlin, T. 39
Malloch, Theodore 25
managerialism 72-3, 78
see also new public management
Mandela, Nelson 97, 99
Mannheim, Karl 155
Manville, Brook 15
Māori education in New Zealand 151-2
Maravelias, C. 43
'market servitism' 71
marketising meta-governance 64, 66-7, 69, 71, 81-2, 158, 162, 164
markets *see* private business/markets model
Marsden, D. 167-8*n*

Marx, Karl 1, 65
material resources 86, 87, 160-1
maximal scope of participation 112*fig*, 121, 126*fig*, 127-8, 132
meaning and participation in organisations 5-6, 9-12
alternative models and adaptive strategies 77-87, 96, 102, 128, 129, 160-1, 162
and degrees of democracy framework 126-9
drivers for 15-30
and entrepreneurialism 40
holistic meaning and organisational democracy 166*n*
substantive meanings of entrepreneurialism 34-40
see also holistic meaning and holistic democracy model
mechanical model of education 7-8
Meill, Augusta 17
Melluci, Alberto 174*n*
meta-governance
and educational policy 63-4
see also marketising meta-governance; organic meta-governance
metaphor and myth 103-4
method of teaching variable 112*fig*, 115-16
Michael Hall school case study 109-11, 113-28, 135
Michalski, W. 15
micro-genesis 101
micro-management 17, 53, 54, 55, 59, 61, 78, 164
militant democracy 155
Miller, L. 7
mindful practice and democratic entrepreneurialism 43
mindset variable 112*fig*, 125-6
minimal (partial) scope of participation 112*fig*, 121, 126*fig*, 127
Mitchell, R. 98, 178*n*
mobilising resources
as adaptive strategy 86-7, 90, 160-1
critical democratic actors 101, 102, 162
and entrepreneurialism 33, 86-7, 90

modernisation agenda and education 52-3
modes of learning variable 116-17
monitory democracy 27-8, 58, 105
Morgan, G. 164
Mulgan, Geoff 28
multiple communication flows 112*fig*, 121-2, 132
multiple rationalities and educational practice 143-4
Murchú, D.O. 24
Murphy, Jo 172*n*
mutualism
  and localism 57, 59, 60-1
  mutual ownership movement 5
  and organic meta-governance 65
myth and metaphor 103-4

N

Namaste Solar 18, 86
National College for Leadership of Schools and Children's Services 48-9, 93
national testing and effect on curriculum 54-5
Native Hawaiian Charter School Alliance 152-3
network governance and education 51, 55
network logic 103
networks
  and critical actors 100, 101, 139, 162-3
  democratising networks 104-6, 162
  and eco-leadership discourse 26-7
  and educational policy and practice 69
  HertsCam Network 137-8
  New DEEL network 162-3
New DEEL (Democratic Ethical Educational Leadership) network 162-3
New Labour *see* Labour Government
'New Localism' 172*n*
new openings theory 79-80, 86, 90, 174*n*
new public governance 28-9, 58, 62, 64, 100

new public management 32, 58, 64
  see also managerialism
New Zealand Māori education 151-2
Newman, Janet 77, 175*n*
Nietzsche, Friedrich Wilhelm 103
nodal systems leaders 100

O

Oakington Manor primary school 38-9
Obama, Barack 173*n*, 176*n*
Ober, Josiah 15, 98, 101, 105, 166*n*
OECD 15
one-way communication flows 112*fig*, 121-2
organic belonging 23, 42, 58, 87
  and degrees of democracy framework 112*fig*, 123-4, 126*fig*, 127, 128
organic change 6-8
  and educational policy 6-7, 63-75, 157
organic meta-governance 63-75, 104, 128, 155-6
  constellation of change for 156-7
organic steering 159
organisational democracy 4, 5-6, 9, 15-19, 22, 26, 29, 43, 58, 98, 131, 165*n*, 166*n*
  drivers for 15-30, 58
  see also empowerment and organisational democracy; innovation and organisational democracy; meaning and participation in organisations
Ormerod, Paul 57, 100, 104
Osborne, D. 32
Osborne, S.P. 28-9, 58, 64
Ozga, J. 81

P

paradigm shift *see* democratic paradigm shift
partial (minimal) scope of participation 112*fig*, 121, 126*fig*, 127
partially embodied learning 94, 95*fig*

participation *see* meaning and
    participation in organisations;
    participative dimensions of holistic
    democracy
participative dimensions of holistic
    democracy 10
  and degrees of democracy
    framework 126*fig*, 127-8
  scope of participation variable
    112*fig*, 120-1, 126*fig*, 127, 132
  spaces for participation variable
    112*fig*, 119-20, 126, 132
  and democratic entrepreneurialism
    41-2
  as drivers for change 19, 22, 27-30,
    58
  and practice in education 131-2,
    133-44
  see also power sharing and holistic
    democracy; transforming dialogue
    and holistic democracy model
participatory democracy 27, 58
partnerships in education 52-3, 79
Peacock, Alison 134-5
pedagogy
  and central control 46, 48
  and degrees of democracy
    framework 115-16
peer-assisted review 161
performance measurement and
    monitoring 32, 54-5
  and competitive performance aim
    113, 114
  data-driven decision making 90
performative and economistic culture
    70-3, 74, 77-8, 90, 132, 156-7, 160
personal change and instrumental
    drive 21
personal reflexivity and new openings
    theory 79
personal variable 112*fig*, 124-5
personalised learning 46, 93
Piers-Mantell, Susan 140, 142
Pillai, Anand 17, 29
plural controlled schooling model 45,
    51-5, 61, 68, 73-4, 78
  and critical democratic actors 101
  and new openings theory 79-80
policy *see* educational policy
Pollard, David 81

Popper, Karl 63-4
postmodernism and
    entrepreneurialism 35
power
  devolution of power 15, 17, 59-60,
    69, 80
    see also power sharing and holistic
    democracy
  renegotiation of power relations
    28-9, 73-4
power sharing and holistic democracy
    9-10, 11, 166*n*
  and building on instrumental drives
    85, 160
  and degrees of democracy variables
    113, 118-21
  and democratic entrepreneurialism
    42
  and democratic governance 68
  in education systems 69-70, 80
  and educational practice 132, 135-7,
    141-3
  and participative drives 29
Prince of Wales 7
principal organisational purpose
    variable 112*fig*, 113-14
private business/markets model
  in education 46, 47, 49-51, 79
  flaws in 2-4, 53, 60
  public sector emulation 32-3, 34, 53
    see also capitalism
professional development 114, 115,
    116, 159, 162
'professional empowerment' and
    schools 51
  profession-led culture of innovation
    61-2
public entrepreneurialism 35, 36,
    37-8, 41
public sector
  and entrepreneurialism 32-3, 34, 53
  need for change in governance 60-1
pyramid structure of authority 112*fig*,
    118, 119, 161

Q

quality control model of governance
    48
Quanta 83

'quasi-autonomous schools' 47, 48, 49

R

'radical collegiality' 139
radical tradition in education in
England 132-4
radicalisation of entrepreneurialism
30, 40-4
Ranson, S. 45, 50, 104
rationality
adaptive rationality 81-7, 90
clash of rationalities critique 70, 74
dominance of rational approaches
90-2
multiple rationalities and
educational practice 143-4
rationalisation of organisational life
23
and entrepreneurial approach 35
substantive rationality 80-1
see also instrumentalism
reciprocal accountability 161, 162
recruitment and organisational
democracy 18-19
reflection 84, 85, 128
reflective leadership and embodied
learning 94
reflexivity 103
personal reflexivity 79
'relational state' 28-9
relational view of entrepreneurialism
39, 40
resource mobilisation *see* mobilising
resources
Reynolds, Christopher 135-7
right-brain approaches and education
92-3
Roberts, Amanda 139
Robinson, Sir Ken 8
Rothschild, J. 2, 27, 176*n*   add 19, 57,
86, 87, 163, 168*n*
'rounded persons' as education goal
124, 174*n*
Rusbridger, Alan 28
Russell, J. 23

S

sacred and expression of 97-8
Sahlberg, P. 69

Saint Benedict Catholic School and
Performing Arts College, Derby
135-7
St George-in-the-East Secondary
School, Stepney 132-4
Salvation Army 37
Sands School case study 109-11,
113-28
Schneider, A. 92
school councils 118, 119, 121, 133-4,
135, 137, 144, 149   make initial
letter of 'school' and 'council'
lower case.
see also student voice
school empowerment governance
model 50
schools
and degrees of democracy 111-128
and entrepreneurialism 33-4, 38-9,
80
and practice of holistic democracy
131-53
see also educational policy; teachers
scope of participation variable 112*fig*,
120-1, 126*fig*, 127, 132
scrutiny *see* accountability
Seel, Richard 57
self-esteem and Academy approach
117, 125
self-governance 67, 68
self-government and holistic
democracy 15, 22
self-improvement systems for schools
61, 174*n*
self-managing school model 51
self-organisation 16, 22, 27
and adaptive strategies 80-7, 160-1,
162
and authority structures 118
and democratic paradigm shift 57-8,
64, 65, 129
change to democratic self-
organising system in education
157-64
and entrepreneurialism 40
and holarchy 79, 103, 141, 157
and participatory democracy 27
and values 158
see also organic meta-governance
Sen, Amartya 85, 94

Sennett, Richard 20, 73
shared action 156
shared awareness 156
Shatkin, G. 181*n*
Shields, Carolyn 84, 101, 178*n*
Shirley, Dennis 5-6, 33, 53, 57-8, 61-2, 73, 90, 124
simulated ownership model 29-30
Singh, Simrita 38-9
Sir Thomas Boughey Co-operative Business School, Staffordshire 145-7
social entrepreneurialism 35, 36-7, 74-5, 83
social knowledge and networks 105
social networks 104
social responsibility and eco-leadership 27
socio-political critiques of democratic paradigm shift 70-5, 77-8, 80
Socrates 99-100, 178*n*
Sørensen, Bent M. 78, 89-90
spaces for participation variable 112*fig*, 119-20, 126, 132
Spangler, David 79
specialist schools 46
Specialist Schools and Academies Trust 55
Spicer, Andre 34
'spiritual bankruptcy' of corporate world 5
spiritual capital/enterprise 25, 100
spirituality and spiritual awareness 23, 24-5, 29, 72
    capability for 94-100
    and degrees of democracy framework 114, 115, 117, 127
    and democracy 98-100
    and educational policy 93
    and educational practice 96-7, 98
    and leadership 26
    and left-brain dominance 91-2
    'life spiritualities' 24-5, 65, 92
    in school curriculum 49
    and Steiner school philosophy 114, 117
sponsorship of schools 46-7, 49-50, 51, 73, 79, 145
    Urbanview Academy case study 109, 119

state
    and capitalism 3-4
    'relational state' concept 28-9
    see also government
steering
    as government role 2, 45
    organic steering 159
Steiner, Rudolf 109, 114, 125
Steiner Hereford Academy 37
Steiner school case study 109-11, 113-28
Steyaert, Chris 31, 32, 40, 41, 43, 103-4
Storey, Val 172*n*
strong identity formation 86
structural change
    and central control in education 49-50, 78
    and democratic paradigm shift 63
    and instrumental drive 21, 84-5
student voice and democracy in schools 61, 80, 115-16, 121-2, 133-4, 134-7
    Learning to Lead project 139-43
    see also School Councils
student-led funding in schools 50
'Students as Leaders' project 139-40, 141-3
Studio Schools 47
substantive aspiration as principal purpose 112*fig*, 113-14
substantive liberty 42, 67, 156, 175*n*
substantive meanings of entrepreneurialism 34-40
substantive rationality 80-1, 87
substantive values 82, 84, 96, 158-9, 160
sustainability and eco-leadership 27
symbolic resources 86, 160-1
synergy and change 161
system leaders in education 100, 162
system redesign 53, 55, 57-8, 62

T

tacit knowledge and expert teachers 93
target-driven culture and education 54-5
Taylor, Charles 91-2

teachers
  collaborative teacher groups 85
  community link teachers and
    Learning to Lead 142-3
  and degrees of democracy
    framework 115-16
  emergent leadership scheme 107-9,
    116, 120, 124
  and right-brain approaches 93
  spiritual awareness 96, 117
  teacher leadership and new
    openings theory 79-80
  teacher-led development work
    groups 138-139
  teacher-led innovation 55, 80, 101,
    120, 138, 139
  see also educational policy; schools
team working 85
technocratic solutions and education
  53, 78
testing in schools and curriculum
  54-5
'third way' approach 60
  in education 5-6, 7, 52-5
Tillich, Paul 97
top-down delivery 59-60, 68
  in education 5-6, 55
Touraine, Alain 1
Training and Development Agency
  for Schools 93
tranformational leadership and critical
  actors 101-2
transactional engagement 112*fig*, 123
transcendent spiritual awareness 94-9
transformation of capitalism 4
transforming dialogue and holistic
  democracy model 10, 11, 160,
  166*n*
  and degrees of democracy variables
    113, 121-3
  and democratic entrepreneurialism
    42
  and democratic governance 68
  and educational practice 132, 134-
    35
  and participative drivers 27, 29, 84-5
transforming understanding and
  purpose of dialogue 112*fig*, 122
Trust Schools 47, 79
  cooperative schools 145, 146-7

U

uncertainty
  and changing schools system 157
  and entrepreneurial approach 35
  and flexibility 73
  and governance 60
  and plural controlled schooling 79
University Technology Colleges 47
Urbanview Academy case study 109-
  11, 113-28
utopianism and entrepreneurialism
  89-90

V

Vacher, K. 55
values
  cooperative schools 144-5, 146, 147,
    148-9
  and democratic consciousness 102
  and entrepreneurial approach 34
  and holistic democracy 9, 12, 18, 25,
    26, 82-4
    in education 158-9
    higher order values 84, 87, 113-14,
      120
  and organic meta-governance 64
  and substantive aspiration 113-14,
    158-9
  substantive values 82, 84, 96, 158-9,
    160
values rational action 83
virtues and democratic consciousness
  102
visionary zeal and bureau-enterprise
  culture 32
visualisation of change 33, 102, 103,
  160, 162
vocationalisation of curriculum
  critique 74
voice *see* student voice and
  democracy in schools

W

Waitere, Hine 151-2
Waldorf schools 111
  see also Michael Hall school case
    study
Weber, Max 23, 32-3, 35, 71-2, 73, 91

Weiskopf, Richard 32, 43, 103-4
welfare state and governance 66
Wenger, E. 178*n*
Western, Simon 5, 26-7
Whitehead, Jack 96-7
Whitney, D.K. 89
Whitt, J.A. 2, 27, 176*n*   add 19, 57,
    86, 87, 163, 168*n*
Wilson, Fraser 18
Wilson, Mervyn 181*n*
Woods, Glenys 109 add 9, 33, 35, 38,
    43, 49, 93, 96, 99, 102, 107, 109,
    114, 117, 124, 125, 151, 160, 165,
    170, 173, 177, 178, 179 [*NB: some
    of the references to Glenys Woods are
    to jointly authored works appearing as
    'Woods and Woods'.*]
Woods, P.A. 11-12   add 25, 33, 35,
    38, 42, 43, 48, 49, 50, 52, 54, 65,
    70, 71, 72, 78, 93, 99, 102, 104,
    116, 117, 119, 120, 123, 124,
    125, 126, 151, 158, 160, 165, 168,
    169, 170,   172, 173, 174, 175,
    177, 178, 179, 180 [*NB: some of
    the references to Philip Woods are to
    jointly authored works appearing as
    'Woods and Woods'.*]
'workforce remodelling' and central
    control 46
Worldblu 5, 15, 16-19, 30, 83, 166*n*,
    167*n*,170*n*, 173*n*, 177*n*, 180*n*

Z

Zappos 19, 177*n*
Žižek, Slavoj 6